#15.95
3/28/11

Zora Neale Hurston

Zora Neale Hurston

A Biography of the Spirit

Deborah G. Plant

ROWMAN & LITTLEFIELD PUBLISHERS, INC.
Lanham • Boulder • New York • Toronto • Plymouth, UK

Zora Neale Hurston/ A Biography of the Spirit, by Deborah G. Plant, was originally published in hard cover by Praeger, an imprint of ABC-CLIO, LLC, Santa Barbara, CA. Copyright © 2007 by Deborah G. Plant. Paperback edition by arrangement with ABC-CLIO, LLC, Santa Barbara, CA. All rights reserved.

Published by Rowman & Littlefield Publishers, Inc.
A wholly owned subsidary of The Rowman & Littlefield Publishing Group, Inc.
4501 Forbes Boulevard, Suite 200, Lanham, Maryland 20706
http://www.rowmanlittlefield.com

Estover Road, Plymouth PL6 7PY, United Kingdom

Distributed by National Book Network

British Library Cataloguing in Publication Information Available

Library of Congress Cataloging-in-Publication Data

The Praeger Publishers edition of this book was previously catalogued by the Library of Congress as follows:

Plant, Deborah G., 1956–
    Zora Neale Hurston : a biography of the spirit / Deborah G. Plant.
        p.   cm.—(Women writers of color, ISSN 1559–7172)
    Includes bibliographical references and index.
    1. Hurston, Zora Neale.   2. Authors, American—20th century—Biography.
3. African American women—Southern States—Biography.   4. Folklorists—
United States—Biography.   5. African American authors—Biography.   I. Title.
    PS3515.U789Z824   2007
    813'.52—dc22   2007021467

ISBN: 978-0-275-98751-0 (cloth : alk. paper)
ISBN: 978-1-4422-0612-0 (pbk. : alk. paper)

♾™ The paper used in this publication meets the minimum requirements of American National Standard for Information Sciences—Permanence of Paper for Printed Library Materials, ANSI/NISO Z39.48-1992.

Printed in the United States of America

Recognizing the power, wonder, and beauty of the spirit, this work is dedicated to the spirit of Zora Neale Hurston and to all my godchildren—Bobby Plant, Jr., Brittany Minor, Felicia Kelley, Jalani Kelley, Shekina Burson, Diego Negrao-Guerra, Leonardo Castro, "Everlasting" Evelinda Watkins, Patrice Thybulle, and Ryan Burns.

Contents

Acknowledgments ix

Introduction 1

One   The Essence of Things 7

Two   The Pathless Path 27

Three   "A Genius of the South": An American Genius 55

Four   "Coming Out More Than Conquer": Spirituality,
Empowerment, Freedom, and Peace 85

Five   Who Was Herod and What Made Him Great? 133

Six   Ancestral Spirit 163

Conclusion: Sankofa 201

Notes 207

Selected Bibliography 225

Index 229

Acknowledgments

I begin by bowing to Source and acknowledging those spiritual forces and families and individuals who were a part of my opening to the spirit of Zora Neale Hurston and her guidance. I have heartfelt appreciation for Tina Baker who told me out of the blue one day, "Zora wants you to write her biography." I was more than skeptical given that writing a second book on Hurston was not on my mind at the time and that Valerie Boyd had just recently published her excellent and wonderful work. Months later, Joanne M. Braxton contacted me to inquire of my interest in writing the Hurston biography. Although I impute everything that transpired before and after this to the spirit of Zora Neale Hurston, I claim responsibility for any and all shortcomings of this work.

For their support, affirmation, encouragement, and spiritual insights, I thank my Ascension and Yoga families, especially Gomati Ishaya, Vasistha Ishaya, Patricia Measal, Catherine Tardif, Magdelena Koob-Emunds, "Coach" Stephanie, and Lily. I am grateful to other members of my various families for our many and often long conversations about Zora Neale Hurston or the writing of this manuscript, particularly Phyllis McEwen, Gurleen Grewal, Jeongwoo Han, Takako Kikuchi, Gloria Plant Gilbert, Rose Ann Carter, Cindy Joe Rossiter, G. Yvonne Carter, and Dayna Christopher. I have profound gratitude for this Earth, the lakes, flora, and fauna of my immediate environment. For as often as I talked with others, I communed with Her. I would walk to the lake with questions, doubt, frustration, and stress. But I always left clear, at ease, and with direction and renewed vigor.

For their support and encouragement, I thank the faculty and staff in my home department of Africana Studies at the University of South Florida (USF): Professors Trevor Purcell, Edward Kissi, Cheryl Rodriguez, Eric Duke, Kersuze Simeon-Jones, and Yvonne Eisenhart. I acknowledge as well Professors Kevin Yelvington, Linda Ray Pratt, Shirley Toland-Dix, and Christine Probes for their ongoing friendship and support. I am most appreciative of Director William Scheuerle of the Humanities Institute of USF for the Summer 2005 Creative Scholarship Grant, which afforded me a full summer to devote to this project as well as funding for travel and purchase of research materials and services. I thank Director Scheuerle and former Associate Dean Sandra Schneider for their assistance with the writing of grant proposals for this project. Their feedback on my work, individually and in workshops, was very helpful to me. I am deeply appreciative of Provost Renu Khator and the College of Arts and Sciences for the Fall 2005 Sabbatical, which gave me an extended period of quality time to focus on my research on Hurston and the writing of this manuscript. I am indebted to the USF College of Arts and Sciences for the Spring 2006 Faculty Development Grant in support of this project.

My students are ever an inspiration to me in all my research endeavors, especially my work on Zora Neale Hurston. In particular I want to thank my "students of excellence" in the Black Women Writers class that I taught in the spring of 2006 on the Lakeland campus and the Zora Neale Hurston class that I taught the same semester on the Tampa campus. Their love of and appreciation for Zora Neale Hurston encouraged me in my efforts to write a spiritual biography. They generously shared their thoughts and feelings in the survey responses presented in Chapter Six, "Ancestral Legacy."

For their assistance, conversation, and direction, I thank the staff of the Special Collections Department of the George Smathers Libraries at the University of Florida in Gainesville, Florida. Among them I thank librarians Florence Turcotte and John Nemmers and student assistant Gilbert Levy who assisted me with the "Herod the Great" manuscript. I am grateful to USF graduates Patrice Thybulle and Evelinda Watkins and Ph.D. student Daphine Washington for transcriptions of audio- and video-taped interviews, assistance with copying of photographs, and their general support and encouragement. I appreciate my sister Gloria Jean Plant Gilbert for her assistance in researching the climactic data during Hurston's birth and death dates.

I am grateful to senior editor Suzanne Staszak-Silva and Joanne M. Braxton who considered me for the undertaking of such an humbling and honorable task. My gratitude for their patience and understanding throughout the entire process of bringing this work to completion is boundless. I extend my appreciation to Elizabeth Potenza and Randy Baldini for their editorial assistance.

For their love and continued support, I thank and am appreciative of my family of origin—my dad Alfred Plant, Sr.; my mother Elouise Porter Plant, whose spirit keeps me strong and safe; and my siblings, nieces, and nephews—and my surrogate family—Mr. Henry and Mrs. Rose Ann Carter and their children Cole and Wendell.

Also, for their spirit of friendship and camaraderie, I am appreciative of my community of Zoraphiles and "Zoraheads," including John Lowe, Valerie Boyd, Robert Hemenway, Lynn Moylan, "Jillie Mae" Bowen, Pamela

Bordelon, Jon Ward, Marjorie Harrell, Margaret Benton, Arlena Benton Lee, Jack Connolly, Herb Ellis, Anita Prentice, and the entire Fort Pierce, Florida, community. I express particular appreciation of Lucy Anne Hurston, who graciously and generously shared her time and her stories and her love of Hurston with me. Looking at her and listening to her, one senses that the spirit of Zora Neale Hurston lives on.

Introduction

lice Walker wrote in *In Search of Our Mother's Gardens* that *"we are a people. A people do not throw their geniuses away.* And if they are thrown away, it is our duty *as artists, as witnesses for the future* to collect them again for the sake of our children, and, if necessary, bone by bone."[1] In the gradual, but dramatic, unfolding of the life-story of Zora Neale Hurston—from Robert Bone (*The Negro Novel in America*), Mary Helen Washington and Alice Walker (*I Love Myself When I'm Laughing …*), and Robert Hemenway (*Zora Neale Hurston, A Literary Biography*), to Karla Kaplan (*Zora Neale Hurston: A Life in Letters*), Pamela Bordelon (*Go Gator and Muddy the Water: Writings by Zora Neale Hurston from the Federal Writers' Project*), and Valerie Boyd (*Wrapped in Rainbows*)—we get the sense that these and a host of other scholars, writers, and artists have, indeed, re-membered Hurston, bone by bone.

In the discipline of literature, Zora Neale Hurston has received a good deal of critical attention, but only since the 1970s. Virtually lost to oblivion after the 1940s, there was little written or known about this seminal author who is touted as one of the major voices of the Harlem Renaissance. As scholars reclaimed her and created a space for her in the African American and American literary canons, the availability and accessibility of her works have generated a growing popular reception of this author and a growing interest in who she was and how she reached the outstanding level of accomplishment that inspired author Alice Walker to describe her as "a genius of the South." My earlier work on Hurston focused on analyses of her texts. This work is offered as a contribution to a more profound understanding of the author herself, the world in which she lived, and the spiritual fortitude that allowed her to face and surmount the social realities of her day. Although Hurston scholars and biographers have alluded to the spiritual dimension of this author and her works and emphasized its significance, none has given any extensive examination or analysis of this aspect of the author. My exploration of Hurston's spiritual thought and practice, its manifestation in her life and work, and its role in her achievements will enhance our appreciation of this author, because it will speak to the matter of the human spirit and our own human possibility.

No longer a woman "half in shadow," as Mary Helen Washington once described her, Zora Neale Hurston's life can now be seen in a fuller light. "Lost years" have been found, birth dates discovered, and the intricacies of relationships with friends, spouses, and family members have been uncovered. We know she loved to cook, she kept a flower and vegetable garden, and she had a pet Scottish terrier named Spot whom she loved. With these new discoveries and recoveries of Hurston's life, relations, and works, we have a clearer idea of what she meant when she wrote in "Looking Things Over," "I have been in Sorrow's kitchen and licked out all the pots. Then I have stood on the peaky mountain wrappen in rainbows, with a harp and a sword in my hands."[2] We have a more profound sense of Hurston's courage and resilience, and a more profound respect for her intellect, ingenuity, creative genius, political activism, and literary production. Aware of the challenges she faced in terms of nagging ill health, personal and professional disappointments, struggles to fund her projects, even the inability sometimes to buy groceries, one wonders at her consistently positive outlook, enthusiasm, and extraordinary productivity. Hurston's life story and circumstances beg the question: How did she do it? How did she accomplish so much with so little revenue? What did it take for her to live through what she experienced in Sorrow's kitchen *and* to stand on that mountain peak? As she wrote in a letter to Annie Nathan Mayer, "To be brave costs something.... It is so much easier to die out of one's troubles than to live with them."[3] What allowed her to live—and not just survive, but thrive?

Hurston lived and worked most of her life in the Jim Crow South, a social system designed to undermine the humanity of African Americans. Yet Hurston considered herself a superior human being. Although compelled to negotiate a racist system, she did not allow that system to define her or determine the focus of her work. Some critics continue to criticize Hurston for not directly or substantively addressing the racial issues of her day, claiming she ignored them or denied them. Hurston did address issues of race, however, subtly in her fiction works and directly in her autobiography and journalistic writings. She considered race consciousness to be the scourge of humanity and observed such dispositions as the preoccupation of little minds. She was inspired by the possibilities of greatness within the human spirit, and how that greatness might be achieved, and focused her attention accordingly. Furthermore, Hurston conceived of the human spirit as a part of a greater, divine, universal spirit. Thus, human beings were always much more than their situations and circumstances and always had the power within themselves to triumph over socially contrived conditions. Hurston, like several of her protagonists, looked within—to her higher, spiritual self—for sustenance, guidance, and an angle of vision on the world that allowed her to engage her external environment in a manner that enabled her to express her creative genius.

Robert Hemenway's literary biography gave us the first comprehensive examination of Hurston's then-known oeuvre in context of her life. Valerie Boyd's general biography expanded the works of earlier scholars, especially Walker and Hemenway, to give readers the most complete biographical narrative of Zora Neale Hurston to date. Even as these works provide a fuller portrait of Hurston, even as the facts gathered can now account for virtually every mark on the timeline of her life, there is still a part of Hurston's life that is not accounted for: that which made Hurston's life work possible—the spirit. When we ask what it is that animated the woman who achieved all that the current biographies detail so well, we must necessarily probe further. Valerie Boyd discussed Hurston's appreciation of Hoodoo and Voodoo and her anthropological interests in these religious practices, and she alluded to Hurston's interests in Eastern philosophy. In the last paragraph of the last chapter of *Wrapped in Rainbows*, she wrote:

> Given her spiritual beliefs—born in Macedonia Baptist, warmed by the fire of hoodoo and voodoo, then finding a resting place in Eastern philosophy—death was not the end for Zora Neale Hurston. Instead, it was a new beginning—of her life as an ancestor, as a spirit. "I know that nothing is destructible; things merely change forms," she once said. "When the consciousness we know as life ceases, I know that I shall still be part and parcel of the world."[4]

This is where Boyd's book ends. This is where mine begins.

Using various critical approaches, I endeavor to determine the configuration of Zora Neale Hurston's spiritual views and beliefs and examine and interpret Hurston's life choices, her texts, and her professional and political activity in the context of her spirituality. What I mean by "spirituality" is best articulated in Akasha Gloria Hull's book *Soul Talk: The New Spirituality of African American Women*. In this work, Hull investigated a spiritual movement, which she conceived as "The Third Revolution." This movement, she wrote, has three dimensions: political and social awareness, eclectic spiritual consciousness, and enhanced creativity. Spirituality, expressing these "three interlocking dimensions," is discussed as "a legitimate way to participate in struggle":

> If being spiritual means meditating to make connection with the larger self that is part and parcel of the greatest whole, and trying to see, feel and know our oneness with it; if being spiritual means going to therapy in order to feel and heal our own pain so that we can identify with and heal the pain of others; if it means traveling to Machu Piccu or Egypt to enlarge our vision of the world beyond our own backyards, money worries, and personal problems; if being spiritual means taking up Tibetan Buddhism to open our hearts and minds so that we are moved to alleviate suffering and misery wherever we encounter it,

in whatever way we can; if it means seeking transcendent merging with the whole so that we no longer name as "other" those who are different from us and those whose life scripts challenge us to get outside of our own comfort zones; if it means doing yoga to reduce the stress and tension ballooning inside us so that we can open our eyes to the world around us and really be present in it; if it means visualizing our health and prosperity as pieces of the health and prosperity of every living being; if being spiritual means all of these kinds of things, then, surely, it is a more-than-legitimate way to participate in struggle.[5]

Hull declared 1981, the year Toni Morrison was depicted on the cover of *Newsweek*, as the year that marked this new spirituality and its parallel literary renaissance. She explained that African Americans of earlier periods, such as Harriet Tubman, Zora Neale Hurston, and Fannie Lou Hamer, manifested this three-pronged aspect of the "new spirituality." But beginning in 1981, an unprecedented number of African American women manifested this dynamic: "It goes beyond individual attainment into the realm of a group phenomenon."[6]

What is also new is the nature of the "struggle." Struggle typically entails passionate engagement with some external, adversarial force. "Passion" means to suffer pain, and "struggle" means slavery in that, as Chögyan Trungpa states in *Cutting through Spiritual Materialism*, "the absence of struggle is in itself freedom."[7] The "new spirituality" entails a letting go of struggle in the conventional sense. In *We Are the Ones We Have Been Waiting For*, Alice Walker wrote that "we can turn our attention away from our oppressors—unless they are directly endangering us to our faces—and work on the issue of our suffering without attaching them to it."[8] That is, African Americans, as with any people who have been subject to unjust treatment, *must* let go of "the oppressor" if healing, wholeness, and joy are to be realized. Freeing oneself requires letting go of the struggle as we have been wont to conceive of it. Hurston uses folklore to express these ideas about struggle in relation to race pride and race consciousness:

> A bear has been grabbed by the tail. The captor and the captured are walking around a tree snarling at each other. The man is scared to turn the bear loose, and his handhold is slipping. The bear wants to go on about his business, but he feels that something must be done about that tail-hold. So they just keep on following each other around the tree.[9]

In previous works, I have described Zora Neale Hurston as a model of resistance. As I have continued to study her legacy, I see her more clearly as a model of freedom, and not so much a *model* of freedom but as the living embodiment of freedom. Walker proclaimed, "We live in a time of global enlightenment." Her optimistic jubilance is not unmindful of the tyranny of human greed, envy, and covetousness that results in cruelty and conquests. Walker stated,

> We will know at least a bit of the truth about what is going on, and that will set us free. Perhaps not free in the old way of thinking about freedom, as literal

escape from enslavement in its various forms, but free in our understanding that our domination is not a comment on our worth. It is an awesome era in which to live.[10]

Hurston is heralded as one of the forerunners of this "new spirituality." As one who always knew her self-worth—in the face of male domination, race domination, and class domination—Zora Neale Hurston is a beacon for those of us who, in this potent era, aspire to freedom.

ONE

The Essence of Things

O n Thursday January 28, 1960, the sun rose on Fort Pierce, Florida, at 7:10 A.M. It set that day at 5:59 P.M. and the vast twilight sky boasted a new moon. At 7:00 P.M., Zora Neale Hurston's sun set and she crossed over.

Like the Biblical David, whom she so admired, she stood on the mountain-top with a harp in one hand and a sword in the other. She had crossed over. Like the mythical Hercules, with whom she was so impressed, she was true to her oath to shun pleasure and "take the hard road to labor."[1] Her searching and searching had come to an end. Like the Moses of *Moses, Man of the Mountain*, she was falsely accused and much maligned, while she was also acknowledged, recognized, and celebrated for her genius and her achievements. But the ever-changing vicissitudes of her mortal life were done—the peaks and the valleys. She had crossed over. Sheltered in the house of a friend and maintained by her community, there was no need to keep "wrassling up a living." She crossed over. American social politics buried her in a Jim Crow cemetery; Percy Peek's Funeral Home laid her body to rest in Genesee Memorial Gardens. Having crossed over, Hurston "left us to act out our ceremonies over unimportant things."[2] She had said her say and sung her song.

On the day of the burial, February 7, 1960, the temperature ranged in the low to mid-sixties. The "yellow line of morning" sprang forth at 7:10 A.M. It was a Sunday. That evening, Hurston "return[ed] with the earth to Father Sun."[3]

Rumors of her having died alone and unknown have been greatly exaggerated. Following treatment for a stroke she suffered October 12, 1959, Hurston had been released from Fort Pierce Memorial Hospital and transferred to Lincoln Park Nursing Home. Although she would have preferred to return to her own home, her limited ability to "manage herself" necessitated her being in an environment in which assistance could be provided. But in this facility administered by the St. Lucie County Welfare Agency, Zora Neale Hurston was not left alone. She was visited regularly by friends and family members. Her brother Clifford Joel, his wife Mabel, and their daughter Vivian also came to see about her. Hurston refused her family's concern and their offering of money and various items bought for her and told them that she was "fine." She was "where she wanted to be" and "didn't want anything from anybody."[4]

The second stroke was fatal. As Hurston had anticipated, she nearly lived her "allotted span of time" (three score and ten), so was granted "a timely death."[5] Afterward, Marjorie Silver Alder's *Miami Herald* article informed readers that money was needed to cover burial expenses. Donations came in from longtime friends, among them Carl Van Vechten and Fannie Hurst, and also the Lippincott and Scribner's publishing houses with which Hurston had been associated. Former colleagues and students from Lincoln Park Academy and members of the community shared what financial resources and services they could. More than $600 dollars was a sufficient sum for the funeral. More than 100 people, including family members Clifford Joel and Mabel, gathered to bear witness to Hurston's home-going and to hear testimonials about her life. Chairs were set out on the sidewalk to accommodate the gathering. Choirs sang and preachers preached. Reverend Jennings delivered a eulogy in which he testified to this profound truth: "They said she couldn't become a writer recognized by the world. But she did. The Miami paper said she died poor. But she died rich. She did something."[6]

JUMP AT THE SUN

Hurston lived a rewarding life even though she stated her life was not easy. She had basked in the sunshine and she had shivered in the shadows of hell's kitchen. Whence this resilience? This enthusiasm for life? This triumphant spirit that continually trumps adversity? Whence this ardent belief in truth? In the dream? Whence this ability "to come out more than conquer"?

The beginning of this was a woman: Lucy Ann Potts "of the land-owning" Potts of Notasulga, Alabama. Born December 31, 1865, she was the daughter of Richard and Sarah Potts. Both of her parents were from Georgia and had experienced America's "Peculiar Institution" called slavery. After emancipation, the couple settled in Macon County, in Notasulga. Richard and Sarah Potts managed to acquire five acres of land on which they built a home for their four children—two boys and two girls—and two grandchildren. Lucy

Ann was the youngest. At age sixteen, small and nut brown, Lucy Ann Potts was considered "the prettiest and smartest black girl" around.

She was singing in the Macedonia Baptist Church choir when she felt the admiring and inquiring eyes of John Hurston upon her. Touched by his glance, she began to ask questions about this "yaller," big-boned and heavy-muscled fellow with gray-green eyes. The report was that he was one of those Hurstons from over the creek, that is, a nobody. "Over-the-creek" Negroes were considered poor—poor in material accoutrements and, even worse, poor in spirit. That is, ambitionless and "don't-carefied." Like Sarah and Richard, John's parents had experienced slavery. John, himself, was born January 1, 1861, just before emancipation. His father Alfred Hurston was originally from Georgia, and his mother Amy Hurston was from Alabama. John was the oldest of nine children and of questionable paternity. It was surmised that "some white man" was his biological father. The postbellum years would find the Hurston family established in Notasulga, Alabama, in Lee County.[7]

Contrary to popular opinion, John Hurston had ambition. He wanted something out of life and he crossed the creek in search of it. Having spied Lucy Ann Potts and having made some assessments from afar, he considered that frequent attendance at Macedonia might allow him to get a little closer. The interest between the two being mutual, they engaged in a surreptitious courtship for some months, slipping each other notes between the pages of hymnals.[8] Zora Hurston fictionalized the marriage proposal of her parents in *Jonah's Gourd Vine*:

> "Lucy, you pay much 'tention tuh birds?"
>
> "Unhunh. De jay bird say 'Laz'ness will kill you,' and he go to hell ev'ry Friday and totes uh grain uh sand in his mouf tuh put out de fire, and den de doves say, 'Where you *been* so long?'"
>
> John cut her short. "Ah don't mean dat way, Lucy. Whut Ah wants tuh know is, which would you ruther be, if you had yo' ruthers—uh lark uh flyin', uh uh dove uh settin'?"
>
> "Ah don't know whut you talkin' 'bout, John. It mus' be uh new riddle."
>
> "Naw 'tain't, Lucy. Po' me Lucy. Ahm uh one wingded bird. Don't leave me lak dat, Lucy."
>
> Suddenly Lucy shouted, "Look, John, de knot is tied right, ain't it pretty?"
>
> "Yeah, Lucy iss sho pretty. We done took and tied dis knot, Miss Lucy, less tie uh 'nother one."[9]

Whereas John Hurston might have been congratulated for "picking from a higher bush," Lucy Ann Potts was condemned for lowering her standards. Being from the "right side of the creek" meant something to Lucy Ann's folks, especially her mother, who could only conceive of John as "dat yaller bastard" from "over de creek." But neither Lucy nor John felt compelled to sacrifice their love on the altar of class and color prejudice. In defiance of violent family opposition, Lucy Ann exchanged marital vows with John on February 2, 1882. Lucy was 16 and John had just turned 21 on January 1. Sarah Potts was irreconcilable and expressed her displeasure of the union by not attending the wedding. Lucy Ann's father Richard, however, softened. He would not allow his young daughter to walk two miles, alone, through the February night to her wedding. He would accompany her. He hitched the horses to the buggy and escorted his daughter to the church.

Forbidden to step one foot on the Potts's family homestead, life for the newlyweds commenced in a little cabin on a Notasulga cotton plantation where the couple worked as sharecroppers. November of the same year, Hezekiah Robert (Bob) was born. A second son, Issac, followed ten months later, but did not survive beyond early childhood. After the first boy child, John Hurston had his heart set on a girl baby. But John Cornelius came in January 1885, and then Richard (Dick) William came in 1887. John Hurston was granted his heart's desire in December of 1889 when Sarah Emmeline was born. "If she were not fore-told, she was certainly fore-wished."[10] In spite of Sarah Potts's continued hostility, or in an attempt to appease it, Lucy Ann named the baby in honor of her mother and sister. John Hurston's joy at her arrival was boundless. He would change and wash Sarah's diapers and listen for her cries. As she grew up, John Hurston anticipated her every wish, so Sarah never wanted for anything.[11]

The attention John Hurston lavished on his first daughter, Sarah, con-trasted sharply with the attention given to his second daughter. When Zora Neal Lee rushed into the world on January 7, 1891, her papa was away from home. Because it was hog-killing time, no adults were at home with Lucy Ann. Everyone was going through the preparations and rituals of butchering their hogs or assisting others in doing so. Lucy Ann sent one of the children to get Aunt Judy, the midwife. But even Aunt Judy was off in a neighboring town eating some of the good cooking that always accompanied this seasonal ritual. Indifferent to the lack of arrangements and preparations for her arrival, the baby eagerly delivered herself. Weak and disoriented from the birthing, Lucy Ann was unable to do more than wait for assistance. Her new-born's cries could be heard "all over Orange County," so the exhausted mother had at least that consolation.

As family lore had it, a family acquaintance, "a white man of many acres and things," happened along a few minutes after the birthing. Knowing John Hurston was out of town, he stopped to bring over a shoat, some sweet pota-toes, and other garden vegetables.[12] Hearing no answer to his hellos, he trailed the baby's cries and saw that his help was needed: "[H]e took out his Barlow Knife and cut the navel cord, then did the best he could about other things." Aunt Judy finally arrived and assumed administration of matters. The old man fussed about Aunt Judy's not being around when needed, and Aunt Judy complained about his birthing handiwork. "[T]he cord had not been cut just right, and the belly-band had not been put on tight enough." Aunt Judy was afraid Zora was going to have a weak back and have trouble holding her water until she reached puberty. And she did.[13]

Hurston explains in her autobiography that a Mrs. Neale, a friend of her mother, named her. "She had picked up a name somewhere which she thought was very pretty. Perhaps, she had read it somewhere, or somebody back in those woods was smoking Turkish cigarettes. So I became Zora Neale Hurston."[14] Hurston never used and, in her narrative, never accounted for the additional middle name "Lee" nor does she explain the "e" added to "Neal." Her name was recorded in the family Bible as "Zora Neal Lee Hurston." "Lee" may have been a reference to the county in which Hurston was born, and "Neale" may have been a merging of her two middle names.[15] John Hurston was not present for the baby's birth or her naming, and he was not pleased to learn that this newest addition to the family was also a girl: "Plenty more sons, but no more girl babies." Although she "looked more like him than any child in the house," one daughter was all he wanted, and Sarah had already fulfilled that wish. "I hear he threatened to cut his throat when he got the news," Hurston recalled, and she pondered whether her father "ever got over the trick he felt I played on him by getting born a girl, and while he was off from home at that." This tension between father and daughter continued throughout their relationship. As Hurston put it, "A little of my sugar used to sweeten his coffee."[16]

John Hurston's work as a carpenter took him far and wide and away for long periods of time. He had been away for months when Zora Neale Hurston was born. It was, perhaps, during this time that he ventured south into Florida, and discovered Eatonville. A new town. A self-governed, all-Negro town. A haven from Reconstruction hostilities. A place where John Hurston could realize his ambitions as an individual, as a husband, and as a father. A place where, to some extent, Jim Crow would be held at bay. The hand-to-mouth existence of plantation life had begun to "irk and bind" John Hurston. Eatonville was the promise of a new beginning.

Eatonville was not "the black back-side of an average town":

> Eatonville, Florida, is, and was at the time of [Hurston's] birth, a pure Negro town—charter, mayor, council, town marshal and all. It was not the first Negro community in America, but it was the first to be incorporated, the first attempt at organized self-government on the part of Negroes in America.[17]

Situated near Orlando, Eatonville was originally "a community founded in the tradition of the race colony." It evolved from a settlement of extended families and friends who were drawn to the area by the hope of plenty of work at fair pay in the newly thriving town of Maitland. Veterans of the civil war and monied whites from the North and Midwest were attracted to the area's picturesque landscapes and chose to cast their fortunes there. The swampy terrain, however, needed clearing and houses and halls needed erecting. The Negro settlement in the area provided much of the labor. Hurston's recounting of the historical unfolding of Maitland describes a harmonious relationship between the whites and the community of Negroes who helped raise the town. When Maitland incorporated in 1884 and held elections, both white men and black men cast their votes. The election results yielded Tony Taylor, a black man, as the first mayor of Maitland, and Joe Clarke, "a dark-complexioned Georgia Negro," as the town marshal. Under their leadership, Maitland continued to thrive, and life in Maitland continued peacefully.

Nonetheless, Joe Clarke still carried the dream of establishing a Freedman's town. Whether his term as the marshal of Maitland encouraged him positively or negatively is speculative. His ambition to realize his dream remained. Clarke had approached Lewis Lawrence, a white philanthropist from New York, with his proposition. Clarke had made an attempt elsewhere in Florida to establish a town, but no whites would sell him land.[18] Lawrence appreciated Clarke's vision and supported his efforts. Of twenty-two acres of land Lawrence had purchased from Josiah Eaton in 1881, Lawrence had deeded ten of them to Negroes for the purpose of building a church. The edifice they constructed was christened the St. Lawrence African Methodist Episcopal Church. The remaining twelve acres, Lawrence sold to Joe Clarke. Those acres and the deed parcel were the beginnings of Eatonville, named in recognition of Josiah Eaton. Joe Clarke, along with other black leaders purchased more than 100 acres of land from Lawrence and Eaton. These leaders, in turn, sold small parcels to other Negroes.[19] By 1887, there were enough landowners to file for the town's incorporation.[20]

On August 15, 1887, Eatonville held its incorporation meeting. At this meeting, Reverend Columbus H. Boger became Eatonville's first mayor. Joe Clarke became its alderman.[21] With capable leadership and a post office and general store, owned by Joe Clarke, Eatonville was poised for growth and greatness.

Two years later, in 1889, Russell and Mary Calhoun founded the Robert Hungerford Normal and Industrial School. The school was modeled from Booker T. Washington's Tuskeegee Institute and was named to memorialize the deceased son of Edward and Anna Hungerford, benefactors of the school.[22] In twenty-four years of freedom, African Americans sought every path to full citizenship and full human expression. Education was a path in which they firmly believed. As the only school for Negroes in central Florida, the Robert Hungerford Normal and Industrial School became a light unto the path of many.

John Hurston saw the progress and prosperity of Eatonville and resolved to settle there. After about a year, he sent for his wife and five children. Around 1892, not long after Hurston's birth, Lucy Ann and the five children joined John Hurston down in Eatonville. Once again the family was all together. John had stuffed burlap sacks with Spanish moss on their arrival. These would serve as the children's bed that night. John and Lucy and baby Zora slept on the feather mattress Lucy brought down from Alabama. The night-blooming jasmine perfumed the air with promise—promises of a better life for the Hurston family, promises of equality and opportunity for black folk. Over time, John and Lucy purchased five acres of land and built an eight-room house Hurston described as "one story and a jump."[23]

As Lucy urged John on in his work as a carpenter, she also urged him to respond to his call to preach. John Hurston had the voice and the figure that made him a successful preacher. Hurston wrote fondly of her admiration for her father's ability with the spoken word. The folk in Eatonville and surrounding areas were likewise enthralled by his "primitive poetry." In 1893, before John had preached his trial sermon at Eatonville's Macedonia Baptist Church, Zion Hope Baptist Church in Sanford, Florida, claimed him as their pastor.

John excelled. The Hurston family grew and became more prosperous. In March of that year, Clifford Joel became the newest member of the family. Benjamin Franklin arrived in December of 1895, and Everett Edward was born in October of 1898. The year prior, John's popularity and civic spirit would win him the town's mayoral election. He would serve a second term in 1912 and another in 1914.

The Reverend Mayor John Hurston was boastful of "his house full of young'uns." Hurston related that "we were never hungry." The five-acre stead yielded plenty vegetables, livestock, and trees heavy with fruit. Chicken and home-cured meat graced the table, and the children had all the eggs they wanted—as food and as missiles to be thrown at each other and at other children in the village. With eight children, "the house was noisy from the time school turned out until bedtime."[24] As John and Lucy Ann Hurston delighted in their children, they also administered discipline.

John was a successful provider who negotiated the world beyond the home and community, and Lucy Ann tended to those matters inside the home relevant to her husband and their children. She provided their nurturance and care. And given that John Hurston was away from home so often and for extended periods, Lucy Hurston did a yeoman's part. She insisted on good behavior and didn't think twice about applying peach hickories to backsides. The children were mindful and respectful of their mother.

While the children were mindful of their mother, they were in awe of their father. He was godlike to them. Their perception of their father was reinforced by his reputation in the community. Admired for his verbal prowess in delivering the Word, he was equally admired for his physical prowess. "He could hit ninety-seven out of a hundred with a gun. He could swim Lake Maitland from Maitland to Winter Park, and no man in the village could put my father's shoulders to the ground," Hurston wrote with pride. The children were convinced of their father's invincibility. When a neighbor scolded Evertt Edward and told him that God would punish him, the two-year old leaned back and countered, "He better not bother me. Papa will shoot Him down."[25]

John Hurston was easily 200 pounds of bone and muscle, and Lucy Ann, described as "frail," wasn't quite 100 pounds. If John was the family hero in form, Lucy Ann was the family hero in essence. Along with inculcating proper home training and overseeing their school studies, Lucy Ann dispensed wisdom that enhanced her children's spiritual development: "Mama exhorted her children at every opportunity to 'jump at de sun.' We might not land on the sun, but at least we would get off the ground."[26]

The phrase, "jump at de sun," has been repeated often in reference to Hurston and in characterizing Hurston's relationship to her mother. In her 1942 autobiographical narrative and in her extended autobiography of letters, the state of Hurston's spiritual condition is expressed through and measured by the presence, the brilliance, the fading, or the absence of the sun. More than scholars and lay readers of Hurston's work might have guessed, the sun is a central, unifying symbol and metaphor throughout Hurston's work and throughout her life. It symbolizes spirit and spirituality in her personal universe, just as the sun symbolizes spirit in the world cosmologies that are reflected in Hurston's thought. In Hurston's belief system, spirit is equated with energy and with consciousness, and sometimes with the human heart. The sun symbolizes Hurston's spiritual self. When her mother exhorted her to "jump at de sun," she, in essence, was advising Zora Neale to immerse in Self—not the lowercase self of human identity and personality, but the capitalized Self of spirit and consciousness. It is not surprising that in her autobiography Hurston referenced "spirit" more than twenty-five times and often did so in contexts that include the sun motif. If Hurston's mother did not articulate this cosmological philosophy in words, she certainly demonstrated it in her actions and her adamant determination to protect Zora Neale from those who would "squinch her spirit."

Lucy Ann Hurston saw in her daughter Zora an extraordinary presence of strength, will, and procreative intelligence. As Hurston was the child who most resembled her father physically, she was the child who was most like her mother spiritually. This didn't sit well with John Hurston. Just as he professed he could break his wife of her headstrong ways if he just wanted to, he promised to break Hurston of hers. Unlike her mama, her papa "did not feel so hopeful. Let well enough alone. It did not do for Negroes to have too much spirit." Because Hurston was high-spirited, "He was always threatening to break mine or kill me in the attempt." Hurston escaped the crime. "My mother was always standing between us."[27]

If John Hurston was prevented from breaking her and her mother would not undertake the task as he thought she should, he was convinced that the white folks would. He warned Zora that "[t]he white folks were not going to stand for it. I was going to be hung before I got grown. Somebody was going to blow me down for my sassy tongue. Mama was going to suck sorrow for not beating my temper out of me before it was too late," and there would be a litany of other dire consequences.[28] Lucy Ann was the safety point between hope and despair, joy and pain, white folks and black folks, and life and death. Hurston's safe haven from her father and his doomsday predictions was behind her mother's rocking chair. Declaring that her daughter would not become "a mealy-mouthed rag doll," Lucy Hurston drew a line: "Zora is my young'un and Sarah is yours. I'll be bound mine will come out more than conquer. You leave her alone. I'll tend to her when I figger she needs it."[29]

Lucy Ann Hurston was born in 1862, the year that the emancipation promised to black folks was officially proclaimed. John Hurston, born in 1861, right before Lincoln's signing of the Emancipation Proclamation, continued to live out plantation life after 1865 along with his parents. It is clear that Zora Neale Hurston's parents' expectations for life were different because of the place and time of their birth, and their spirits reflected this. Hurston wasn't sure whether her father really feared for her future, living in a society that was openly hostile to their race or whether her father felt affronted by the observations her mother made.[30] In any case, John Hurston envisioned privilege and power as perquisites of whites. The idea that his younger daughter could conceive of herself as an equal in American society with entitlement just like everybody else baffled and angered him. When young Zora announced that she desired "a fine black riding horse with white leather saddle and bridles" for a Christmas present, John Hurston was nonplussed.

> "You what?" Papa gasped. What was dat you said?"
> "I said, I want a black saddle horse with...."
> "A saddle horse!" Papa exploded. "It's a sin and a shame! Lemme tell you something right now, my young lady; you ain't white.... Riding horse!! Always trying to wear de big hat! I don't know how you got in this family nohow. You ain't like none of de rest of my young'uns."
> "If I can't have no riding horse, I don't want nothing at all...."
> "I'll riding horse you, Madam!"

Hurston noted in her text that "you ain't white" was "a Negro saying that means 'Don't be too ambitious. You are a Negro and they are not meant to have but so much.'"[31] John Hurston jumped to his feet to apprehend the offending daughter and to impress upon her just how much ambition she was supposed to have. But Zora was sitting at the far end of the dinner table opposite her father. She sped out of the back door of the kitchen with her father in hopeless pursuit. Zora Neale's fearless innocence and free-spiritedness marked her as an atavist of sorts as far as John Hurston was concerned: "How you got in the family nohow," he wanted to know. "You ain't like none of de rest of my young'uns." What were the rest of his young'uns like and how did young Zora differ? For one thing, she had a wonderful imagination and an unquenchable curiosity. For instance, her request to her Papa for the riding horse was to make possible her desire to go to the horizon and "see what the end was like"[32] She had asked her childhood friend Carrie Roberts to go with her. Afraid that they might not get back before sundown, and so would get a whipping, Carrie figured they should postpone the venture until they were both old enough to wear long dresses. The disappointment was upsetting to Zora who, in retrospective regret, hit her friend "to keep my heart from stifling me ... and went on home and hid under the house with my heartbreak." Not to be dissuaded, Zora decided to delay the quest until she had something to ride on, and could then go alone. "So for weeks I saw myself sitting astride of a fine horse. My shoes had sky-blue bottoms to them, and I was riding off to look at the belly-band of the world."[33] The saddle horse that was denied her, she made up. "No one around me knew how often I rode my prancing horse, nor the things I saw in far places," said Zora who rode off to imagined worlds with her puppy Jake.[34]

Zora combined her colorful imagination with her natural surroundings to create vivid stories. Only in her fantasies could she ride off to the end of the world, but she could actually walk into a fantastic world at Joe Clarke's store. The general store was "the heart and spring of the town," and Lucy Ann would send her to the store on errands. Once at the store, her imagination and curiosity were both whetted and appeased. She would drag her feet in and out of the store, lingering here and there, listening to the townfolk pass "this world and the next through their mouths," and allowing the town's gossip to hang in her ears.[35] Hurston wrote that what she liked best were the "lying sessions," wherein the men folk strained against one another in the telling of folktales: "God, Devil, Brer Rabbit, Brer Fox, Sis Cat, Brer Bear, Lion, Tiger, Buzzard, and all the wood folk walked and talked like natural men."[36] These tales about God and the Devil and animals and elements "stirred up fancies" in the child Zora. The wind and the trees would talk to her. One tree in particular, "the loving pine," became a good friend and playmate with whom she could talk "about everything in my world." A variegated rainbow of a bird allowed her to walk up its long tail into a tree where the two engaged in lengthy conversation. The lake, promising not to drown her, invited Zora for a walk. Whereas her mother indulged her playfulness, her maternal grandmother, Sarah, was not enchanted: "I vominates (abominate) a lying tongue," she spat, and tried to coerce Zora's mother to punish her.

> Luthee! (She lisped.) You hear dat young'un stand up here and lie like dat? And you ain't doing nothing to break her of it? Grab her! Wring her coat tails over her head and wear out a handful of peach hickories on her back-side. Stomp her guts out! Ruin her!

Hurston wrote, though, "Mama never tried to break me." In a sweet reverie, she recalled that her mama would "listen sometimes, and sometimes she wouldn't. But she never seemed displeased."[37] The child knew she could disregard her grandmother's threats. Nonetheless, more often than not, she kept her inventions to herself. She would play under the house for hours, transforming ordinary objects into personages with histories and future plans. There was a Miss Corn-Shuck, a discarded shuck of corn, which was betrothed to Mr. Sweet Smell, a bar of soap. A Reverend Door-Knob, who rolled off the kitchen door. A Miss Corn-Cob, who was generally invidious and disturbed everybody's peace. And there were the Spool People who hopped off Zora's mother's sewing machine and were a kind of sentimental church choir. The drama of this cast, centered around Miss Corn-Cob and

Mr. Sweet Smell, was a veritable soap opera, with almost marriages, funerals, and good times and bad times. The imagination that transformed inanimate objects into people also transformed people into fantastic creatures. Zora re-created Mr. Pendir into a terrifying 'gator. The innocuous old man lived, alone, on the outskirts of town near Lake Belle. But Zora imaged him as a mutant who, under cover of darkness, grew reptilian claws, a knotty green-ish hide, and a long snout with jutting teeth. Her powerful storytelling had her chums inspecting Mr. Pendir for "'gator signs."[38]

Zora differed from "de rest of [John Hurston's] young'uns" in other ways as well. She was scared of nothing on "God's dirt-ball" of which "a little col-ored girl" was supposed to be frightened: adults, boys, snakes, and white folks. The protection of her mother likely encouraged Zora to speak her mind and stand her ground. To her father's and her grandmother's dismay, she was "of the word-changing kind," and they were sure her "tendency to stand and give battle" would be her undoing. They never considered that it was probably just the thing that might help her survive in the world—in Eatonville and beyond. No doubt their warnings were well founded. And in reality, their fear makes one wonder just what was the nature of America that even in the safe bosom of Eatonville, free and economically independent, black adults sought to break the spirit of this girl-child and instill in its place a subservient humility. But there was nothing humble about Zora Neale Hur-ston. She was as physically tough as she was psychologically and spiritually unflappable. She was "extra strong," she happily discovered and was proud that she could dish it out to the boys as well as "take a good pummeling without running home to tell." All her parents, including her mother, frowned on this behavior: It wasn't "lady-like." Her folks queried, "What was wrong with my doll-babies? Why couldn't I sit still and make my dolls some clothes?"[39] Zora found the doll-babies, like her female playmates, to be timid, weak, and helpless.

"Without knowing it," Hurston realized later, "I wanted action." Her inside urge for action created omnipotent figures in her imagination. The dolls she made up could do "everything." Sometimes this urge would take her wandering in the woods, the only place she felt happy, especially when springtime came, "trance-glorifying the world." This tendency distressed her mother, but Zora felt perfectly safe in the woods. She nibbled sweet oat stalks and befriended flora and fauna alike, even snakes. She wrote, "I was not afraid of snakes. They fascinated me in a way which I still cannot explain. I got no pleasure from their death."[40]

Next to the woods, there was no place Zora liked better than her perch atop the gatepost of her house. She saw the movement of carriages and cars stream by on their way to Orlando, and that made her feel glad. She would exchange greetings with the travelers, most of whom were white, and some-times ask them, "Don't you want me to go a piece of the way with you? They always did." If she were caught, this behavior guaranteed her a whipping. And she would get caught: "Git down offa dat post! You li'l sow, you! Git

down! Setting up dere looking dem white folks right in de face! They's
gwine to lynch you yet.... Youse too brazen to live long," her grandmother
said. These chastisements and whippings never dampened her spirits. She'd
go a piece of the way whenever she could make it.[41]

Zora Neale Hurston's childhood urgency to reach the horizon—"where
the sky meets the ground"—was spurred by a desire to know "about the end
of things." For, she "had no doubts about the beginnings. They were somewhere in the five acres that was home to me. Most likely in Mama's room."[42]
But on September 19, 1904, Lucy Ann Potts Hurston died, just shy of 39
years. She had returned from the Alabama homestead, having tended to her
sister whose illness had ended in death. Lucy Ann had developed a chest
cold that only got worse. Hurston speculated that the illness, coupled with
long-standing family wounds—such as the grudge still alive over her marriage to John and conflicts over family property—and John Hurston's continuous marital infidelity was more than her mother could bear. She became
more frail and had taken to bed. The night before her death, she had sol-
emnly given her daughter Zora certain instructions: "I was not to let them
take the pillow from under her head until she was dead. The clock was not
to be covered, nor the looking-glass." These were among the traditional African American folk rituals of death that Lucy Hurston preferred to forgo.
With the strength of her thirteen years, Zora vowed that she would see to
her mother's wishes. Noticing the women of the village going into her mother's room but not coming out, Zora entered to find them executing the very
rites her mother spoke against. Her promise propelled her to intervene and
shout out her mother's will, "Don't cover up that clock! Leave that looking-
glass like it is! Lemme put Mama's pillow back where it was. But "Papa held
me tight and the others frowned me down."[43]

Crushed by the weight of loss and the grief of a promise unfulfilled, Hurston remembered the momentousness of her mother's death as the end of a
phase in her life: "Mama died at sundown and changed a world. That is, the
world which had been built out of her body and her heart. Even the physical
aspects fell apart with a suddenness that was startling." All eight siblings had
gathered in mourning: "grubby bales of misery, huddled about lamps."[44]
Some in inconsolable grief, others with plaintiff tears, all helplessly trying to
pacify one another. It would be the last time the family was all together.

Shortly after Lucy Potts Hurston was carried to Macedonia Baptist Church
for the last time, the Hurston family, "the world which had been built out of
her body and her heart," began its dissolution.[45] Robert, the oldest returned
to Florida Baptist Academy in Jacksonville. Sarah was also sent to the boarding school, and Zora followed her older sister and brother two weeks later.
When Sarah, too aggrieved and homesick, returned home, she found that
her father had married twenty-year-old Mattie Moge, in February 1905,
Mattie was three years younger than John's oldest child. Mattie's affection for
John Hurston, however, did not extend to his children. And when Sarah
commented on how quickly the two married, Mattie set John Hurston

against his favorite daughter. The young wife influenced her husband to strike Sarah, something he'd never done, and to put her out. Shortly after, Sarah married John Mack and the couple moved to Palmetto.[46]

In Jacksonville, without her sister, the bereaved Zora adjusted as best she could. Jacksonville was not home. It was a strange place, and she felt like a stranger. The warmth and acceptance she enjoyed in Eatonville and its environs, from both blacks and whites, was replaced with coldness and distance and funny-acting white folks. With its segregated streetcars and segregated stores and palpable racism, Jacksonville let Zora know she was "a little colored girl." At the Florida Baptist Academy in Jacksonville, she excelled in her studies, even winning the citywide spelling bee championship for the school. Her transition into the academic life of the school was smooth in contrast to her social transitioning. She was labeled as "sassy" for giving "back talk" to the school's authority figures, and the cliques of girls complained of Zora's perceived intrusive listening in on their conversations. She broke up many of their "'He said' conferences," Hurston confessed. But it was unintentional. She only wanted to listen to the stories, the way she did on Joe Clarke's storefront in Eatonville.[47] Her social discomfort may have intensified with Sarah's leaving only two months into the term. Also, the dubious economic situation in which she found herself exacerbated her discomfiture. Her father had discontinued paying her room and board. The "Second in Command" administrator demanded to know what the thirteen-year-old Zora was going to do about it. Then she stopped calling Zora into the office and started yelling her demanding question out of the window into the schoolyard where Zora might have been playing. "That used to keep me strunk up inside," Hurston wrote. "I got so I wouldn't play too hard. The call might come at any time. My spirits would not have quite so far to fall."[48]

The school was compensated by Zora's physical labor. She was assigned to scrubbing the stair steps every Saturday, cleaning the pantry, and assisting where needed in the kitchen after school. In between her compensatory duties and her schoolwork, Zora found time to write secret love letters fantasizing a "torrid love affair" with Mr. Collier, the school's president, on whom she had a big crush. This "affair," of course, required her to take the competition down a "button hole low." She must pull the prank of placing a wet brick in the bed of the teacher she suspected of horning in on her "husband-in-reserve." When it was discovered that she was behind the prank, the real life President Collier "lifted up my skirt in the rear and spanked a prospective tall, beautiful lady's pants."[49]

The end of the school year found Zora Neale looking out the office window, waiting for her papa. Her brother Bob had immediately left school to take a job. He instructed his younger sister to stay there, at the school until their father sent for her. John Hurston did not come for his daughter. Weeks later, he sent word in a letter that the school could have her. The same administrator who demanded to know how Zora would pay her room and board, had the repugnant task of not only telling this child that her father had given the school permission to adopt her, but also that the school "had no place for a girl so young." Much later, Hurston was to describe her year spent at Florida Baptist as "one of those twilight things. It was not dark, but it lacked the bold sunlight that I craved." "Twilight" is defined as the soft glowing light from the sky when the sun is below the horizon, especially in the evening. It is figuratively defined as an intermediate condition or period; a condition or period of decline or destruction; also, a condition or period of a state of imperfect knowledge or understanding. The twilight cast by Lucy Hurston's "sunset time" initiated an intermediate period of decline in Hurston's life—socially, economically, physically, psychologically, and spiritually. Although she had experienced visions of future life events, her knowledge and understanding of what they entailed, or even why they occurred, was imperfect. How could this now fourteen-year-old adolescent, who had just recently lost her mother, understand this out-and-out rejection by her father? "It was crumbling news for me." Hurston remembered.[50] What crumbled? What expectation died? Did she belong to anyone? Would no one claim her? As with Janie and Jody Starks in *Their Eyes Were Watching God*,[51] was there an image of her father that fell off the shelf?

Hurston reported in her autobiography that she had begun to have visions around nine years of age. "Like stereoptican slides, I saw twelve scenes flash before me." Each in vivid detail foretold her fate:

> I knew I would be an orphan and homeless. I knew that while I was still help-less, that the comforting circle of my family would be broken, and that I would have to wander cold and friendless until I had served my time. I would stand beside a dark pool of water and see a huge fish move slowly away at a time when I would be somehow in the depths of despair. I would hurry to catch a train, with doubts and fear driving me and seek solace in a place and fail to find it when I arrived, then cross many tracks to board the train again. I knew that a house, a shotgun built house that needed a new coat of white paint, held torture for me, but I must go. I saw deep love betrayed, but I must feel and know it. There was no turning back. And last of all, I would come to a big house. Two women waited there for me. I could not see their faces, but I knew one to be young and one to be old. One of them was arranging some queer-shaped flowers such as I had never seen. When I had come to these women, then I would be at the end of my pilgrimage, but not the end of my life. Then I would know peace and love and what goes with those things, and not before.[52]

Two weeks after her mother's death, Zora was sitting on the buckboard next to her brother Dick. He was driving her to the station in Maitland to board the train to Jacksonville, where she would attend Florida Baptist Academy. When Dick approached the curve in the road that skirted Lake Catherine, Hurston wrote that she experienced a flashback: "I saw the first picture of my visions. I had seen myself upon that curve at night leaving the village home, bowed down with grief that was more than common." John Hurston's letter to the school foretold the unfolding of Zora's second vision. Although he did not send for her, she went home anyway. The school administrator paid her $1.50 boat passage. The *City of Jacksonville* side-wheeler docked her at Sanford where she boarded the train for the fifteen miles into Maitland.[53] But the place that was home when her mother was alive was now her father's house, and it was unwelcoming. "The very walls were gummy with gloom." It disturbed her, when she returned home, to find her younger siblings in dire conditions. Raggedly and dirtily clad, they were undernourished with "hit-or-miss meals." It disturbed her to see Mattie Moge, her stepmother, asleep on her mother's feather bed. Lucy Ann had bequeathed the feather bed to Zora. Seeing her stepmother so reclined, recalled a lot of hurt and ignited a lot of repressed anger and resentment. What to do but take the mattress off the bed, reclaim *something* for herself. So much had been taken away. The incident made real the household divide that everyone was tiptoeing around. Mattie refuted Zora's claim and called on her husband John to protect and defend her claim, and to give Zora a thrashing in the process. The siblings sided with their sister and her brother John Cornelius stood toe-to-toe to his father in Zora's defense. It was a standoff pregnant with imminent violence. "Papa had an open knife in his hand," and John Cornelius had defiance in his eyes. John Hurston dropped his hand and ordered his son to leave the house. Mattie Moge lost her privilege "to rack her bones on Mama's feather bed," and the children lost the Papa of their childhood.

> Papa's shoulders began to get tired. He didn't rear back and strut like he used to. His well-cut broadcloth, Stetson hats, hand-made alligator-skin shoes and walking stick had earned him the title of Big Nigger with his children. Behind his back, of course. He didn't put and take with his cane any more. He just walked along. It didn't take him near so long to put on his hat.[54]

After the altercation, the children, one by one, shifted to the homes of their mother's friends. The four older children had already left for good. "So my second vision picture came to be. I had seen myself homeless and uncared for." From late 1906 to 1911, Zora lived from pillar to post. As Hurston put it, "My vagrancy had begun in reality."[55] Even as friends and relatives opened their doors to her, Zora "found comfort nowhere." She was a maturing young woman who, from the point of view of her hosts, should also be contributing to the household. But Hurston longed to be back in school. Not only had she lost her anchor and the stability of family life, she was without books, which had become a great comfort to her. The community consensus, however, was that "[p]eople who had no parents could not afford to sit around on school benches wearing out what clothes they had." Hurston was still only fourteen when she began her attempts at self-support. Looking younger than her years, potential employers were reluctant to hire her. "Does your mother know you're out looking for work?" they queried. She sought domestic work as a maid, nurse, or babysitter. She would find employment, but then soon lose the job. It wasn't that she was lazy, she explained. It was that she was more interested in the reading material she came across than in dusting or dishwashing.[56] Some jobs ended because of family dynamics within the employer's family. Hurston surmised that the $2.00 per week babysitting job she finally landed was terminated because of a husband's insecurity. If the wife was home taking care of their children, the husband had less of her time about which to be suspicious. After being fired from that job, she was hired to attend to a Mrs. Moncrief who was ill. Although the house and its several inhabitants were somber and unsmiling, Zora might have been able to work there a while but for the "chuckle-headed" husband. Mr. Moncrief "took to waylaying me down the street a piece and walking with me." Moncrief told Zora he was "sick and tired of that house full of sour-looking women" and had decided to run off to Canada—with Zora.[57] Zora made her excuses and even threatened to inform Mrs. Moncrief, which she did. Mr. Moncrief, however, was neither distressed nor deterred. He continued with his plans and assumed Zora's complicity:

> I'll come get you. Don't you fool me, now. Just be there. I'm not the kind of man that stands for no fooling. I'm not the kind of man to be worried with so much responsibilities. Never should have let myself get married in the first place. All I need is a young, full-of-feelings girl to sleep with and enjoy my life. I always did keep me a colored girl. My last one moved off to Chicago and sort of left me without. I want a colored girl and I'm giving you the preference.[58]

When Mr. Moncrief came to get Zora, she had moved. She didn't even return for her pay.

Out of that job, Hurston was out of many more jobs that offered more of the same. Her third vision of aimless wandering was upon her when she heard from her brother Richard William. Richard had settled down, married, and sent for her. Finally, Hurston had a ray of hope. "I wanted family love and peace and a resting place. I wanted books and school." Zora went to Sanford, Florida, to join her brother. When she got there, her father "ordered" her to come back to his house.[59] Zora went back to her father's house, but it proved to be an unholy reunion. Maybe John Hurston finally wanted to try to set his compass toward his younger daughter. Maybe he thought he could appease his conscience by making amends with the one child who was closest to his beloved wife. Maybe Zora thought that finally her Papa would acknowledge her and care for her. Maybe Zora thought that she could regain something of her former ease and stability. But, again, there was a woman standing between Zora and her Papa, and this one had neither Zora's welfare nor John Hurston's at heart. Whereas Hurston's mother would prevent John Hurston from chastising Zora, her stepmother, at every opportunity, urged him to beat her. By the time Zora returned home, she was twenty years old. She was a woman grown. After some occurrence or other, Mattie Moge threatened to beat Zora for being a "sassy, impudent, heifer." The threat was only a threat; she assumed John Hurston would naturally intercede and complete the job, as he had done with his older daughter Sarah. Mattie was mistaken. But Mattie didn't know that. So she threw a bottle at Zora's head.

And missed. Unfortunately for Mattie Moge, Zora visited upon her every pent-up frustration, disappointed expectation, unconsoled grief, repressed desire, deferred dream, and lewd and lascivious insult she had to bear from the lowering of Lucy's body into the ground up to that present moment. Mrs. G, a neighbor, who was also a friend of Mattie's, heard the commotion and came to investigate. Hurston's response to Mrs. G's concern was a hatchet she let fly in the direction of the neighbor's head. The hatchet, having struck the wall too close to Mrs. G's head, ended the inquiry. Mrs. G, in turn, flew down the steps, screaming the alarm that Zora "had gone crazy." John Hurston managed to gather his wits about him and pull Zora off of a battered Mattie Moge. Afterward, Mattie commanded John to have Zora arrested. He responded that "he didn't have to do but two things—die and stay black. And then, he would never let [Zora] sleep in jail a night." Her papa's stance must have done something for her soul. For once, her father was in her corner, even though the circumstances in which he finally stood *with* Zora were unfortunate. Mattie took the matter before the church, but the church heard her not. The members were friends of Lucy.[60]

Zora left her wreck of a father and the wreck of his house and sought work in another town. Her job searches were interspersed with leisure hours spent stretched out in the woods, slowly reading Milton's *Paradise Lost*, a volume she found that had been discarded. She eventually found work as a receptionist in a doctor's office. A young woman she met was taking a two-month vacation, and asked Zora to fill in for her. Zora "became so interested and useful" in the office that the doctor was inclined to hire her on a permanent basis and have her trained as a practical nurse should his current receptionist choose not to return. Zora was heartened by her prospects. The possibilities they held, however, paled in light of the letter she received from her brother Bob. Newly graduated from Meharey Medical School, Bob wanted Zora to join him and his wife Wilhemina and their three children Wilhemina, Edgar, and Winnifred. The most thrilling part of his letter was his promise to help Zora return to school. "Nothing can describe my joy," Zora wrote. "I was going to have a home again. I was going to school. I was going to be with my brother! He had remembered me at last. My five haunted years were over!" Boarding the train, Zora waved a good-bye, "not to anybody in particular, but to the town, to loneliness, to defeat and frustration, to shabby living, to sterile houses and numbed pangs, to the kind of people I had no wish to know; to an era." It was near nightfall when Zora sank into the cushioned seat of the train. That night emblazoned itself on her memory: "I shall never forget how the red ball of the sun hung on the horizon and raced along with the train for a short space, and then plunged below the belly-band of the earth. There have been other suns that set in significance for me, but *that* sun!" she exclaimed. "It was a book-mark in the pages of a life. I remember the long strung-out cloud that measured it for the fall."[61]

"*That*" sun, for all its significance, was yet another setting sun, ushering in another intermediary period of misunderstanding and disappointment. Bob rationalized that putting his sister in school immediately would "cause trouble" and inspire resentment in his wife. In the meantime, Zora should help her sister-in-law, look after her nieces and nephew, and generally make herself useful around the house. Upon rising early, she was to make a fire in the kitchen range without disturbing her sister-in-law. After all, she was a mother of three. She needed her rest and deserved the best that her brother could give her. Though Zora enjoyed being with the children and the embrace of the family circle, she "was not happy at all" with Bob's arrangement. "I wanted to get through high school. I had a way of life inside me and I wanted it with a want that was twisting me." Her dream seemed as far off as ever. Not only was she subjected to more domestic labor, but this time she would not even be paid for it. What Bob said to her "didn't sound just right," and what he was doing didn't feel right either. "I was not the father of those children, and several months later I found out what was wrong. It came to me in a flash. She had never borne a child for me, so I did not owe her a thing. Maybe somebody did, but it certainly wasn't I."[62]

Hurston's narrative suggests that there were other unpleasant occurrences, but she preferred not to disclose them. The situation, in any case, compelled her to take her leave. It seems as though Zora was in somewhat of a compromised situation as regards her ability to move about freely. Her communication with a friend who helped her to get her next job is characterized as furtive and surreptitious. This friend "slipped" Zora a message one day to meet at her home. "We had a code. Her son would pass and whistle until I showed myself to let him know I heard. Then he would go on and as soon as I could I would follow." The friend had told Zora about a job as a lady's maid. A singer in the Gilbert and Sullivan Theater Company was in need of a maid since the one she had had left her service to marry. The singer, Miss M, was enchanted with Zora. And though she thought Zora rather youngish, she hired her anyway at $10.00 per week plus expenses. Zora was impressed and elated: "Ten dollars each and every week! Was there that much money in the world sure enough? Com-press-ti-bility!!"[63]

Zora never returned to her brother's house. "I was afraid he would try to keep me," she said. Zora stayed with her friend for the week the company remained in town. When the company moved on, Zora moved with them. "I was the only Negro around," she observed. After a lot of teasing, joking, and "backstage gags," she was a fully initiated member of the group. When their run ended and Miss M had a two-week interval between shows. Zora accompanied Miss M to her home in Boston. They then traveled to Reading, Pennsylvania; Bridgeport, Connecticut; northern Virginia; and Baltimore, Maryland. In 1916 Miss M decided on marriage and encouraged Zora to return to school. "She said she thought I had a mind, and that it would be a shame for me not to have any further training." In Baltimore, Miss M inquired about schools, gave Zora some money, told her to keep in touch, then hugged her good-bye.[64]

Zora had been in Miss M's employ for a year and a half. She realized that all the while she had been in school, though informally. She had learned so much in the areas of literature and music. A member of the company would loan her books to read and she became knowledgeable about light and grand opera and European classical music. She even gained insights into notions of "race" and race relations. The company consisted of more than thirty people of differing races and classes, yet they were all living a communal life. Within her nuclear group were people of Anglo-Saxon, Irish, and Jewish backgrounds. This experience gave Zora an approach to racial understanding, and discouraged in her any racial sensitivity and racial consciousness.

> I found out too that you are bound to be jostled in the "crowded street of life." That in itself need not be dangerous unless you have the open razors of personal vanity in your pants pocket. The passers-by don't hurt you, but if you go around like that, they make you hurt yourself.[65]

Hurston wrote affectionately of her time with the theater company: "I had been sitting by a warm fire for a year and a half and had gotten used to the feel of peace." As her run with the troupe came to an end, seven of her twelve visions also ended. She was relieved that the seventh vision, depicting the shotgun house that represented torture, had come and gone. What next, she pondered. "It was not all clear to me how I was going to do it, but I was going back to school."[66]

TWO

The Pathless Path

Zora Neale Hurston did not love school—but she loved learning. She received her formal, academic training from Hungerford Normal and Industrial School. It was a model school, it was progressive, it was in the South, and, like Eatonville, it was "all-Negro."

The school attracted a stream of northern, white visitors. Some wanted to satisfy their curiosity. Others wanted to extend their philanthropic support. And some aspired to both. Mrs. Johnstone and Miss Hurd were two among the stream of visitors to the school. Accustomed to such visits, the school's founders and principals Mr. Russell and Mrs. Mary Calhoun would admonish the students to be scrubbed, coiffed, shod, and prepared in their lessons. The students then would greet the visitors with a spiritual, led by Principal Calhoun. Mrs. Johnstone and Miss Hurd, however, appeared unannounced. After a bit of scrambling about and regrouping, Mr. Calhoun called the fifth-grade class, Zora's class, to the front of the room.

The fifth graders had recently begun a new lesson in their readers. It was the Greco-Roman story of Pluto and Persephone. Each student took a turn in reading successive paragraphs. They stumbled over words or spelled and sounded out the words under their breath, testing them before presenting them to the ears of their audience. Hurston allowed that the story "was new and hard to the class in general."[1] Her schoolmates put forth the best effort they could under the circumstances. But Mr. Calhoun saw nothing to be proud of until Zora Neale Hurston recited.

Alerted by the reading of the student next to her, Zora stood poised to read her paragraph:

Yes, Jupiter had seen her (Persephone). He had seen the maiden picking flowers in the field. He had seen the chariot of the dark monarch pause by the maiden's side. He had seen him when he seized Persephone. He had seen the black horses leap down Mount Aetna's fiery throat. Persephone was now in Pluto's dark realm and had made her his wife.[2]

She practically sang the story she knew it so well. As soon as Zora's father had gotten her the reader, she read it "from lid to lid." Of the myths she read, Jupiter and Persephone was one of her favorites. "I was exalted by it," Hurston wrote, "and that is the way I read my paragraph."[3] Zora's audience was exalted, too. Mrs. Johnstone and Miss Hurd looked at each other. They were impressed, and Mr. Calhoun smiled his pride. Thrilled by her musical reading of the tale, Mr. Calhoun asked Zora to read to the end of it, which she did happily.

Mr. Calhoun then dismissed the class and talked with the two visiting philanthropists. After a flurry of words, he sent for Zora. She was introduced to the guests who asked if she loved school. "I lied that I did. There was *some* truth in it," Hurston explained in her autobiography. She liked geography and recess, but "[w]hoever it was invented writing and arithmetic got no thanks from me." She also found the institution's power dynamic problematic. Who authorized teachers "to sit up there with a palmetto stem and lick me whenever they saw fit," she complained. It was an arrangement in which she felt powerless, and that did not sit well with this spirited youngster who was affectionately and enviously referred to as "Old Smarty." Old Smarty "knew better than to air such grievances before guests, so, yes," she said, "I *loved* school."[4]

So impressed were these guests that they invited Zora to their Park House hotel room in Maitland. Testing her with a paragraph from a copy of *Scribner's Magazine*, these guests found Zora's reading and comprehension skills authentic and incredible. Her reading of the material they'd selected convinced them. On that day, in recognition of her intellectual gifts, they gave her a cylinder of 100 "goldy-new pennies." On the next day, Zora received a white leather-bound Episcopal hymnal, a copy of the *Swiss Family Robinson*, and a book of fairy tales. A month later, they sent from their Chicago home, "a huge box packed with clothes and books." That first day when she returned home with the cylinder, her mother allowed her to play with her golden mountain of pennies. They "lit up the world." In the clothes, second-hand but very good, "I shone like the morning sun." If the clothes made her external appearance radiant, the books excited her internal brilliance. *Gulliver's Travels*, Grimm's Fairy Tales, Dick Whittington, Greek and Roman Myths, and Norse Tales were among the trove she received and absorbed. The Norse Tales stirred her most deeply. With all the maturity of her youthful years, she resonated with the "great and good Odin" whose purchase of a drink from the well of knowledge was the price of an eye: "Odin drank deeply, then plucked out one eye." "That," said Hurston, "held majesty for me." But it was Hercules whom she resolved to be like. Hercules, but a youth himself, put his hand in the hand of duty. Pleasure looked on as Hercules followed duty's "steep way to the blue hills of fame and glory."[5] Zora pledged to travel her own path into those blue hills.

Zora also read the Bible enthusiastically. Once she was locked in her mother's room as punishment for repeating something she overheard a neighbor say. The only thing to read was the Bible. "I happened to open to the place where David was doing some mighty smiting, and I got interested." Of all the personages in the Old Testament, David was outstanding: "David went here and he went there, and no matter where he went, he smote 'em hip and thigh. Then he sung songs to his harp a while, and went out and smote some more." In company with her friend Carrie Roberts, Zora ventured into Leviticus. "There were exciting things in there to a child eager to know the facts of life."[6] The curious Zora moved on to "the Doctor Book," which elaborated on those facts gleaned from Leviticus.

During these early years, she developed an unquenchable thirst for knowledge and for experiences that excited and gratified her soul's longing. "In a way this early reading gave me great anguish through all my childhood and adolescence," Hurston wrote. "My soul was with the gods and my body in the village."[7] When young Zora chose to leave Memphis with the Gilbert and Sullivan Theater Company, she had already left the village, and she had left family members who were a reminder of the restrictions and constraints of the village. What never left her were the thirst for knowledge and the desire for expansive and enlightening experience.

She was "[b]lack, out walking on fly-paper again," Zora winced when she parted company with Miss M. Yet she wanted to get into school. For, she knew, even without Miss M's telling her, that she would benefit from further formal academic training. School meant tuition, registration fees, books, and general living expenses. But Zora had only what little money Miss M could spare her. She had not saved any because "theatrical salaries being so uncertain," Zora said, "I did not get mine half the time." Zora got a job waiting tables. It was not an emotionally or intellectually rewarding job. Patrons were either "at the old game of 'stealing a feel'" or, if "educated," regarded her with incredulity if she "seemed to listen" to the conversation. During this time, Zora was diagnosed with appendicitis and admitted to the free ward of the Maryland General Hospital. On her way to the operating room, Zora wasn't too concerned about dying, "Nobody would miss me," she thought, and she "had no treasures to leave behind." Living was the question. So Zora made a wager with God: "I bet God that if I lived, I would try to find out the vague directions whispered in my ears and find the road it seemed that I must follow. How? When? Why? What? All those answers were hidden from me."[8]

The answers to at least two of Zora's questions would manifest themselves: The how was school; the when was *now*. Waking up later than expected in the recovery room, Zora scared the doctor and nurses. As she regained consciousness, she remembered her promise. "I was alive, so I had to win my bet with God."[9] Back on her feet, she got another job as a waitress and tried other means to earn enough money to return to school. She operated a confectionery, selling items such as soft drinks and cigarettes out of the house she shared with Martha Tucker. Zora likely worked with her sister Sarah also. Sarah and John Mack had recently moved to Baltimore where Sarah set up an in-home dining service.[10] All Zora's efforts at earning the money to go to school came to naught. "My clothes were practically gone. Nickeling and dimering along was not getting me anywhere." It was 1917. Zora was twenty-six. She was frustrated with "jumping up and down in my own foot tracks." She decidedly pulled out. "I just went."[11] What made her decision possible was her willingness to tell the lie that would allow her to live her truth. In Maryland, "all colored youths between six and twenty-six years of age" were allowed free admission into the public schools. Zora's youthful appearance did not call attention to the 1901 birth year she entered on her application form. It was "a quiet act of revolution."[12]

Zora went to night school in Baltimore. One of her teachers was Dwight O. W. Holmes, whom she described as "a pilgrim to the horizon." Everything about him made the way seem clear and encouraged her to stay the path that led to the horizon. Night school, "did something for my soul," Hurston recollected. With Dwight Holmes's tacit corroboration of her intellectual capabilities, Zora was spurred on to register in the high school department of Morgan College. Still with no money and not even a notable family reference to recommend her, Zora "just went" to this elite black institution, too. She met with Dean William Pickens who gave her an assessment examination, credited her with two years of high school, and on September 17, 1917, admitted her to Morgan Academy, a black prep school.

The dean and his wife assisted Zora in securing employment and housing. She would be employed by Dr. Baldwin, a white clergyman and trustee of Morgan College. Baldwin's wife had broken her hip, so needed assistance dressing and undressing and general attention. Zora would provide the service. In turn, Dr. Baldwin would give Zora room and board and $2.00 per week. And, in addition to a tuition waiver, she had the bonus of the Baldwins's library. Her hungry eyes feasted. Committing Gray's *Elegy in a Country Courtyard* to memory, then *Ballad of Reading Gaol*, then *The Rubayiat*, "I acted as if the books would run away." With social and economic stability, Zora could finally apply herself to her studies.[13]

Zora entered Morgan Academy with "one dress, a change of underwear, and one pair of tan oxfords." Her enthusiasm, however, tipped the scale. The well-heeled students of her class took no notice of her wardrobe, except to extend it by loans from their own. What they recognized more was her brilliant mind. Old Smarty was newly dubbed "old Knowledge Bug" by a newfound and less intellectually oriented friend, Bernice Hughes, who observed Hurston's depth and breadth of knowledge. Zora's English and history teachers, as well, recognized her abilities and entrusted their classes to her in their absence. Her brilliance shone also in the school's oratorical contest, in which she placed second.[14]

Hurston excelled in history and English, did comparatively well in science and music and was routinely given a "C" in math. "Why should A minus B? Who the devil was X anyway?" These were questions that she did not feel compelled to answer. "I was at last doing the things I wanted to do. Every new thing I learned in school made me happy." Zora's self-declared first literary publication "was on the blackboard in the assembly hall at Morgan. I decided to write an allegory using the faculty members as characters."[15]

While Hurston was busy with her studies in Maryland, the summer of her 1917–18 academic year, her father died. He had moved to Memphis where Zora's brother Bob still lived. On August 10, 1917, an oncoming train struck his automobile, and he was killed.

At the end of her first year at Morgan, Zora anticipated completing her high school curriculum and remaining at Morgan for undergraduate study. However, Mae Miller, first cousin of Bernice Hughes, convinced Zora that she was "Howard material." Buoyed by the willing support of her friends and their families, Zora was persuaded. "You can live at our house, Zora! Bernice offered.... Then you won't have any room and board to pay. We'll all get together and wrestle you up a job to make your tuition."[16]

The summer of 1918 found Zora in Washington, D.C. She had secured a job as a waitress at the Cosmos Club, a Jim Crow establishment servicing "Washington's intellectual aristocracy."[17] She took her earnings and tips to the Registrar's window at Howard. To enroll in Howard for that first quarter, however, required more money than she had and more credits than what she had acquired at Morgan. Disappointed, Zora was ready to "give up and call it a day."[18] Dwight Holmes, now a teacher at Howard, happened to be there. He gave her encouragement and advice. "He saved my spirits again," Hurston said. She made the Promethean effort to stay the course. On December 2, 1918, Zora enrolled in Howard Academy and was graduated in May 1919 with her high school diploma. She eagerly began her Howard University courses that fall.[19]

Zora sat in her first college assembly. Her heart was full of the knowledge and appreciation for Howard University and what it represented: "the capstone of Negro education in the world. It was to the Negro what Harvard was to the whites." It was the place where "gather[ed] Negro money, beauty, and prestige." Zora felt gratitude and privilege. "I was so exalted that I said to the spirit of Howard, 'You have taken me in. I am a tiny bit of your greatness. I swear to you that I shall never make you ashamed of me.'" She pledged to do her class work and "be worthy to stand there under the shadow of the hovering spirit of Howard." To support herself and her studies at Howard, Zora worked at the G Street Barber Shop as a manicurist, a trade she learned while in the employ of Miss M. The G Street Shop was one of a chain of racially segregated barbershops owned and operated by George Robinson, an African American businessman. The downtown Washington, D.C., shop where Zora worked catered to whites only. She worked daily from 3:30 to 8:30 P.M. Realizing that she was an aspiring student who needed to work, her customers tipped her accordingly. With an average weekly income of $12 to $15, Zora could support her studies at Howard and dress for success.[20]

Work and school demanded most of Zora's attention. She carried a full schedule of classes during the day and studied at night after work. At Howard, it was literature professor Dr. Lorenzo Dow Turner who stimulated her imagination. "Listening to him, I decided that I must be an English teacher and lean over my desk and discourse on the 18-century poets, and, explain the roots of the modern novel." The energetic Zora found time for socializing and for extracurricular activities. She met Herbert Arnold Sheen of Decatur, Illinois, in 1920. A handsome and vigorous twenty-three years old, Sheen was the son of a Methodist minister who, like Zora, was working his way through school at Howard. Sheen "could stomp a piano out of this world, sing a fair baritone and dance beautifully." Zora noticed him. "He noticed me, too, and I was carried away," she recounted. It was a mutually respectful and warm embracing. It was the first time since her mother's death, Hurston reflected, that she felt close to someone.[21] Zora balanced out her social agenda with membership in the Zeta Phi Beta Sorority and in the Howard Players, the school's theatrical troupe. Perhaps inspired by Dr. Turner, Zora pursued her literary interests in a more formal manner. She submitted a poem, "O Night," and a short story, "John Redding Goes to Sea," to *The Stylus*, the journal of the literary society of the same name which was cofounded by Professors Montgomery Gregory and Alain Locke. The society had nineteen members, and membership was determined on a competitive basis. Semiannual contests were held, soliciting short manuscripts. Successful participants became members. The society's purpose was that of "stimulating and producing authors and artists within the race."[22]

Hurston's publication in *The Stylus* and her membership in the society led her to ever-widening literary circles. She became a participant in Georgia Douglas Johnson's literary salon. In the living room of Johnson's Washington, D.C., home was a meeting of minds that would later become part of the New Negro Movement. Among those who attended the Saturday night soirees were Sterling Brown, Angelina Grimke, Jean Toomer, Richard Bruce Nugent, Rudolph Fisher, James Weldon Johnson, W.E.B. Du Bois, and Alain Locke. Georgia Douglas Johnson's meetings foreshadowed Charles Spurgeon Johnson's March 21, 1924, meeting at the New York Civic Club. The dinner, which brought together New Negro writers and pundits and white writers, editors, and publishers was a kind of "dress rehearsal of what was soon to be known as the 'Harlem Renaissance.'"[23]

At Alain Locke's urging, Charles Johnson read Hurston's "John Redding Goes to Sea." The story might be considered an excellent example of the adage advising beginners to write about what you know. It is the story of protagonist John Redding who lives in a rural village in Florida near Jacksonville. John's character is modeled after the young Zora and the setting reflects Hurston's hometown of Eatonville. Described as "an imaginative child and fond of day-dreaming," even John's desires recall the expressed wishes of the child Zora. John Redding, too, would ride "away to the horizon" on a "fiery charger."[24] The story revolves around John's wish to explore the world beyond his little village, where the "indolent atmosphere" was stifling to him. Years later John seemed determined to leave. But his mother's refusal to consent to his leaving and his wife's insecurities made John a "home-tied" man. He was like the little ships he made from dry twigs in his childhood. John would set them afloat on the St. John's River only to see them caught, not very far downstream, among the weeds that prevented them from going out to sea. In an accident caused by storm-raised waters, John is killed and his body is allowed to float freely "away toward Jacksonville, the sea, the wide world—at last."[25]

Hurston's characters are early casts of "the folk," the rural people who speak in the black vernacular and repair to the natural world and the spiritual world to explain and influence the lives they live. Much to Alfred Redding's chagrin, his wife Mattie believes that John's desire to see and explore the world beyond his village was due to conjure. Mattie Redding was convinced that "ole witch Judy" put travel dust in her yard when John was born. She speculated this act to be Judy's revenge for Mattie marrying Alfred, whom Judy wanted as a husband for her own daughter. Both Locke and Charles Johnson saw the potential in Hurston's work. As "press agent" of the New Negro Movement and as a member of the "advance-guard" of the Harlem Renaissance, Alain Locke encouraged "the younger writers" to explore the folk roots of African American culture. Formerly shunned and stigmatized as backward and inferior, African American folk culture was to be examined and reevaluated, and African American history was to be investigated and embraced. Harlem Renaissance pundits argued that America's "only genuine folk tradition" was to be found in the life and lore of marginalized Negroes.[26] The only distinctly American contribution to world culture and civilization was that produced by black folk whose origins were African—not European. This phenomenal and distinctly racial contribution to American society was to be the New Negro's entrée into full citizenship and equal social status in a society that was dominated by a "whites only" mentality. Thus the Harlem Intelligentsia encouraged the exploration and artistic adaptation of the black folk ethos. The mandate was to "promote poetry, prose, painting, and music as if their lives depended on it."[27]

As editor of *Opportunity,* the journal of the National Urban League, Charles Johnson sought to create a venue designed to give voice to the New Negro. *Opportunity,* like *The Crisis* (published by the National Association for the Advancement of Colored People), *The Negro World* (organ of the Universal Negro Improvement Association), and *The Messenger* (edited by

A. Philip Randolph and Chandler Owen), sought to address "The Negro Problem," to bear witness to racial injustice and violence and seek social, political, and economic parity and equal opportunity for Negroes. The editors of these publications equated value and worth with the perceived richness or bareness of their culture. They saw art as a tool for social and political propaganda and, therefore, championed artistic expression. No matter how competitive these journals were or what political strategies each advocated, in the matter of art, they were all on the same page.

Charles Johnson saw Hurston's story as an example of "Negro life as it is." He inquired whether she might have materials to submit to *Opportunity*. Hurston sent him "Drenched in Light." More closely autobiographical than "John Redding," "Drenched in Light" was the humorous story of lil' Isis Watts who, like the author, sat atop the gate post, hailing travelers going up to Sanford, Florida, or down to Orlando. Isis, the joyful, was compelled to maintain her post as well as walk along, drive along, or ride along on horseback with the travelers. This tendency drove her Grandma Potts to distraction. In addition to this "brazenness," Isis's behavior was not that befitting someone "of the female persuasion." Playing with boys, romping with dogs, sitting with knees apart, and whistling were actions that demanded Grandma's best excoriating criticism and invited the ever-threatening peach hickories. Trying to shave her grandma and dancing and prancing at the town's barbecue, draped in her grandma's just-bought, never-been-used red tablecloth shifted Grandma's aggravation from distracted to "frackshus." "You're gointuh ketchit f'um yo' haid to yo' heels m'lady," Grandma promised. As fate—or joy—would have it, Helen, a kind lady traveler who had befriended her, saved Isis from this abomination. Helen paid Grandma $5 for her $1 tablecloth and requested Isis's company at her Orlando hotel: "I just want a little of her sunshine to soak into my soul. I need it."[28]

This story continued the folk aesthetic present in Hurston's first story. The characteristic dialect and humor would become signature aspects of Hurston's writing. Charles Johnson published "Drenched in Light" in the December 1924 issue of *Opportunity*. Hurston reflected, "He wrote me a kind letter and said something about New York. So, beginning to feel the urge to write, I wanted to be in New York." Hurston had completed a year and a half at Howard when she became ill. Consequently, she had no money for tuition and could not continue with her classes. Johnson's invitation created another option for her: "Being out of school for lack of funds, and wanting to be in New York, I decided to go there and try to get back in school in that city. So the first week of January, 1925, found me in New York with $1.50, no job, no friends, and a lot of hope."[29] At the very least, though, Hurston had the support of Charles Johnson and his wife who invited her over for home-cooked meals and gave her fare for transportation. Johnson encouraged Hurston to enter *Opportunity*'s first annual literary contest, which she did.

That spring on May 1, 1925, Hurston attended the *Opportunity* award banquet. She had won the second-place award in fiction for "Spunk" and an honorable mention for her short story "Black Death." She also won second-place in drama for *Color Struck* and honorable mention for her play *Spears*.[30] Against the backdrop of the folk community, its funeral rites and beliefs concerning death and the hereafter, Hurston develops in "Spunk" the theme of heterosexual relationships and marital infidelity. As his name implies, Spunk Banks is brash, bold, and "ain't skeerd of nothing on God's green footstool"[31] That includes Joe Canty, the husband of the woman he is seeing, Delia Canty. Although afraid to trembling, Joe Canty confronts Banks and is killed in the act. At work in the sawmill, Banks falls on the blade and is killed. With his dying breath, he tells the men around him that Joe's spirit had come back from the grave and pushed him. In *Color Struck*, Hurston presents the theme of intraracial color prejudice. The play dramatizes a young woman's insecurities about her dark skin pigmentation. She is jealous and envious of light-skinned blacks and loathes her own dark-skinned self. Given her inferiority complex, she can't imagine that anyone could find her color beautiful. This belief causes her to lose someone who loves her.

At the party that followed the *Opportunity* award banquet, Hurston met and mingled with the contest judges, guests, and other award winners. Several of these guests would prove instrumental in helping Hurston to establish herself in New York. Among them were author and Barnard College founding trustee Annie Nathan Meyer, popular novelist Fannie Hurst, and author and "man-about-town" Carl Van Vechten. Charles Johnson's award ceremonies were designed to bring about such happy consequences: "White critics whom everybody knew, Negro writers whom nobody knew—meeting on common ground."[32] Meyer facilitated Hurston's admission to Barnard and helped her secure funding. In September 1925, she enrolled as an English major. Hurston wrote her thanks and enthusiasm to Meyer. "I am tremendously encouraged now. My typewriter is clicking away till all hours of the night. I am striving desperately for a toe-hold on the world.... No, no, the little praise I received does not affect me unless it be to make me work furiously. Instead of a pillow to rest upon, it is a goad to prod me. I know that I can only get into the sunlight by work and remain there by more work." Fannie Hurst also sought Hurston out and, at Meyer's suggestion, offered Hurston employment and a place to stay. "I have been with Miss Hurst one week today," a letter from Hurston to Meyer read. "I am very happy with the arrangement and I think that she is satisfied, too. I answer letters for her, the telephone, go errands and anything she wants done.[33] This arrangement ended after a month, but it was the beginning of an enduring friendship.

Of Barnard, Hurston "had no lurid tales to tell."[34] Sometimes her classmates teased her about her French pronunciations. But Hurston had learned from her childhood and her days with the Gilbert and Sullivan Company how to take teasing. Besides, she had prepared her recitations so well, that one of the students who joked at her expense "asked to quiz with me. I know getting mad would not help me. I had to get my lessons so well that their laughter would seem silly." "I strive so much harder now for those things that I want," she wrote to Annie Meyer. "You see, being at Barnard and measuring arms with others known to be strong increases my self love and stiffens my spine."[35]

Hurston met Barnard's academic challenges and fell in with the "Social Register crowd," accepting and receiving invitations for lunch and tea and other such affairs. She described herself as Barnard's "sacred black cow." Although always preoccupied with financial arrangements and making ends meet, she was, nonetheless, intellectually productive, and she was having a ball. "I suppose you want to know how this little piece of darkish meat feels at Barnard," she queried Constance Sheen, Herbert Sheen's sister. "I am received quite well. In fact I am received so well that if someone would come along and try to turn me white I'd be quite peevish at them.[36] Hurston's popularity among the Barnard folks was quite likely enhanced by her affiliation with best-selling author Fannie Hurst. But Hurst's attention could only have enhanced what was already there.

Hurston also got on well with the New Negroes of the Harlem Renaissance. She became one of a core group of "the younger Negro artists," whom she and Wallace Thurman affectionately and defiantly dubbed "the Niggerati." The constant luminaries of this group included Hurston, Thurman, Langston Hughes, Dorothy West, Richard Bruce Nugent, Countee Cullen, Gwendolyn Bennett, Aaron Douglass, and Augusta Savage among others. Hurston's New York flat was often a gathering place and sometimes a home for the growing and changing members of the gang. Among her Harlem crew, Hurston was an engaging raconteur who was "full of side-splitting anecdotes, humorous tales, and tragicomic stories.... She could make you laugh one minute and cry the next."[37] Bruce Nugent warmly remembered Hurston as someone who could glance the inside track of a person. She knew when you were hungry, he reminisced. "She always knew when you were and always did something about it. Not just food, but anything that you might be hungry for." Very clear, Hurston knew her own mind and spoke it. She was "one of the most alive people" he knew.[38]

At that time, Zora's ambitions lay in becoming a writer and a professor of English. But anthropology caught her attention, or rather a paper she submitted in Dr. Gladys Reichard's class caught the attention of the Anthropology Department and that of Franz Boas. Boas recognized Hurston's genius immediately. He anticipated the contributions she could make in the newly burgeoning field of anthropology and immediately began to cultivate her skills. By the summer of 1926, Hurston was conducting fieldwork in Harlem, measuring the heads of African Americans for anthropometric studies. Also, under the supervision of Melville Herskovits, a former student of Boas, she was engaged in social anthropological research, involving a study of families. Even though Hurston continued her literary pursuits, she became more and more drawn to anthropology.

At the same time, like other Harlem Renaissance artists, she was becoming more articulate about her political and aesthetic ideology and her role as

a writer. The established Black Intelligentsia, "the older Negroes," had definite concepts about the New Negro and how he was to be portrayed.
Endowed with a genteel morality, the New Negro was to be representative of
"the Race." Writers and artists were to use ideas and images to solve the
"Negro Problem." Hurston and her compeers protested the directives. They
believed art to be the independent expression of the artist, not social or
political propaganda in service to a determined cause. At the same time, they
made the folk, not the bourgeois talented tenth, the center of their artistic
expression.

Discussions of such issues led to collaboration on *Fire!!*, which would
express the views of the Harlem Renaissance artists. Hurston, Wallace,
Hughes, Bennet, Douglass, and John P. Davis broke rank with their 1926
publication of *Fire!!* Described as "a Negro quarterly of the arts," *Fire* was
created with the intention to chart a new course:

> [*Fire!!*] would burn up a lot of the old, dead conventional Negro-white ideas
> of the past, *épater le bourgeois* into a realization of the existence of the younger
> Negro writers and artists, and provide us with an outlet for publication not
> available in the limited pages of the small Negro magazines.[39]

Hurston's contribution to the quarterly was her play *Color Struck* and the
short story "Sweat," the story of the church-going washerwoman Delia Jones.
Delia triumphs over her cruel and unfaithful husband, Sykes. Desirous of
taking the house that has been paid for with Delia's sweat and giving it to
his woman Bertha, Sykes plots his wife's death. He puts a rattlesnake in the
house, assuming it will eventually bite his wife. But "whatever goes over the
Devil's back, is got to come under his belly."[40] By a twist of fate, it is Sykes
who is bitten by the serpent and dies as Delia looks on.

Hurston also began to explore and more actively develop her interests in
dramatic production. More specifically, she was interested in creating an
authentic Negro theater. In addition to writing plays at this time, she also
worked in collaboration with W.E.B. Du Bois who had comparable ideas.
"Do you think Krigwa [*sic*] would be interested in a play with music?" Hurston wrote him. "I have been absent by necessity, but I am working for the
project just the same."[41] The project was the Little Negro Theatre, called
originally the Crigwa Players (Crisis Guild of Writers and Artists), which
produced propagandistic drama and influenced similar productions by
others.

The 1926 fall term brought Hurston closer to completing her Barnard
studies. Hurston's course work and research were bringing her recognition
in the field of anthropology. Her achievements were acknowledged and honored by membership in the American Folk-Lore Society, the American
Ethnological Society, and the American Anthropological Society.[42] She had
but a few courses and an exit examination in French remaining when Franz
Boas informed her that she had received a $1,400 Fellowship to collect folk-
lore. Carter G. Woodson, founder and director of the Association for the

Study of Negro Life and History, granted $700 that was matched by the American Folklore Society. The fellowship was to support Hurston for a six-month period while she researched beliefs and customs, for both Boas and Woodson, and investigated historical sites and materials for Woodson. She would also conduct an interview with Kossola Cudjo Lewis. Hurston and Boas both reasoned that Hurston should begin her expedition by collecting lore in the familiar territory of the South, in Florida, at home, in Eatonville, "the city of five lakes, three croquet courts, three hundred brown skins, three hundred good swimmers, plenty guavas, two schools and no jail house."[43]

In February 1927, Hurston headed South, stopping first in Jacksonville where her brother John Cornelius lived. She and her brother discussed the practicalities of her project and concluded that it would be best for Hurston to purchase a car and avoid travel by common carrier. Not only were Jim Crow accommodations for blacks unseemly and objectionable, the places in which Hurston would be collecting lore were not accessible by public transportation. And all the things of which a little colored girl was supposed to be afraid still loomed large in America for the adult black woman traveling alone. But whatever trepidation Hurston may have experienced, her courage was stronger. She bought a chrome-plated pistol to keep courage company.

"Well if it ain't Zora Hurston!" the crowd uttered as they gathered around Sassie Susie to meet and greet. The homefolks were glad to see that "the world had not been all together unkind to Mama's child."[44] They welcomed Hurston with open hearts and open doors. Her childhood friend Armetta Jones and her husband Ellis made room for her at their place. Hurston was pleased to know that they were still full of the "[s]ame love of talk and song" she remembered from her youth. For some fresh-baked gingerbread and buttermilk, they were willing to recount those "big ole lies" she wanted to record, although they were doubtful as to who would "want to read all them old-time tales about Brer Rabbit and Brer Bear."[45]

Hurston was happy to be basking in the warmth of home and in the radiance of the Florida sun. She felt proud that Franz Boas, America's leading anthropologist whom she revered as the "King of Kings," had such confidence in her as to send her into the field alone. An exacting scientist who had tolerance only for clearly substantiated objective facts, he obviously believed in her abilities. Initially, Hurston was satisfied with what she was collecting. Personal letters from the field to friends in New York might be enhanced with excerpts from her field notes, describing speech patterns, lexical items, transcriptions of jokes, or proverbial expressions. She would write to Langston Hughes, "Getting some gorgeous material down here, verse and prose, *magnificent*." With an eye toward a folk opera on which they were to collaborate, she wrote, "Shall save some juicy bits for you and me." Her letter to Boas reporting her activities and her progress also shared her professional observations. "You see, the Negro is not living his lore to the extent of the Indian. He is not on a reservation, being kept pure. His negroness is being rubbed off by close contact with white culture." She believed it fortuitous "that it is being collected now." Hurston alerted Boas to the materials she was sending him "under separate cover," informed him of conjure items she had collected for the museum, addressed some financial matters, and indicated the next towns on her itinerary: Armstrong, Palatka, Sanford. She could be reached by general delivery.[46]

"When I pitched head foremost into the world," Hurston wrote in her introduction to *Mules and Men*, "I landed in the crib of negroism. From the earliest rocking of my cradle, I had known about the capers Brer Rabbit is apt to cut and what the Squinch Owl says from the housetop."[47] With the "spy-glass of anthropology," Hurston had acquired the psychological distance necessary to examine and study her culture and, in reality, herself. The discipline of anthropology gave her the objectivity to realize the value of the black folklore she knew so intimately and the great contribution to social sciences she was making in the collecting of the material. But she was also a novice, an apprentice collecting lore. The approach she was instructed to use rendered the collecting process impersonal and awkward for her. In observing the customs and cultural expressions of the folk, she was to emphasize form, method, and processes versus content. She was to be the objective, scientific observer.

This methodology, along with inexperience and her Barnardese mannerisms, resulted in an unsatisfactory yield. Toward the end of her fieldwork, Hurston did not feel so pleased. Also, she had felt pressured. She complained to Annie Meyer that "both Dr. Boas and Dr. Woodson are rushing me like thunder along. I need at least a whole year to do what I am doing in six months."[48] "I got a few little items," she sighed. "But it was not enough to make a flea a waltzing jacket." Reflecting on her field research experiences in *Dust Tracks*, Hurston wrote, "My first six months were disappointing." Though dissatisfied with the quality and quantity of material she gathered, Hurston enjoyed her time in the field. In addition to her Eatonville homecoming and the opportunity to test herself as a social scientist, she took advantage of her time in the South to visit with her brothers, Bob and Ben. They updated each other on family matters, and she and Bob reconciled. He regretted not realizing his sister's passion for school and not being more supportive. It was a "happy interval" for Hurston, who left feeling, once again, the "warm embrace of kin and kind."[49]

On May 19, 1927, midway through her six-month expedition, Hurston and her Howard University sweetheart promised each other connubial bliss. "Yes, I'm married now, Mrs. Herbert Arnold Sheen, if you please," Hurston confided to Dorothy West and Helene Johnson whom she warmly referred to as her "Little Sisters."[50] Herbert had taken some time away from his medical studies at the University of Chicago to meet Hurston in St. Augustine, Florida, for their marriage. It "should have been the happiest day of my life," Hurston contemplated in *Dust Tracks*, but "this was not the expected bright dawn." Herbert Sheen had been the main attraction throughout Hurston's collegiate years, and except for two "fallings-out," the couple had had a pleasant relationship. Yet, "I was assailed by doubts," she wrote. "For the first time since I met him, I asked myself if I really were in love, or if this had been a habit."[51] When Zora Neale Hurston experiences "lifeprints,"[52] she is conscious of something deeply moving or personally profound—such as her mountain of goldy-new pennies, the moment of her mother's death, learning of her father's abandonment of her, the train ride to her brother's home to be finally reclaimed. With such lifeprints, with Hurston, there is always a symbolic image of light, indicating that she has been deeply touched emotionally and spiritually. But her wedding day?

> The day and the occasion did not underscore any features of nature nor circumstance, and I wondered why. Who had cancelled the well-advertised tour of the moon? Somebody had turned a hose on the sun. What I had taken for eternity turned out to be a moment walking in its sleep.[53]

The image most consistent in Hurston's vivid depiction of personally profound experiences is the sun. How the sun is depicted gauges her emotional and spiritual state. In relation to her marriage to Herbert, she wondered who had "turned a hose on the sun." Instead of sunrise, "some vagrant ray cloaked as dawn had played a trick on the night."[54]

In spite of the doubts and "dark shadows," Hurston said, "I do," and Herbert joined his wife in her fieldwork. Herbert Sheen, however, was not interested in the Florida backwoods, so he wasn't an ideal companion for a wife who "was full of her work."[55] In Hurston's correspondence to her Little Sisters, she instructed them to "write me still by my maiden name as I don't want my mail balled up." Her statement seems also to have had reverberations for her life. Although she indicated to them that her husband pleased her and boasted of "having a hubby to look out for me now," Sheen went back North and Hurston remained in the South and continued with her work.[56]

In Mobile, Hurston interviewed Kossola Cudjo Lewis, the last living captive of the *Chlotilde*, the reputed last ship to bring Africans to the United States. Afterward, while investigating the environs of New Orleans, she had a chance run-in with Langston Hughes. Hughes had been invited to read his poetry at Fisk University's June commencement ceremony. He was on an impromptu tour of the South and happily accepted Hurston's invitation to join her on her drive north, taking the back roads. Unlike Sheen, Hughes was interested in Hurston's work, particularly, and in the Southern folk, generally. Thus, Hurston had in Hughes a congenial companion. On their trip back north, they stopped at jook joints, attended country church services and musical performances, met with conjurers, and supped with turpentine and dock workers. They had the fortune of catching a performance by Bessie Smith, who just happened to be staying at the same hotel in Macon, Georgia. They gave a few lectures at Tuskegee and visited Jean Toomer's farm.[57] Sassy Susie crisscrossed the back roads leaving the South. In the intimacy of the car, the miles behind and the miles ahead syncopated with laughter, collaboration, and confidences shared. They became friends. In early September, they drove into New York.

One of the confidences Hurston shared with Hughes was that she was a new bride. One that Hughes shared with Hurston was that he was the "godson" of Charlotte Osgood Mason. Charlotte Mason was the wealthy widow of Rufus Osgood Mason. She had a keen interest in Native American and African American culture and was a patron of the arts. Inspired by a lecture given by Alain Locke on African art, Mason, with Locke as her advisor, became a patron of New Negro artists. Among the artists Mason supported, in addition to Hughes, were Aaron Douglass, Richmond Barthé, Hall Johnson, Miguel Corravarubias, and Claude McKay.[58] After a meeting with Mason, Hurston reported to Hughes that she and Mason "got on famously."[59] Hurston was a budding scholar and researcher, and Mason had spent time among the Plains Indians as an amateur anthropologist. Given Mason's growing interest in black folk culture, she and Hurston had some things in common and much to discuss. Charlotte Mason's spyglass had a primitivist's lens; she honored the spirituality of people of traditional cultures, but believed "civilization" to be a distinctly Western phenomenon, a phenomenon from which the "primitives" could save them. In many ways, she was like the white woman who befriended lil' Isis Watts: she wanted some sunshine to soak into her soul.

For as much as Charlotte Mason felt herself and the West to be in need of salvation, she also wanted to control the prescription. She entered into a contract with Hurston on December 8, 1927. Mason agreed to fund Hurston's folklore collecting for a year. As Valerie Boyd points out, the terms of Mason's contract with Huston were uncharacteristic. Whereas Mason's monies supported her other "godchildren" so that they could focus on their work, she wanted to fund Hurston to do work that Mason would covet as her own. Hurston was employed "to seek out, compile and collect all information possible, both written and oral, concerning the music, poetry, folklore, literature, hoodoo, conjure, manifestations of art and kindred subjects among Negroes in the South."[60] Hurston was regarded as an agent, working in service to Charlotte Mason and undertaking research that Mason was unable to undertake herself. Mason was seventy-three, white, and a widow who lived in a penthouse with Swedish maids. It is doubtful that she was going into the Southern backwoods, or to jook joints, sawmill camps, Hoodoo doctors, and the like, to collect Negro folklore.

Although Mason was dictatorial with Hughes, Douglass, and other artists and influenced the content of their work, she did not claim their work as her own. But whatever Hurston collected, contractually speaking, belonged to Charlotte Osgood Mason. In addition to Mason's racial prejudices, perhaps sexist compunctions may have been at play, as well as professional envy. Hurston, nonetheless, signed the contract. But Zora Neale Hurston could always read between lines. And in spite of what Mason intended,

Hurston had her own intentions. And for as much as Mason may have considered Hurston to be the perfect Howard-Barnard-Columbia trained "primitive," Mason's stereotypes and ideas were not uppermost in Hurston's mind when she signed the contract.

However Hurston read Charlotte Mason, she obviously had some assurance that she would eventually control the materials that she herself collected. Not only was Mason a patron of several members of her New Negro circle, Mason in Hurston's interpretation, was the realization of the last vision she experienced in her childhood. The big house was a New York, Park Avenue penthouse. The two women awaiting her, one young and one old, were Cornelia Chapin and Charlotte Mason. The queer-shaped flowers were calla lilies. This scene portended a period of peace and love and those things that were essential to peace and love: financial security, freedom, self-identity, and self-direction. Following the Christmas of 1927, Hurston penned her appreciation to Mason. "You have given me the happiest Christmas season of all my life. For the first time ever, I was among friends and well fed and warm." Hurston felt grateful to be able to give as well as receive gifts. "It was nothing expensive that I had to give, but I could give something.... I had love." Mason's largesse afforded Hurston her "first Christmas. I mean the first Yule season when reality met my dreams. The kind of Christmas that my half-starved child-hood painted."[61]

Hurston didn't get her black prancing pony with white saddle and bridles, but she was provided with the means to get a shiny gray Chevrolet that was "all paid for." Her long-awaited trip to the horizon stood before her. A more mature and a seasoned researcher, Hurston longed to be back in the South doing what she liked best—being in nature and listening to lies. Aware of the value of her cultural heritage, now her "poking and prying" had a purpose. She described her research as "formalized curiosity" and defined it as "a seeking that he who wishes may know the cosmic secrets of the world and they that dwell therein."[62] Through her seeking into the cosmic secrets of black folk culture, and the folk therein, Hurston simultaneously unfolded the secrets of her own life. She had bet God that she would try to find out the vague directions whispered in her ears and find the road it seemed she must follow. Having attained her formal education, the how and when of her queries were answered. The what—that is, the road she must follow—was now clear. The collection, preservation, interpretation, and celebration of African American folklore was her calling, her path.

Hurston departed New York for Mobile on December 14, 1927, to interview Lewis a second time. As Boyd surmises, perhaps it was to redeem the rather superficial interview she had conducted the first time and the unprofessional article she had submitted to Woodson. Perhaps, too, she wanted to engage in a more significant investigation that might uncover fresh information.[63] Having spent sufficient time with Lewis to write a book manuscript, she returned to Loughman, in the Florida Everglades. Hurston secured a room in the quarters of the Everglades Cypress Company Lumber camp and set up shop.

She had abandoned Boas's objective-observer method of collecting lore for the participant-observer approach. She knew that she had to gradually remove social barriers to become one of the group. Hurston had myriad techniques to accomplish her purpose. She would speak in the language and rhythm of the folk, not the off-putting, cultivated Barnardese. She would tell a lie that was believable and that would render her acceptable to her potential informants—at Loughman's, for a while, she was a bootlegger's woman and on the lam. And she would sponsor "lying contests" to encourage participation in the telling of stories and tales.

Of necessity, she would have to secure protection. Loughman was an environment in which the law was lax. The camp harbored many who were lawless and many who were on the run from the law. Hurston described the folk at the Loughman settlement as "quick to sunshine and quick to anger. Some little word, look or gesture can move them either to love or to sticking a knife between your ribs." Whatever happened to Hurston's chrome-plated pistol, she didn't say. At Loughman's, she was unarmed: "I had no gun, knife or any sort of weapon. I did not know how to do that kind of fighting."[64]

Some may have looked to a two-headed doctor for protection, but Hurston looked up the row of houses where she lived and spied Big Sweet—the most feared person on the place, "uh whole woman and half uh man."[65] That morning, Big Sweet had her foot up on somebody, signifying in a most particular manner that she had one foot on the step of her enemy, and her elbow on her knee playing the dozens. Such actions were not taken unless one was thoroughly prepared to stand one's ground. "Tain't a man, woman nor child on this job going to tackle Big Sweet," Hurston's landlady told her, not even the white "Quarters Boss." Hurston had found her protection. With laughter, gifts, and rides in her Chevy, Hurston won the friendship of Big Sweet. "You sho is crazy!" she told Hurston. "I loves to friend with somebody like you. I aims to look out for you, too. Do your fighting for you. Nobody better not start nothing with you, do I'll get my switch-blade and go round de ham-bone looking for meat."[66]

With Big Sweet, Hurston hit the mother lode. Big Sweet became Hurston's means of protection and collection. Not only did Big Sweet have Hurston's back, Hurston wrote,

> Big Sweet helped me to collect material in a big way. She had no idea what I wanted with it, but if I wanted it, she meant to see to it that I got it. She pointed out people who knew songs and stories. She wouldn't stand for balkiness on their part.[67]

Having established a rapport with the quarters' residents and a sense of security, Hurston went about colleting myths, fables, legends, work songs, stories of Ole Massa and John, preacher tales, sermons, spirituals, children's games and songs, blues, and love letters.

In *Dust Tracks*, Hurston wrote beautifully and appreciatively of "These poets of the swinging blade!" Of these fellers of great trees, engaged in a graceful dance of body with ax lifted high over head in a fluid arc, suspended, dancing in the air before the swing down into the bark of a tree. Of the men attached to tall pines, bleeding gum from trees with swift strokes of a blade. Of men perched atop ladders, picking oranges. Of men in the bowels of the earth with wet dust wrung from ancient bones by time. Death was sometimes the price paid for this poetry.[68] All the while, talk and story and song steadied their hand, sharpened their eye, quickened their step, and stiffened their spine. Their words road the breath of air that inspirited their bodies and sharpened their minds. The words made sense of the senseless, and their words created realities that respected and responded to their existence. "Sweating black bodies, muscled like gods, working to feed the hunger of the great tooth." Their labor contributed to the life of a nation. The sublime American reality, Hurston subtly interjects, was that they would not share equally in the terrific boon. From the gum of the pine trees came "[p]aint, explosives, marine stores, flavor, perfumes, tone for the violin bow, and many other things which the black men who bleed trees never heard about." Because "[t]he world must ride," they swung ninety-pound hammers that spiked the ties that joined the rails of steel. "Another offering to the soul of civilization whose other name is travel," but those who spiked the ties would travel second class, if at all.[69] Hurston's black-muscled gods were more than able laborers with a penchant for lying. They were human beings. And in listening to and participating in, and recording the rites and realties they created, she discovered "that which the soul lives by."[70]

Hurston corresponded with few of her friends and associates while in the field. Her contract with Mason forbade it, as it also forbade Hurston from revealing Mason's name to anyone. Nevertheless, she wrote frequently to Langston Hughes, whom she regarded as an artistic collaborator and confidante. Her letters to Hughes were filled with exuberance for her continuous discoveries. "Langston, Langston, this is going to be big." Hurston had begun to extrapolate from the various forms of black expression some essential qualities, and she enumerated them for Hughes: (1) "The Negro's outstanding characteristic is drama." (2) Irreverence. "God, Church, and heaven are treated lightly." (3) "Angularity in everything, sculpture, dance, abrupt story telling." (4) "Redundance." Repeated features in stories—usually three times. (5) "Restrained ferocity in everything. There is a tense ferocity beneath the casual exterior." (6) Various laws of dialect.[71] Hurston was percolating with ideas about how she—and Hughes—might make use of the material. Certainly, she would draw on the material for "the new, the real Negro art theatre" she had envisioned.

In her excitement, Hurston was collecting folklore "like a new broom." That is until Lucy tried to "steal" her, bringing Hurston's sweeping to an abrupt halt. Lucy was one of the women in the quarters whose personal insecurities overrode concern for her personal well-being. Her man Slim had left her some time ago, but Lucy elected to blame Hurston for it. Lucy's jealousy was activated by Hurston's easy rapport with the men, in general, and with Slim, in particular. To facilitate collection of the lore, Hurston would treat her informants to drinks and rides in her car to get it. But truth has never had anything to do with what one wants to believe. Besides, Lucy and Big Sweet were adversaries. Harming Hurston would be like hitting a straight lick with a crooked stick. Thus, one evening, assuming Hurston was alone at the local jook joint, Lucy made her move. With an open knife, she was headed toward Hurston who was leaning against the wall in proximity to Slim.

Big Sweet, who unexpectedly pounced from a far corner of the joint, preempted Lucy's intentions. Feet were kicking, blades were flying, and Jim Presley, a sympathetic informant, advised Hurston, "Run you chile! Run and Ride! Dis is gointer be uh nasty ditch ... Run clean off dis job! Some uh dese folks goin' tuh judgment and some goin' tuh jail. Come on, less run!" With some help from Slim, who used his guitar to clear the path for her escape, Hurston "fell out of the door" and "was in the car in a second and in high just too quick. Jim and Slim helped me throw my bags into the car and I saw the sun rising as I approached Crescent City."[72] Polk County may be the place "where the water tastes like cherry wine," but Zora Neale Huston didn't have to think twice about leaving Polk County behind.

Just short of the Crescent City, Hurston spent time in Magazine, Alabama, until mid June. She did more collecting, took stock of her materials, and outlined some plans:

> 1 volume of stories. 1. children's games. 1. Drama and the Negro 1 "Mules & Men" a volume of work songs with guitar arrangement 1 on Religion. 1. on words & meanings. 1 volume of love letters with an introduction on Negro love.[73]

By August, Hurston wrote Hughes, "I have landed in the kingdom of Marie LaVeau and expect to wear her crown someday." She continued, "I am getting on with the top of the profession. I know 18 tasks, including how to crown the spirit of death, and kill."[74] In New Orleans, Hurston devoted most of her energies to the collection of materials on religion, conjure, and Hoodoo. By actually going through the initiation rites to become an apprentice or a practitioner, she learned spells for those things with which people wanted a little extra help—attracting a mate, preventing a mate's infidelity, influencing judges, cursing some one or removing a curse, punishing or killing enemies. She learned the composition of potions and medicinal cures. Hurston studied with several two-headed doctors, each one with a different initiation rite. With one, Hurston had to sit at the crossroads and invite the "King of Hell." With another, she had to go through the ritual of getting the black cat bone. She sat in a circle around a boiling cauldron, with other initiates, while the cat was thrown in.

The experience that moved her the most was that with Luke Turner, the nephew of Marie LaVeau, "queen of conjure." A nine-day preparation preceded the initiation ceremony; for, "no one may approach the Altar without the crown, and none may wear the crown of power without preparation. *It must be earned.*" Prepared for the initiation, Hurston lay face down on a snake skin cover for three days, silent and fasting. At the end of this time, she had a new name. She was to be called Rainbringer. Her symbol was the lightning and her mode of communication with Spirit was through storms. When she was dressed, "a pair of eyes was painted on my cheeks as a sign that I could see in more ways than one. The sun was painted on my forehead." Later, after these and other rituals, Luke Turner crowned her with power. For five months, Hurston studied with Turner. She was the last Hoodoo doctor Turner would make.[75]

As Hurston told Hughes, on November 22, 1928, she was "knee deep" in the collection of Hoodoo materials "with a long way to go." By the end of the year, Hurston sought Boas's guidance in the content and organization of her material as a book manuscript. She was forbidden to publish *any* materials without Mason's expressed consent, she was to work with no one else—not even her colleagues in anthropology—and she was to be in contact with no one. Zora Neale Hurston, however, consistently thwarted Mason's efforts to restrain and control "every little detail" of her work and life. She confessed to Hughes that Mason's heavy-handedness was utterly demoralizing and undermined her self-respect. Hurston was resilient. She had her own mind, and she followed it.[76] "This is confidential," she wrote to Boas. "I accepted the money on the condition that I should write no one. It is unthinkable, of course, that I go past the collecting stage without consulting you, however I came by the money." In a later letter, she reported, "I am through collecting and I am sitting down to write up." She had amassed a great deal of material, more than 95,000 words of stories and religious matter and a lot of photographs. Through several interrogatory statements, she discussed her ideas and conclusions with Boas and solicited his opinion:

> Is it safe for me to say that baptism is an extension of water worship as a part of pantheism just as the sacrament is an extension of cannibalism? Isn't the use of candles in the Catholic church a relic of fire worship? Are not all the uses of fire upon the altars the same thing?[77]

Hurston's bold and innovative fieldwork took her deeper and deeper into the cosmic mysteries shrouded in the symbols and rituals of African American folk magic belief practices. As her expertise in collecting expanded, her understanding of Africana culture grew in sophistication. As a social scientist, she was motivated to engage in comparative studies of various African cultures, analyzing the ways in which they diverged from or retained elements of their common African origin. To this end, she collected material in the Bahamas, Jamaica, and Haiti. Her first trip to the Bahamas, on October 12, 1929, yielded three reels of folk dances, twenty Bahamian songs, artifacts such as a Congo drum, and a promise to return. Because a hurricane slowed her pace, she had just found the island's Hoodoo doctors the day before her departure. With only her return ticket and twenty-four cents, she reluctantly left. Back in Jacksonville, Florida, Hurston continued revising the folklore manuscript she had tentatively titled *Folk-Tales From the Gulf States* and spent part of the summer of 1929 collecting lore in Miami. That fall she went to the Bahamas. In her correspondence with Boas, she made some general comparative observations: "The Negroes there are more African, actually know the tribes from which their ancestors came. Some still speak the dialects."[78] Hurston made her second trip to the Bahamas in December, during the carnival season. One result of her work there was the article "Dance Songs and Tales From the Bahamas," published in the July-September 1930 issue of *Journal of American Folk-Lore.*

Impressed with Hurston's talent, perception, and industry, Boas sought funding for Hurston's doctoral studies at Columbia. "She is an unusually gifted person with a good deal of literary skill" and is "well fitted" for doctoral study he wrote in recommending her. Unsuccessful in acquiring an assistantship for her, Boas suggested Hurston approach her "patron." Hurston did so, conveying later to Boas that Mason was "cold toward the degrees, but will put up more money for further research."[79]

In the meantime, Hurston worked on the book manuscript. Still on Mason's payroll, she was not severely affected by the 1929 stock market crash that ushered in the Great Depression. With a steady eye toward the New Negro Theatre, Hurston also continued to work, sub rosa, on a play she had conceived of called *Mule Bone.* Early on, she shared the idea with Langston Hughes and intended that the play be a collaborative effort. But, in a November 1930 correspondence, Hurston sent Carl Van Vechten a draft of the play. She disclaimed that, this being her "first serious whack at the play business," the draft was "tentative." Explaining the play's origins she wrote, "Langston and I started out together on the idea of the story I used to tell you about Eatonville, but being so much apart from rush of business, I started all over again while in Mobile and this the result of my work alone."[80] *Mule Bone* would have been one of the first authentic black folk comedies to be produced. But Hurston and Hughes disagreed about authorship and about what role their stenographer, Louise Thompson, should claim. It was never staged during Hurston's lifetime.

Hurston's folklore materials resisted being melded into book form. She had submitted her Lewis manuscript to a publisher for consideration, but without success. Perhaps, as Hughes wrote in *The Big Sea*, Negroes were "no longer in vogue, publishers politely rejected new manuscripts, and patrons found other uses for their money."[81] Mason's purse strings were being drawn more tightly as well. No matter the current circumstances, Hurston vowed, "I shall wrassle me up a future or die trying." Mason had become less controlling of Hurston's life and career, even encouraging her creative efforts. Frustrated with the progress on her folklore and Hoodoo materials, Hurston explored more fully her dramatic interests. She began with skits for the musical revues *Fast and Furious* and *Jungle Scandals.* These both met with negative reviews and the second revue was cancelled. Hurston believed the show met such a fate because the "stupid and trite" producer, Forbes Randolph, "squeezed all Negro-ness out of everything and substituted what he thought ought to be Negro humor."[82]

Hurston knew she could do better. Mason wholeheartedly agreed. She recognized Hurston's "natural creative impulse" and its rarity. "God knows you are about the only person left among the Negroes who can translate that impulse into exact Negro language."[83] The shows brought Hurston some degree of success in that "they are making the public know me and come to me," she told Mason. In the same letter, Hurston dryly stated, "I hear that my husband has divorced me." Far from being upset, she expressed relief. Hurston saw marriage to Sheen as an "obstacle." But now that he had divorced her, she was "playing on her harp like David."[84]

In September 1931, the newly divorced Hurston was enthusiastically "planning a Negro concert of the most intensely black type."[85] She intended to bring to the stage a troupe of sixteen Bahamian dancers to perform the ritual Fire Dance she had filmed there. The dance had three parts: The Jumping Dance, The Ring Play, and the Congo. She sought to combine her dancers with Hall Johnson's singers. Respecting Johnson's musical talent and his contributions to successful musical productions such as *Green Pastures* (1930), Hurston made a genuine effort to collaborate with him.

Johnson, however, neither believed in Hurston's original Bahamian material nor saw the beauty in folk artistry. "The public only wanted to hear spirituals, and spirituals that had been well arranged," he told Hurston.[86] Hurston went it alone. Amid subterfuge designed to "throw her off," mean-spirited African Americans who voiced their prejudices against West Indians, and egotistical Bahamians who played the intraracial card and tried to undermine her efforts, Hurston persevered. She would produce and direct the concert herself. She organized her performers, including Bahamian and African American dancers and singers, and directed their rehearsals. She put all her monies into the production, even selling her car and radio. "I am willing to make any sacrifice, meet any terms, to give it a chance of success," Hurston wrote. This included asking Mason for a loan, which Mason granted.[87] Hurston's concert, *The Great Day*, "A Program of Original Negro Folklore," opened on Sunday, January 10, 1932, at the John Golden Theater in New York City. The play dramatized a work day at a Florida railroad camp. The script included work songs, a sermon delivered by an itinerant preacher, spirituals, and children's games, and ended with the Fire Dance.

From the reveille of the shack rouser in the first scene of the play, the audience was with the performers, Hurston reported.[88] When the last note was sung and the last step danced, the house applauded and applauded. So did the critics. "The evening was altogether successful, and carried off with a verve, a lack of self-consciousness, and obviously spontaneous enjoyment as eloquent as it was refreshing." Audience and critics alike experienced the genuineness of the performance. In comparing *The Great Day* to other black dramas and musicals, the critic wrote that *The Great Day* "was the real thing; unadulterated and not fixed and fussed up for purposes of commerce."[89] After the performance, Hall Johnson congratulated Hurston. Although he admitted that he really came to see Hurston "do a flop," he also admitted the performance "was swell! and that she proved her point."[90]

The Great Day was an artistic and professional success, but left Hurston in a financial bind. Although it wasn't "fussed up" for commercial purposes, Hurston and Mason both hoped that a producer with adequate funding would pick up the play. Hurston's debt to Mason gave Mason another opportunity to dictate what Hurston could and could not do with Mason's folk collection. These unfortunate circumstances also dictated the terms of Hurston's negotiations with Mason. Of the material Hurston was permitted to use, she produced the concert again, on March 29, 1932, at the New School for Social Research. Invitations for her productions continued to come in, and she staged the concert again at the Vanderbilt Hotel, for The Folk Dance Society, and at other venues. It was déjà vu: critical acclaim, but no monetary gain.

Bankrupted by the productions, Hurston could not afford to continue living in New York, and Mason was not interested in continuing to subsidize her living expenses. Spiritual and insightful, Charlotte Mason was also besotted with the paternalistic and prejudiced attitudes of her times. So Zora Hurston went home to Eatonville. In spite of Mason's controlling and manipulative hand, Hurston was genuinely appreciative of Mason and her support. As Hurston herself, wrote, Mason was deeply human. In her generous funding of Harlem Renaissance artists, she made a valuable contribution.

Although Zora Neale Hurston accepted Mason's patronage and her conditions, Hurston never lost her sense of self. She knew the value of compromise, and the world she lived in was a world in which the playing field was not even and the deck was always stacked. As appreciative as she was, Hurston was happy to leave New York and told Mason so: "Somehow a great weight seems lifted from me. I have been trying to analyze myself and see why I feel so happy. But I do." A later letter from Eatonville declared, "I am happy here, happier than I have been for years." She had been working nonstop for several years, running about collecting folklore, "with my tongue hanging out," as she once put it. Although still working and writing in her retreat home, she experienced a sense of renewal. It was May. Flowers were in full bloom and Hurston was blooming with creative ideas:[91]

> I have finished one short story that I had had in mind to write for the last four years and tomorrow I shall resume work on the story book. That does not seem to me to be hard work at this stage of its construction. Mostly polishing and trimming. Then to the novel that I have wanted to write since 1928.[92]

In Eatonville, Hurston was "renewed like the eagle." The rush and clamor of New York dissolved in Florida's humidity. "I am so glad to be here. I awake with the sun and go to bed early."[93]

The following month, Hurston introduced herself, by letter, to Edwin Osgood Grover, a professor at Rollins College, in Winter Park, Florida. She gave him a brief biography of herself and an overview of her professional work, highlighting her recent concert productions. The purpose of the letter was to interest Grover (and Rollins College) in staging a folk concert.

> Now the material used in these concerts was gathered for the most part in Orange County. All of it came from Florida and so I thought that it would be fine to give a series, or one at least in the native habitat of the songs and tales. And I wondered if Rollins College ... would not like to assist in putting the world right on Negro expression.[94]

Grover introduced Hurston and her ideas to Robert Wunsch, Rollins's theater director. Wunsch, a new recruit to Rollins, desired to generate in his students "a genuine interest in American folk material." A collaboration with Hurston would prove useful to both parties. Hurston would be able to promote her authentic Negro theater and Wunsch would benefit from the materials Hurston had collected and would also find in Hurston an access to the community.[95]

In a letter to Rollins's president, Hamilton Holt, Wunsch outlined his objectives for the year: "to make the students sensitive to the lyric beauty of swamp and citrus grove, sense the pageantry of the Ponce de Leon exploration, find the drama in the life of fisherfolk and sponge diver and cowboys." He could think of no better way to accomplish his objectives, he informed Holt, than to have this "honest-to-the-soil material" presented to the students in a program of folk songs and dances performed by a group from Eatonville, under the direction of Zora Neale Hurston. Wunsch paid Hurston the complement of acknowledging her as "a national authority on Negro ways [who] has an enviable place for herself in American dramatics."[96] Hurston had succeeded in gaining the support she needed. With the College's financial backing and assistance from Grover and Wunsch, *The Great Day* was performed at Winter Park's experimental community theater, The Museum in Fern Park, on January 20, 1933. Its success warranted another performance the following week and then was staged at Recreation Hall, Rollin's major theater, on February 11. Hurston's production was entertaining; but more important, some of the audience understood the profundity of the work.

Described as the "most dramatic entertainment" given in Winter Park, the *Winter Park Herald* reviewer also wrote,

> What the Negro has brought to America is too vital to be allowed to vanish from the earth. His barbaric color adds patterns to the Nordic restraint about him. America needs this because its civilization, like Minerva, sprung full grown from the head of Europe, and so there is not the wealth of native folklore as in Europe, Asia, Africa, and other continents where civilization had to grow through long ages.[97]

The performances evoked repeated encores, praise, and more praise. Yet, no matter the vitality of the play or how much the American Nordic needed this vitality, the audience at Rollins remained white only—in spite of Hurston's protests against it. She, therefore, staged a special performance in Eatonville. Afterward, Hurston and her Eatonville troupe took *The Great Day* to several sites around central Florida, including the Bok Tower at Lake Wales; Sanford; Daytona Beach Auditorium, Daytona Beach; and Bethune-Cookman College also in Daytona Beach. By November, Hamilton Holt was wandering whether Hurston "had more things to put on at Rollins."[98] On January 5, 1934, she graced Rollins with *All De Live Long Day*.

That spring, Mary McCloud Bethune hired Hurston to found a drama department at the College, so Hurston moved to Daytona Beach. Hurston's ideas for Bethune-Cookman, however, did not pan out. Hurston found that she had neither the artistic license nor the financial support she needed. In May, Hurston took a troupe to St. Louis for the National Folk Festival. Later, in the fall, she was invited to direct a folk concert in Chicago, where she staged a version of *The Great Day*, called *Singing Steel*. On her way up to Chicago, she stopped at Fisk University, in Nashville, Tennessee, to speak with Thomas Jones, the school's president. With a view toward hiring Hurston as a full professor and establishing an experimental theater at Fisk, Jones proposed sending Hurston to Yale to undertake additional formal training. Having seen Hurston's Chicago production, representatives of the Julius Rosenwald Fund invited her to apply for a fellowship and also discussed subsidizing a chair for her at Fisk University.

Edwin Embree of the Rosenwald Fund decided, instead, to offer Hurston a fellowship for doctoral study: "The Rosenwald Fund, the organization that had previously proposed me for a chair at Fisk Univ. now feels that they want to do something bigger. I am asked to fill out an application blank for a fellowship so that I may take my doctor's degree."[99] Hurston considered the benefits of a doctorate and was excited by the prospects. She had considered studying for her doctoral degree a few years earlier, but did not have the means, and Franz Boas was unsuccessful in acquiring funding. But here, again, was the possibility.

Hurston's literary ambitions sprouted right alongside her theatrical ambitions and her academic work. The story she had completed while in Eatonville was "The Gilded Six-Bits." Bob Wunsch had read the story and submitted it to *Story Magazine*. The editors, Martha Foley and Whit Burnett, published the piece in the magazine's August 1933 issue. Hurston believed they did some "missionary work" on her behalf, because she received four letters of inquiry from publishers asking whether she had any book-length work. Bertram Lippincott of J. B. Lippincott and Company was one of the publishers to whom Hurston responded. Although she didn't have the first word on paper, she said that, yes, she was writing a book. "But the very next week I moved up to Sanford where I was not so much at home as at Eatonville, and could concentrate more and sat down to write *Jonah's Gourd Vine*."[100] *Jonah's* was published in May 1934 and Hurston then turned her attention to completing revisions of the folklore manuscript titled *Mules and Men* that would also be published by Lippincott.

While Hurston was successfully publishing both in the areas of fiction and folklore, Edwin Embree, was backpedaling on the fellowship offer to Hurston. His justification was that she had submitted an unacceptable plan of study. Yet, Franz Boas had personally devised this plan: "I was to learn routines and methods with him for two semesters. Then the third term (Spring 1936) to go to Herskovits at Northwestern and work under him as he has done more in the Negro field than any one else." Hurston pointed out that most of the anthropologists in the country had specialized in Native American culture, and that consequently there was a dearth of college courses on the Negro. Besides, as Boas had concluded, "I am not being trained to do a routine job. I am being trained to do what has not been done and that which cries out to be done."[101]

Boas's program for Hurston addressed each of Embree's concerns. Embree, nonetheless, would not be satisfied. Letters of recommendation from Ruth Benedict and Fannie Hurst may have influenced Embree's about-face. But some other unknown factor was also at play. Ruth Benedict was Boas's student. Why would her letter weigh more than Boas's mentorship and unconditional support? Fannie Hurst was neither an academic nor an anthropologist. Whatever the cause, the situation demonstrated that Columbia, premier American university that it was, had no formal structural support for doctoral study in cultural anthropology emphasizing African American life. No American doctoral program did. Boas's configurative study plan is suggestive of what Hurston said point blank to Herskovits:

> I got the grant from the Rosenwald and they rushed me off to talk with Dr. Boas and arrange things. But lo and behold when I get here it turns out that there is nothing here to prepare me for my special field. You see, what you have done and what I have collected is all that there is to this Negro phase.[102]

The discipline of anthropology, itself, was new to the American academy. So new, in fact, that an anthropological focus on "the Negro" barely existed except for the articles and insights from Melville Herskovits and the mass of materials collected by Zora Neale Hurston. Hurston acknowledged the Uncle Remus tales, which she described as "true in spirit and wonderfully done," but that they only "scratched the surface." She described Howard Odum and Guy Johnson's 1926 publication *The Negro and His Songs* as inaccurate. "They have made six or seven songs out of one song and made one song out of six of seven."[103] Nothing substantial had been undertaken in cultural anthropology emphasizing African American life until the advent of Zora Neale Hurston—a pioneer who cut a path where none had existed. Even public transportation had not made inroads to the places she went to collect the cultural artifacts and signs by which the black soul lived. No one before her had conceived of black folklore with the depth of understanding that Hurston had. No one had understood or publicly performed and articulated the true soul of black folks—in the work camps, in the jook joints, on the shrimp boats, in the Sanctified Church, in the pulpit, on the mourner's bench, in the schoolhouse, on the playgrounds, in the parlor of Hoodoo doctors, on the porch of general stores, or at the crossroads. Nobody had ever done that for black people. Zora was the first.

Out of these places, what she had brought back was soul-stuff, vitality, humor, creativity, imagination, style, strength, resilience, music, laughter, movement, vibration, wisdom, ancient wisdom, ancient ancient wisdom—so old it was original. It was the stuff of humanity. It was what inspired the being-ness of black people. What Hurston found was vast and vital. There was no double consciousness for Hurston. She recognized what she experienced as an African American and what she observed as an anthropologist to be at once black and American—this was one consciousness with multiple manifestations. But how to make known this cultural wealth? Hurston chose theatrical presentation. The stage was as ancient as Africa and as old as the Greeks. It was an organic outgrowth of the recognition of drama as one of the major attributes of black peoples. Ritual drama. This sensibility was part and parcel of African American genius. Zora Neale Hurston saw that and published it to the world.

Zora Neale Hurston had discovered the How, When, and What of the "vague directions whispered in her ear." And she discovered the Why: This Pathless Path was hers to walk because she was the only one who had the genius to do it.

THREE

"A Genius of the South": An American Genius

I n 1973 Alice Walker took her legendary journey in search of Zora Neale Hurston's unmarked grave. She had read Robert Hemenway's essay, "Zora Neale Hurston and the Eatonville Anthology," which revealed that this significant, but unread author, had died in obscurity and was buried, "by subscription," in an unmarked grave in a segregated cemetery in Fort Pierce, Florida. A resting place, Hemenway bemoaned, that was "symbolic of the black writer's fate in America.[1] Walker, as indignant as Robert Hemenway about this matter, had determined to find and mark Hurston's grave. "[A]s a black person, a woman, and a writer," Walker saw this undertaking as her natural duty.[2]

On August 15, 1973, she arrived in Eatonville. Posing as Hurston's niece, she searched out anyone who may have known Hurston. She was directed to Mrs. Mathilda Moseley, then 82 years of age. Whether a consequence of her recent surgery, or balked by the presence of Walker's white associate Charlotte Hunt, or from natural disposition, Mrs. Moseley was uneasy, wary, and reluctant to speak about years so far in the past.

Mrs. Moseley was the niece of Joe Clarke, the town-maker and entrepreneur who operated the general store that drew in the townspeople who swapped "lies" and "passed nations through their mouths." Mrs. Moseley was also Hurston's age-mate. They were schoolgirls together at Robert Hungerford Normal and Industrial School. When Hurston left to continue her education, said Mrs. Moseley, who began to warm toward Walker, "she never really came back to live." Except for occasional returns to gather folk material, Hurston spent most of her time in South Florida. After laughs and reflection over old photos and a detailed accounting of Mrs. Moseley's recent surgery, to which Walker respectfully listened, Walker and her associate took their leave. Walker asked a parting question, disclosing the actual motivation for her trip: "Why is it that thirteen years after Zora's death, no marker has been put on her grave?"

"The reason she doesn't have a stone," explained Mrs. Moseley, "is because she wasn't buried here." The real answer to Walker's question was revealed in Mrs. Moseley's last statement: "She was buried down in South Florida somewhere. I don't think anybody really knew where she was."[3]

The "somewhere" was Fort Pierce. Walker, disturbed by this apparent oblivion that shrouded the death, if not the life, of Zora Neale Hurston, ventured to Fort Pierce. There she found it convenient to continue her "profoundly *useful* lie," of introducing herself as Zora Hurston's niece. It helped to prevent "foot-dragging," from those who might know something but feel uncertain about sharing it, Walker explained.[4] It also prompted the opening of closed files and facilitated the viewing of photographs and documents that otherwise might not have been forthcoming.

At the Lee-Peek Mortuary, in Fort Pierce, Walker solicited information on the location of Hurston's grave. Mrs. Sarah Peek Patterson, director of the Mortuary, told her that the grave could be found in the middle of a circle that is just beyond the gates of the Garden of the Heavenly Rest Cemetery, located at the end of Seventeenth Street. "Hers is the only grave in that circle," Mrs. Patterson asserted, "because people don't bury in that cemetery anymore."[5]

In search of her foremother's garden of heavenly rest, Walker stood at the site and surveyed the cemetery with incredulity. It was not a garden. The grass, high and in alliance with the weeds and bushes, had overrun the boundaries that once had been set for it. Greeted by the buzz of hungry and curious insects, Walker hesitantly but determinedly waded through the grasping stems and leaves and blades of grass, feet uncertain in the uneven, sandy soil. Scanning the area, her countenance drawn into a perplexed look, Walker called, "Zo-ra!" Summoning Hurston's hurried assistance in locating her grave: "I hope you don't think I'm going to stand out here all day, with these snakes watching me and these ants having a field day." Then, "my foot sinks into a hole," Walker recounted. "I look down. I am standing in a sunken rectangle that is about six feet long and about three or four feet wide. I look up to see where the two gates are."[6] She measured the distance from the gates, checking the circumference from the possible center. She further investigated the immediate surrounding area, looking to see whether there were any other graves. There were none. She concluded, with some assurance, that she had found the forgotten and unattended grave of Zora Neale Hurston.

The next step in Walker's momentous effort was to have the gravesite marked. At the Merritt Monument Company, she experienced some despondency when she realized that the "Ebony Mist" stone—a stone befitting a Hoodoo Queen—was too exorbitantly priced. It was their "finest." Discouraged by the price—it "would feed a dozen Sahelian drought victims for three years"—Walker selected an affordable "plain gray marker" and handed the engraver a piece of paper with the following inscription:

ZORA NEALE HURSTON
"A GENIUS OF THE SOUTH"
NOVELIST FOLKLORIST
ANTHROPOLOGIST
1901–1960

Walker explained in "Looking for Zora" that the epigraph "a genius of the South" comes from a poem penned by Jean Toomer.[7] The line is taken from "Georgia Dusk," which appears in Toomer's *Cane*. From the first two stanzas of the poem's seven stanzas, one can appreciate the context in which the line is written and can interpret Walker's intention in using the line:

The sky, lazily disdaining to pursue
The setting sun, too indolent to hold
A lengthened tournament for flashing gold,
Passively darkens for night's barbecue,

A feast of moon and men and barking hounds,
An orgy for some genius of the South
With blood-hot eyes and cane-lipped scented mouth,
Surprised in making folk-songs from soul sounds.[8]

Jean Toomer is numbered among the first New Negro writers, given that he was present at the soirées of Georgia Douglas Johnson and at Charles Johnson's Civic Club's "dress rehearsal" of the younger Negro writers.[9] His *Cane*, a collection of poetry and fiction, was published in 1923 and heralded as the harbinger of the Harlem Renaissance Movement.

Although labeled a New Negro, Jean Toomer identified himself, first and foremost, as an American. He described himself as being of mixed ancestry with allegiance to no one element of the admixture. But even as Toomer was consciously determined not to be caught in America's artificial, arbitrary, and oppositional classification of races, and later in his life denied any black ancestry, he was deeply moved and enthralled by the beauty and richness of African American life, as that life expressed itself in the feast of moon and men and as it infused itself into the lush, fecund rural Southland.

In 1921, Jean Toomer accepted a position as the acting head of a Negro school in Sparta, Georgia. There, in the quaint hours of dusk, he heard, for the first time, folksongs and spirituals. The poignancy of timbre and word, image and promise stimulated Toomer's own creativity. To the editor of *The Liberator*, who published some of his work, Toomer wrote,

[M]y growing need for artistic expression has pulled me deeper and deeper into the Negro group. And as my powers of receptivity increased, I found myself loving it in a way that I could never love the other. It has stimulated and fertilized whatever creative talent I may contain within me. A visit to Georgia last fall was the starting point of almost everything of worth that I have done. I heard folk-songs come from the lips of Negro peasants. I saw the rich dusk beauty that I had heard many false accents about, and of which til then, I was somewhat skeptical. And a deep part of my nature, a part that I had repressed, sprang suddenly to life and responded to them. Now, I cannot conceive of myself as aloof and separated. My point of view has not changed; it has deepened, it has widened.[10]

Walker's selection of an epitaph from *Cane* is ingenious. The line, the stanza, the poem, the book at once recall the budding promise of the Harlem Renaissance and the genius of Africana peoples, expressed through the night's orgy of "moon and men." The general definition of "orgy" describes an occasion of observances of secret rites or ceremonial practices. Toomer's witnessing of these "secret rites" that came alive in the soft, Southern night air, foreshadowed the coming of Zora Neale Hurston, who, with her stories and novels surprised us with the literary renderings of the souls of black folk, and who, as a social scientist with a knowing eye and heart, investigated these ritualistic secret rites and documented that which the black soul lives by. The two stanzas from "Georgia Dusk," cited above, depict the setting wherein the collective mood and activity of a group, a people, a folk, give birth to a story, a song that gives voice to and formalizes the thought and feeling of those gathered. This storyteller or these song-singers are the channellers of the spirit, the genius, of the group.

Beneath the epitaph "a genius of the South," are the descriptives "novelist," "folklorist," and "anthropologist." Zora Neale Hurston is recognized anew as a major writer, a brilliant novelist. Critics have wrested for her a place in the African American and American literary canons. Her tremendous work as a social scientist, as a folklorist and anthropologist, begs recognition and requires fuller exploration and examination. Widely identified as a Harlem Renaissance writer, Hurston wrote all her books after this period. Nonetheless, her six short stories, two plays, and four essays, which were published during the Renaissance era, were significant contributions to the New Negro Movement.[11]

Of equal significance is Hurston's folklore fieldwork, much of which was conducted during the heyday of the Harlem Renaissance. Hurston's work as a writer was preempted, so to speak, by her anthropological interests. In 1926, just about a year after the launching of the New Negro Movement, Hurston had begun fieldwork for Franz Boas in Harlem. In February 1927, she went south, to Florida and Alabama, to collect materials under the auspices of Franz Boas and Carter G. Woodson. By December 1927, she was under contract with Charlotte Mason to act as her agent in the field. Hurston remained under contract with Mason, in one form or another, until April 1932. For as much as she was a presence in New York and a vital spirit amongst her New York friends, she spent most of her time in the South, engaged in field-work. The writing she produced during this time included her copious anthropological field notes and letters from the field. In spite of Mason's attempts to control Hurston and suppress her communications, Hurston wrote Langston Hughes often, and less frequently, she wrote to other associates and colleagues. Although she was not publishing her stories, she would return from her field collecting expeditions and regale her compeers with impromptu performances of the stories and songs she had learned.

After the decline of the Renaissance Movement, which coincided with the 1929 stock market crash, Hurston continued with her folklore field-work. As Toni Cade Bambara remarks in her foreword to *Sanctified Church*, "The Depression, funding sources dried up, blacks out of favor, the Renaissance played out. She never skipped a beat. Went right on collecting, maintaining, celebrating the genius of Blacksouth folks."[12] In the early 1930s, Hurston organized and revised her *Mules and Men* manuscript, while writing and staging dramatic presentations and folk concerts based on her field-work. In 1935, she returned to the South on a collaborative collecting fieldtrip. And in 1937 and 1938, she conducted field research in Jamaica and Haiti. Yet, for Hurston, there was no conflict between her creative and scientific selves, although her critics took issue with her tendency sometimes to fuse the two.

Hurston was bent on becoming a writer. As she confidently told Charlotte Mason, "I firmly believe that I shall succeed as a writer."[13] And she was equally dedicated to her anthropological objectives. Often enough, however, one pursuit would hold predominance over the other. For instance, while in the field, in Haiti, "in a hot-bed of what I want," Hurston's first masterpiece *Their Eyes Were Watching God* was published. Unfortunately, she would miss the event of the coming out of her novel. Hurston was focused on tying up loose ends and verifying her material before leaving Haiti. "So I am skipping about wherever I think I need a re-check," she wrote to Henry Allen Moe, Secretary-General of the Guggenheim Foundation. "Planning to sail Sept. 22. Wish that I could be there for the coming out of my new book Sept. 16, but that is not possible because something big is coming off here on the 18th that I would not miss for anything."[14]

Eventually, as Valerie Boyd makes clear, Hurston elected to express her scientific knowledge through literary versus scientific writing. On the Guggenheim application, Hurston had to respond to the question, "In what field of learning, or of art, does your project lie?" On the 1934 application, she responded "anthropology." On the second application in 1936 she responded "literary science."[15] This description seems to embrace both of Hurston's main areas of interest: She would create literary works, and those literary works would be informed by scientific investigations. Because Hurston was totally committed to a representation of black folk that was true to life, her folklore research was the sine qua non of her writing.

Hurston's *Mules and Men* and *Tell My Horse* are the two collections of folk-lore with which most readers of Hurston's work are familiar. Alice Walker first became acquainted with Hurston's work through *Mules and Men*. She was in the process of "writing a story that required accurate material on voodoo practices among rural Southern blacks of the thirties," but found no sources she trusted. "A number of white, racist anthropologists and folklorists of the period had, not surprisingly, disappointed and insulted me," wrote Walker. "They thought blacks inferior, peculiar, and comic." The perspectives these writers took in their work rendered the material useless to her. "Fortunately, it was then that I discovered *Mules and Men*, Zora's book on folklore, collecting, herself, and her small, all-black community of Eatonville, Florida."[16]

Walker was delighted by this "perfect book!" She "tested" the book on her relatives, and their warm, positive, and knowing response to the material that was read to them and that they read to one another authenticated the text for Walker. "This was my first indication of the quality I feel is most characteristic of Zora's work," wrote Walker: "racial health; a sense of black people as complete, complex, *undiminished* human beings, a sense that is lacking in so much black writing and literature." This characteristic quality of Hurston's work, as observed by Walker, is notable and inviting of both analysis and appreciation. For, Zora Neale Hurston was the first social scientist to not only recognize the *undiminished* humanity of Africana peoples, but also to extensively document the cultural expressions that were indicative of their particular and original genius. The work she did and the material she collected are invaluable contributions to Africana peoples, to American society, and to humanity.

Robert Hemenway forthrightly stated that Hurston is "the most important collector of Afro-American folklore in America."[17] As an American genius, Hurston's collection, preservation, interpretation, and presentation of African American folklore was one of her greatest acts of genius. When one considers the ill-conceived social science theories and pronouncements of the nineteenth and early twentieth centuries and the hostile social policies they engendered, one begins to see the heroic nature of Zora Neale Hurston's work as an anthropological folklorist. Hurston devoted more than twenty years of her life to activities directly or indirectly related to anthropological fieldwork. Her time, energy, effort, and courage call for critical attention.

To appreciate the import of Hurston's genius as an American social scientist and collector, it is necessary to have some understanding of the state of the fields of folklore and anthropology before she entered them. In addition, awareness of the genesis and avowed purpose of early American folklore and anthropological studies create a context in which one can better comprehend the interests and actions of individuals like Charlotte Osgood Mason and other like-minded "Nordics" who were "interested in *the Negro*."

The scientific community of nineteenth-century Euro-America was greatly influenced by Darwinian ideas of origin, survival, natural selection, progress, and development. Applying the theoretical framework and the classificatory schemes of the natural sciences to American society and culture, early American folklorists conceptualized an evolutionary social pyramid that progressed upward from savagery to barbarity, then from semicivilization to civilization, and from there to Enlightenment. The indigenous Native American populations and the African populations in America were not only objectified as the bottom dwellers of this human pyramid, they also were presumed to be poised for extinction. Folklore, a new science, "was basically survivalistic. That is, oral traditions were seen as fossils of an earlier day still preserved and functioning, though rapidly disappearing. If not as dry as the bones of extinct or ancient species of animals, they were just as far removed from the world of civilization." This belief in the "rapidly disappearing" culture of the "rude nations" generated the urgency with which folklorists began to gather materials. Their interests were not motivated by a respect for and honoring of "the past." The intention of these collectors was to retrieve materials "for thought and reflection for the future."[18]

The future they envisioned, however, was exclusive to Euro-Americans who believed themselves naturally selected to reach the pinnacle of Enlightenment. The future did not include Africana peoples who were perceived to be brutes without the civilizing spirit of humanity within them.

"Genius" refers to spirit—the spirit that attends an individual at birth, that is, a genie, or the prevailing spirit or character of a people, a nation, or an age. In the nineteenth century and early twentieth century, this was not a term most American scientists associated with blacks. It was assumed that Africana peoples had no genius, no characterizing spirit, and thus had no civilization and no humanity. Therefore, they had no worth and no value to human society. This mind-set, supported and confirmed by America's scientists, permeated the American consciousness.

This mind-set influenced the discourse of a racial hierarchy, with whites as the supremely positioned group, and it led some of the greatest leaders and intellectuals of American history to not only doubt black ingenuity, thus black humanity, but also to declare black creativity as nonexistent.

Thomas Jefferson, for instance, was of the general opinion that blacks were incapable of abstract thought. "Never yet could I find that a black had uttered a thought above the level of plain narration, never see even an elementary trait of painting or sculpture." He wrote of Phyllis Wheatley, the first African poet published in America, that her work was imitative and unoriginal, and therefore, of no significance. He dismissed her poetry as mere plaint, consequent to the miserable state of blacks as chattel. "Among the blacks is misery enough, God knows, but not poetry.... The compositions published under her name are below the dignity of criticism."[19]

Abraham Lincoln, "the Great Emancipator," like many of his contemporaries, ascribed to the European-created, thus European-favored, hierarchy that castigated African peoples to an inferior place:

> There is a physical difference between the white and black races which I
> believe will forever forbid the two races living together on terms of social and
> political equality. And inasmuch as they cannot so live, while they do remain
> together there must be the position of superior and inferior, and I as much as
> any other man am in favor of having the superior position assigned to the
> white race.[20]

Of the many possible options Lincoln conceived of in response to problems
engendered by America's imminent civil war, he proposed to solve the
problems by supporting the emigration of African peoples to Haiti and
Liberia.[21]

Henry Ward Beecher, brother of Harriet Beecher Stowe, went a step
further. He imagined the possibility of a world, altogether, without Africa
and without Africans. In her 1892 publication *A Voice from the South*, Anna
Julia Cooper quoted these words from Beecher:

> Were Africa and the Africans to sink to-morrow, how much poorer would the
> world be? A little less gold and ivory, a little less coffee, a considerable ripple,
> perhaps where the Atlantic and Indian Oceans would come together—that is
> all; not a poem, not an invention, not a piece of art would be missed from the
> world.[22]

African Americans may have been the first group of peoples who felt compelled to justify their very existence, to prove their worth as human beings,
and to establish their contribution to world civilization. The Harlem Renaissance was, in a sense, a response to Beecher's call for proof of the humanity
of Africans in America. What would be indicative of African civilization?
What would be expressive of African genius? That is, what would evidence
that genie that attended the birth of *African* Americans?

Whatever African Americans thought and believed privately, these were
public and political questions that required a response. Many American
political and social policies were based on the conclusions that black people
were intellectually and culturally inferior and, as the European evolutionary
model of culture and civilization would have it, destined for extinction. Harlem Renaissance leaders perceived that they were engaged in a culture war.
The Harlem Renaissance Movement, in spite of all its perceived faults, shortcomings, and failings, was a resounding response to supremacist Euro-
American queries: Are you human? Are you worthy of our glance? Why
should you continue to live?

With such an uninspiring socio-historical context for black life in
America, one begins to understand Alice Walker's delight and relief upon
her discovery of Zora Neale Hurston's *Mules and Men*. Therein was a testament to the value of black culture, thus to black life. This was no insignificant find. Just as Alice Walker, Robert Hemenway, and other artists and
scholars retrieved Hurston from oblivion, Hurston had, decades before,
worked to rescue black folk from an oblivion imposed by racist social scientists and lay scientists who believed that the oral traditions of "pre-literate"

societies were but relics, survivals from the primitive stages of humanity, with no greater utility than to be mined for the benefit of the self-proclaimed more evolved group. These ideas, prevalent in American culture, also seeped into the mind-set of African American intellectuals. Hurston, unlike many of her contemporaries, saw black folk culture as worthy of study for its own intrinsic value, for its own complex statement on human existence, for its own unique expression of divinity.

Zora Neale Hurston's pioneering efforts in the fields of folklore and anthropology stand out even more clearly when seen in light of the fact that, save for Native American populations, there was no scientific focus on other ethnic minority groups before the 1900s. "Two major assumptions prevalent in American society contributed to this scholarly neglect: that the black man was incapable of any thought or expression meriting serious study; and that whites knew everything worth knowing about the slaves who lived inside white society."[23] During the latter part of the nineteenth century, in the fervor of proslavery and antislavery arguments, African people increasingly became a subject of scientific curiosity. Even as these scientists elected to include African peoples in their purview, their belief in the static quality of "primitive" cultures and the inherent barbarity and, therefore, eventual disappearance of so-called primitive peoples was constant. William W. Newell, for instance, the founding member of the American Folk-Lore Society and first general editor of its publication, the *Journal of American Folklore*, encouraged the collection of lore of the "culturally inferior folk." As with most of his colleagues, his purposes were more oriented toward confirmation of old assumptions rather than edification: "The habits and ideas of primitive races include much that it might be thought well to leave unrecorded," wrote Newell. "But this would be a superficial view. What is needed is not an anthology of customs and beliefs, but a complete representation of the savage mind in its rudeness as well as its intelligence, its licentiousness as well as its fidelity."[24]

Clearly, although these early scientists became more inclusive in their research subjects and emphasized more extensive fieldwork, they had little inclination toward scientific objectivity and little respect for the people among whom they carried out their research. Franz Boas would prove to be different. By the time Franz Boas had begun his work in the United States, evolutionary scientists had generated theories of cultural assimilation and had developed the pseudo-science of eugenics. These theories were integrated into American social and economic policy, and eugenics became a practice sanctioned and supported by the federal government. In the interest of a white nationalism that sought to preserve Anglo-Saxon heritage and a spurious white racial purity, Euro-American leaders of medical institutions and business corporations instituted policies reflecting the dogma of scientific racism. In the face of American interest to realize the beliefs inherent in the Great Race theory (the notion of the supremacy of Nordic whites), Franz Boas's ideas were revolutionary. Zora Neale Hurston was a part of that ideological revolution.

Anthropology had become a formal academic discipline in U.S. universities around the turn of the twentieth century. Franz Boas created the first Department of Anthropology at Columbia in 1899. Earlier scholars and practitioners had already constructed a wall of ignorance that supported the ascendancy of Europeans in the human "chain of being" and relegated all other groups below them. Boas, considered the father of American anthropology, was one of the first American social scientists to question and refute the evolutionary school of thought. To a great extent, Boas's ideas that a culture was to be investigated and understood on its own terms rather than as part of an evolutionary schema of human social development began to create fissures in the racial and social hierarchical wall that Americans were up against. His theories evinced a respect for those cultures, which through the lens of scientific racism had been denigrated.

Whereas his colleagues tended to impose their preconceived ideas and theories on the people and material they collected, Boas was wary of facile theorizing and demanded extensive collection of material and thorough comparative analyses. These were particular aspects of Boas's methodology that impressed Hurston. She admired "his insatiable hunger for knowledge and then more knowledge." And she respected "his genius for pure objectivity. He has no pet wishes to prove," Hurston wrote. "His instructions are to go out and find what is there. He outlines his theory, but if the facts do not agree with it, he would not warp a jot or dot of the findings to save his theory. So knowing all this," as she prepared for her first fieldwork expedition in the South, alone, Hurston said, "I was proud that he trusted me. I went off in a vehicle made out of Corona stuff."[25] Boas's research and publications, along with those of his students and like-minded colleagues, exploded the tenets of biological determinism, which were at the scientific heart of the Great Race theory. Boas's research revealed that there was no superior or inferior race or culture. His work demonstrated that although social behavior and language were key attributes of culture, they were learned and neither race based nor heritable. Through anthropometric studies—the measurement of living humans—Boas showed that even so-called racial types were not fixed, as human physicality tended to change in a changed environment. Thus, the concept of "race," itself, was redefined to describe only general physical features of human beings, to the exclusion of cultural phenomena.[26]

Although revolutionary in the scientific community, these ideas were not new to Zora Neale Hurston. Actually, her appreciation of people as individuals and the relativistic nature of cultures seemed to be just a part of who she was. This natural disposition encouraged her sitting atop the gatepost to hail white passers-by, in spite of the warnings against doing so. It is what allowed her an easy adjustment among her associates of the Gilbert and Sullivan Company, all of whom were of different ethnicities or cultural backgrounds. Her friend and erstwhile roommate, Bruce Nugent, described Hurston as "an integrated person." She was "an extraordinarily multifarious woman," said Nugent, "who had the capacity to understand and appreciate human diversity in all its complex forms."[27] She "had great scorn for all pretensions, academic or otherwise," Langston Hughes recalled. "That is why she was such a fine folk-lore collector, able to go among the people and never act as if she had been to school at all. Almost nobody else," Hughes observed, "could stop the average Harlemite on Lenox Avenue and measure his head with a strange-looking, anthropological device and not get bawled out for the attempt, except Zora, who used to stop anyone whose head looked interesting, and measure it."[28] Alice Walker reflected that Hurston "had a confidence in herself as an individual that few people (anyone?), black or white, understood." Hurston's own positive sense of self was mirrored in her respect for Africana peoples and culture. "Zora's pride in black people was so pronounced in the ersatz black twenties that it made other blacks suspicious and perhaps uncomfortable," noted Walker.[29]

It was Hurston's ability to recognize her oneness with all humanity, in general, and with African peoples, in particular, which made the greatest difference between her work as a social scientist and the work of others in the field. Being one with the African American folk, she understood them. This was a key element in her ability to penetrate the various self-protective layers of folk society to plumb its rich substrata. To understand, to comprehend someone or something, is paramount in any honest attempt to communicate. In his preface to *Mules and Men*, Franz Boas recognizes Hurston's skills and her gifts both as an effective scientist and an effective communicator.

> It is the great merit of Miss Hurston's work that she entered into the homely life of the southern Negro as one of them and was fully accepted as such by the companions of her childhood.... Added to all this is the charm of a loveable personality and of a revealing style which makes Miss Hurston's work an unusual contribution to our knowledge of the true inner life of the Negro.[30]

More than anything else, Hurston's egalitarian spirit was confirmed by her tutelage under Boas. Her innate ease with people was a part of her personality that facilitated her work as an anthropologist. As Hurston's recognition of common humanity preceded her academic training, so, too, her love of and recognition of the genius of black folk was already present. She experienced the bravery, will-to-power, and genius inherent in an all-black town and basked in the warmth of a village whose oral traditions were expressive of a rich, vibrant humanity. "I was glad when somebody told me, You may go and collect Negro Folk-lore." This statement opens Hurston's introduction to the material she published in *Mules and Men*. Then she proceeds to inform the reader about the inner knowingness that was the source of her appreciation of the black folk.

> In a way it would not be a new experience for me. When I pitched headforemost into the world. I landed in the crib of negroism. From the earliest rocking of my cradle, I had known about the capers Brer Rabbit is apt to cut and what the Squinch Owl says from the house top.[31]

Admittedly, as Hurston told the reader, "it was fitting me like a tight chemise."[32] But, with the "spy-glass of Anthropology," she could then view herself and the culture into which she had been born with the objectivity needed to scientifically observe and study the folk and the folk life of their creation.

Another common definition of "genius" is the natural aptitude, ability, or talent for something or to do something. Unlike Jean Toomer, Zora Neale Hurston had been listening to and absorbing African American folklore all her life. This *folklore*, for her, was not the ossified survival of some "fast-vanishing" culture, but her cultural history as well as her everyday life. Over time, she also came to understand that it was not Toomer's "swansong." It was the psycho-spiritual substance of the only individual in America, at that time, who was one of the folk and who had the natural ability—the genius—to document, interpret, and present African American folk culture with authenticity.

Folklore is the lore of folk. "Folk" is a Germanic term that means a people, nation, or race. "Lore," also a Germanic term, refers to the dynamic of learning. Modern society continues to conceive of folklore as something quaint and curious, interesting, maybe, but irrelevant to modern life. But the largely archaic definitions of "lore" tell us something more of the substance, function, and significance of the concept inscribed in the word: The act of teaching; the condition of being taught; instruction, education; a piece of instruction, a lesson. That which is taught; doctrine, precept, teaching. A creed or religion. Advice, counsel, scholarship, erudition. It is treacherously ironic that ideas of "the folks" typically conjure up images of *simple,* uncultured, and unlearned persons. The folklore—what these people know and what they do, that is, their customs—is typically viewed as backward and superstitious, that is, ungodly. Yet, the meanings embedded in the terms "lore" and "folklore" contradict such reductive definitions.

"Folklore" is the science, art, worldview, and wisdom of a people—a folk. It is the collective thought and expression, organically generated and re-created in various cultural forms, which, through ritualistic traditions, are transmitted orally from the older to the younger generation of folk. The few lines in a dictionary or in an introduction-to-folklore reader cannot capture the true meaning and significance of folklore. Popular definitions of "folklore" tend to list various forms of cultural expression, such as customs, songs, and tales, and indicate that these expressive forms are preserved and transmitted through oral tradition. This superficial definition has led to a superficial conception and appreciation of folklore and, thus, of "the folk." The songs, proverbs, dances, cures, beliefs, and so on that are the objects of collection and investigation of folklorists are but the tip of a vast breadth of human understanding that, at its base, is eons old. With only nature itself as a guiding text, indigenous peoples around the globe had to decipher this Ur-text, or very first text, and *learn* how to survive. What did that surviving entail and how was it done sufficiently and efficiently enough to secure continuation? What did they have to know to succeed continually? Out of their will to survive and continue came a complex of sciences, philosophies, and religions that is at the common core of what makes human beings human and out of which humans create societies. And for every people, for every folk, that understanding is unique, aboriginal—that is, *ab origine*: "From the beginning; from the creation of the world."[33] Each aboriginal understanding of life that reflects a folk's coming to terms with life is expressive of the genius of that folk.

Zora Neale Hurston had an intuitive knowing that infused her intellectual pursuits at Barnard and Columbia. The methodological skills she developed at those institutions empowered her to make magnificent contributions to anthropological science, specifically, and to the humanities as a whole. Most of Boas's research, as with those before him, was focused on the indigenous American populations. In the early twentieth century, Zora Neale Hurston was the only African American, from the South, who also had the professional credentials and training to conduct field research among "the American Negro folk."[34] This, in itself, distinguished Hurston from others in the field. Compared with her contemporaries, she had all the attributes for success. In addition to having an insider's knowledge, Hurston, recognized the expressive culture of the African American folk as unique and original. In her investigations of various spiritual expressions of the traditional black church, such as song, sermons, prayers, and shoutings, she concluded that "the Negro has not been Christianized as extensively as is generally believed. The great masses are still standing before their pagan altars and calling old gods by a new name." The shouting expressed in the sanctified churches she wrote, "is nothing more than a continuation of the African 'Possession' by the gods." Hurston saw the rites of the sanctified church as a revitalizing element in black religion, designed to restore "those elements which were brought over from Africa and grafted onto Christianity." In her comparative analysis of African American religious traditions, Hurston contrasted the dynamic sound and motion of the black church with the "staid and restrained" service of "the white man." She compared the "'Possession' by the gods" in African American churches with similar expressions in Haitian practices. Hurston expounded, "These stages can be seen in Haiti when a man or a woman is 'mounted' by a loa, or spirit."[35]

The African American and African continuum may be self-evident today, but many earlier social scientists believed the mind of Africans in the diaspora to be a sort of *tabula rasa*, because of the uprooting of Africans and their dispersion in the Americas and elsewhere. Even beyond that, it was believed that African peoples were bereft of human ingenuity or creativity, so these scientists denied African origins as a source of African American expression. Cultural expression among African Americans was attributed either to Europeans or to Native Americans. To contend that Negro folksongs, for example, were of African origin, was a highly controversial issue. Most agreed, however, that Negro folktales were African in origin. In his

Uncle Remus: His Songs and His Sayings, published in 1880, Joel Chandler Harris stated that, "the folktales of blacks were of remote African origin and did not betray European influences, and that Negro folktales had not been influenced by those of the American Indian, as John Wesley Powell and others had suggested."[36]

Many of the early Euro-American folklorists, like Joel Harris, had no formal anthropological training. Harris, for instance, was a journalist and did not consider himself to be a folklorist. The relatively new field of folklore study had mass appeal and fast became an "interest" of upper-class whites. The new science of folklore, contextualized within an evolutionary model, "confirmed the Victorians' lofty opinion of themselves." It predicted a future civilization of enlightened Nordics, governed by reason and industry. According to Bronner, "It was equally a palliative for what they called 'neurasthenia,' a brand of nervousness and unease caused by the stresses of 'overcivilization.'"[37] Insight into this dis-ease of neurasthenia is helpful in understanding Charlotte Mason's peptic patronage of Harlem Renaissance artists and writers. It also puts into perspective the contradictory behavioral patterns of those who professed progressive social politics, but who were staunch defenders of racial segregation. Whites of that ilk presumed themselves superior, but at the same time, they felt incomplete. As the *Winter Park Herald's* columnist stated, the Negro's "barbaric color adds pattern to the Nordic restraint about him." Americans (i.e., Euro-Americans) needed this color the columnist explains, because America's civilization had "sprung full grown from the head of Europe"; so it was without a wealth of its own native folklore with which to temper its stoic existence.

Zora Neale Hurston's achievements become even more admirable as we realize her ability to negotiate intolerant social and professional terrains to, nonetheless, present black folklore, in text and on the stage in all its integrity. Franz Boas praised Hurston's authentic rendering of black folk life in *Mules and Men*, noting that "since the time of Uncle Remus," attempts had been made to capture black folk life, "but in all of them the intimate setting in the social life of the Negro has been given very inadequately."[38] In Hurston's presentation of the stories, songs, and sayings she compiled in *Mules and Men*, she created a framework that reflects the antiphonal quality of traditional African American storytelling. Her recounting of the dynamic interplay among the characters depicted in the text points up the communal aspect of African American folk culture. And as she describes scenes of the folk at work, at worship, and at leisure, she emphasizes the functionality of the lore—the customs and traditions—in the everyday lives of the people who created it. The folks who people the text speak in cadences of their rich vernacular expression. In her effort to effectively approximate the language of her informants, Hurston rendered their dialogue and their songs and tales phonetically and used italics, elongated syllables, and exclamation points to suggest the rhythm of the speech and the mood or emphatic attitude of a speaker.

In her analysis of the material she amassed, Hurston extrapolated principles of black folk expression. As she indicated in her August 12, 1928, letter to Hughes and as she later wrote in her essay "Characteristics of Negro Expression," "The Negro's universal mimicry is not so much a thing in itself as an evidence of something that permeates his entire self. And that thing is drama." The language is replete with action words and picture-making metaphors, and "every hour of life," whether joyful or sorrowful, invites some drama, some ceremony.[39] Compelled by the cultural impulse of black folks toward drama and toward action, Hurston was inspired to see black folklore enacted on stage. In the dramatic presentation and performance of folklore, Hurston was again ahead of her colleagues in the field of anthropology. Early collectors conceived of folklore as literary and, therefore, focused solely on the written transcriptions of tales, songs, riddles, and other oral expressions. By the mid-nineteenth century, the mode of collecting expanded to include the situational context of stories and songs as well as the musical settings of the songs. The chapter in Hurston's *Mules and Men*, which includes musical notations with the song lyrics, exemplifies this practice, as do the appendixed chapters in *Tell My Horse*. Folklorists gradually came to understand that "folklore, in all its many forms, is *performed*."[40]

Folklore scholar Jack Santino came to this conclusion when discussing myths and was told, "If you ever actually see—as well as hear—someone tell a myth, you'd understand that there is much more to it than universal archetypes." Santino noted that the study of folklore as performance "was a somewhat radical departure from that of a previous generation of scholars, who tended to study folklore as transcribed texts or as items isolated from the original context in which they were collected." Santino traced his breakthrough to the work of Milman Parry and Albert Lord who began their research in the 1930s, which culminated in the 1960 publication *The Singer of Tales*. The upshot of this text and others that followed was that "the study of a folkloric event requires that attention be directed not only to the text, but also to the texture of the performance and the context in which it occurs."[41]

This was precisely Hurston's insight, for example, regarding Negro spirituals. Musicians and singers had taken the songs out of context, defying the natural, organic process out of which spirituals are sung and created what she called "holler singing," "a sort of musical octoroon" that was presented to the public as Negro spirituals. In her 1932 concert performance at the John Golden Theater, Hurston presented folk materials, including spirituals, work songs, and dances, within their genuine contexts. "I did not have the singers stand in a stiff group and reach for the high note. I told them to just imagine that they were in Macedonia and go ahead." Long before she staged performances of folklore for the public, Hurston performed the material for the smaller audiences of her New York friends as well as for her employer Charlotte Mason and her entourage. "I must tell the tales, sing the songs, do the dances, and report the raucous sayings and doings of the Negro farthest down."[42]

HURSTON AS A NATIVE AMERICAN GENIUS

To consider Hurston's genius only in context of the U.S. South and her contributions to the Harlem Renaissance period is to miss the depth and breadth of an extraordinary human being. Alice Walker not only considered Hurston a genius of the South, but also "a native American genius."[43] Hurston's work as an anthropological folklorist had national as well as regional significance. During the years between the World Wars, the interest in folklore became nationalistic. Whereas formerly the official American position was that folk culture represented elements in American society that were best obliterated, the American public and the American government gradually began to embrace folk culture as a valuable part of an authentically American identity. Individuals like Sara Gertrude Knott saw the presentation of various American folk cultures to mass audiences as a means to preserve American folk traditions and to promote cultural diversity. To realize her vision, Knott founded the National Folk Festival Association (NFFA), and Paul Green, with whom she had collaborated, became the association's first president. Under their leadership, members of the organization worked to educate the public about its diverse cultures and to reduce and forestall the "disintegrating influences of the 'American Melting Pot.'"[44]

Columbia University, along with Rollins College, University of North Carolina, Harvard University, Fisk University, and several other institutions were part of the academic "advance guard" of the national folklore movement. Popular and academic interests in American folk culture merged with those of the federal government. President Franklin Delano Roosevelt, for instance, recognized the significance of folk culture in forging a more democratic American identity. In his communication of these ideas to folklorist and dramatist Paul Green, a playwright associated with the University of North Carolina, Roosevelt wrote, "We in the United States are amazingly rich in the elements from which to weave a culture. We have the best of man's past on which to draw, brought to us by our native folk and folk from all parts of the world."[45] The NFFA along with its academic arm worked to identify the varied cultural strands from which American culture was woven. Franklin Roosevelt's conceptualization of folklore as functional and valuable to a modernizing American society contrasted sharply with Theodore Roosevelt's eugenicist notion of racial and cultural "others." As some American cultures were faced with imminent extinction, others were being assimilated into Anglo-Protestant society, and modernity itself was reshaping the cultural patterns of virtually everyone. Genuine folk culture and material culture of early America was disappearing.

Like Paul Green, Zora Neale Hurston was also associated with the NFFA and several institutions within its academic advance guard. Her renown as a producer and director of folk concerts, her membership in the NFFA and participation in its annual festivals, and her research and publications on African American folklore and Hoodoo made her a nationally recognized figure and an asset to both the popular national movement and the various enterprises of the federal government. Hurston contributed her expertise to the government's Federal Theatre Project. As a part of Franklin Roosevelt's New Deal for the country, the Works Progress Administration, later renamed the Work Projects Administration (WPA), was designed to include projects to bring economic relief to professionals in the arts and humanities. To that end, the Federal Art Project, Federal Music Project, Federal Theater Project, and Federal Writers' Project were created. In October 1935, Hurston joined the "Negro Unit" of the WPA's Federal Theater Project in New York as a drama coach at $23.66 per week. Among other activities with the Theater Project, which was directed by John Houseman and Orson Welles, she assisted in the production of *Walk Together Chillun!* and wrote a play. In a letter to Edwin Osgood Grover, she wrote, "I have been called upon to write a play within a week and believe it or not, I did it and got it accepted."[46] The play was accepted, but it was not produced. Hurston's black folk adaptation of *Lysistrata* was considered too scandalous for "both the Left and the Right."[47]

Although poised for a promotion and salary increase in March, Hurston tendered her resignation. After six months, she resigned to accept a Guggenheim award that would take her to the Caribbean—but this time to Jamaica and Haiti. "I humbly and gratefully accept the fellowship granted me by the John Simon Guggenheim Memorial Foundation," Hurston wrote to the foundation director, Henry Allen Moe. She expressed her hope and determination to "add something to human understanding and to art."[48]

Hurston's excitement over receiving the award was infectious. "Hurrah! Zora got her Guggenheim Fellowship," Fannie Hurst reported to Carl Van Vechten. Both had written letters of recommendation on her behalf. "Can't you see the Caribbean heaving with anticipation?"[49] When she received the official announcement, Hurston wrote Moe, "[I] saw my name thru a mist. I go to perform my vows unto God."[50]

Whatever difficulties or trials may have darkened Hurston's back door, she was never short on joy and enthusiasm. "Enthusiasm" from "entheas," formed from "en" plus "theos," means to have god within, which translates as spirit, to be inspired or possessed by a god. Enthusiasm is an elemental aspect of genius; it quickens one's life force, one's vitality—of which Hurston had an abundance. At any given moment, Hurston was actively managing multiple projects. For instance, in her letter to Grover, telling him about her work with the Federal Theater Project, Hurston also thanks him for his letter of recommendation to the Guggenheim Foundation, apologizing for her "long silences." She explains,

> I am doing the most intensive stretch of labor ever.... A whole suit-case full of unanswered mail.... Must keep working on "Moses" for my publishers and another book [*Tell My Horse*] besides. I am requested at public places and make some of them besides getting some reading done and some work on another play which I think is all set so far as acceptance is concerned.[51]

Hurston was of the attitude that hard work "is what folks were born for I reckon." She was working harder than she ever had, she told Annie Nathan Mayer, but proclaimed that she liked it. "So no complaint. I stay tired, but that is not bad. I only feel badly when I feel that I have wasted a day."[52]

In his work *Genius: A Mosaic of One Hundred Exemplary Creative Minds*, Harold Bloom described enthusiasm and vitality as attributes of a literary genius. We read an author "in search of more life," Bloom stated. Thus, "vitality is the measure of literary genius."[53] Reading Hurston's life through her work and her writings, we become aware of the remarkable vitality not only within her writings, but also within the author herself. As Bambara noted, "the woman did not play." Hurston's enthusiasm for the work she was called to do was equaled by her capacity to do it. Hurston once declared to Mason, "I am on fire about my people."[54] That fire never died. The more refined her folklore collecting skills became, the more ambitious were her goals. The nets she would cast stretched wider and wider. Indiscriminate and extensive collections of lore was part of the Boasian field methodology: "amassing data with no particular problem in mind and with no clear idea of what was to be gained in the end," ensured a measure of objectivity. This method resulted from his belief that each culture possesses its own concepts, categories, and biases, and to arrive at a true understanding of another culture, "it was essential for scholars to collect vast quantities of reliable material in the native language."[55] So Hurston always exerted herself to collect everything she could in a given area of field study.

We have some appreciation of the breadth and scope of Hurston's fieldwork when we note that, until recently, most of the material she collected was never published. The material in *Mules and Men*, for example, represents but a portion of the results of her early collection in the South. What was omitted was enough material to compile another book—which has been done. *Every Tongue Got to Confess: Negro Folk-tales from the Gulf States*, edited by Carla Kaplan, was published in 2001. Kaplan stated in her introduction to the book that material from Hurston's early expeditions in the South "eventually found its way into *Mules and Men* and some reappear in Hurston's contributions to the FWP's book-length study 'The Florida Negro.' But together they account for less than a third of the 'gorgeous' stories Hurston originally vacuumed up."[56] *Every Tongue*, a compilation of nearly 500 tales, is still only a partial representation of the entire lode.

We gain an even greater appreciation of Hurston's physical and spiritual vitality when we also consider the conditions under which she did her research and the extended periods of time during which she stayed in the field. "Folklore is not as easy to collect as it sounds," Hurston informed her readers in *Mules and Men*. She always collected in out-of-the-way places where the "underprivileged" lived and worked, "shy" folk, who were the best sources.[57] In a letter posted from Jacksonville, Florida, to her friend Lawrence Jordan, Hurston toyed with him about joining her in the field: "I cannot imagine an ultra like you forsaking the creature comforts of New York for these shacks that suffice in the sub-tropics. I cannot see you forsaking the classic halls of Universities for the songs and tales of camp and road-chain gangs and what-not. I challenge you," she baited him, "*I dare you to try it!*"[58] The "what-not" entailed many possible challenges or mishaps, such as mosquitoes, hurricanes, no public accommodations, and broken-down automobiles. In addition to the arduous nature of research work, Hurston had to negotiate the tensions associated with her work: the tensions relevant to the social dynamics of being a lone black woman among blacks; the social and political dynamics of being a lone black woman in white supremacist environments; and the social and economic dynamics of being a black woman with a patronizing white employer. The hard work and the stress under which she labored would sometimes result in fatigue, depression, or bodily ailments. The ongoing negotiations with an authoritarian patron-employer were a persistent source of nervous tension. Hurston confided to Hughes, for example, that Mason "exploded" when Hurston bought a car. The one she had was continually in the shop and draining her already limited budget. She needed a reliable vehicle. Although Mason paid for the car in the end, she accused Hurston of being untrustworthy and extravagant. "It destroys my self-respect and utterly demoralizes me for weeks," she told Langston Hughes. "I know you can appreciate what I mean."[59]

As a child, Hurston marveled at her physical strength—she could play with boys and not cry. As an adult, she maintained her youthfulness and her physical stamina. From the field she wrote Hughes, "Been working two years without rest, [and] behind that all my school life with no rest, no peace of mind. But the Bahamas trip did me a world of good. I got rested while working hard." Hurston could sometimes even be boastful of her vitality and her energetic spirit. When she returned to New York from her two-year collecting expedition, she conveyed to Franz Boas that she was "working furiously" on the folklore manuscript and other projects. In another letter to Jordan, she wrote,

> I was in Harlem yesterday for the first time. Some of my friends are all tired and worn out—looking like death eating crackers. All of them cried to me to come and put some life into the gang again. I don't feel any older or tired a bit. Perhaps the hectic life of Harlem wore them out faster while I was in the South getting my rest as well as getting some work done.[60]

Although hale, Hurston had to deal with regular maladies such as tonsillitis, toothaches, and stress, and earlier on she was hospitalized for appendicitis. Traveling frequently and oftentimes living in the most spare accommodations and eating and drinking unusual fare, she became susceptible to alimentary ailments. These health conditions persisted throughout her life. Once in 1939, she was hospitalized for digestive problems, but more often than not, Hurston would turn to folk remedies such as agar-agar. Whatever illness Hurston dealt with, she tended to be resilient. The heartiness and enthusiasm that made Hurston an intrepid field researcher in the

American South prepared and emboldened her to go further south, into the West Indies and Haiti to conduct field research. The certificate of health she had to submit to the Guggenheim Foundation before leaving indicated that "all was well."[61]

The letters that recommended Hurston to the Guggenheim Foundation attested to her efficacy as a folklorist as well as an artist: "She has an amazing talent," wrote Van Vechten, "perhaps even genius, for the collection, selection, and creative application of folk material." Edwin Grover, with whom Hurston had worked at Rollins College, stated that "Miss Hurston is a thorough and scientific investigator and reliable in every way. I know of no one of her race who is more likely to do more original or valuable research and creative work in the next ten or fifteen years."[62] Hurston got off the steamer to the British West Indies on April 13, 1936. After a brief stop in Haiti to introduce herself to officials, she proceeded to Jamaica where she settled in and dispatched some correspondences. To Henry Allen Moe she expressed again her excitement and her commitment to the project:

> I am very happy about every thing and I shall work very very hard. It hardly seems possible that my chance has come. I have looked and yearned so long for the chance [to] work as hard as I could at what I wanted to do, I've never really extended because I couldn't before.[63]

It is hard to imagine that, with all Hurston had achieved up to that point, she felt she hadn't really "extended" herself. The statement is suggestive of the passion and capacity she had for her work.

As outlined in her fellowship proposal, Hurston's objectives were to collect all aspects of Negro folklife for scientific scrutiny and to draw on the material for creative fictional work that "shall give a true picture of Negro life at the same time that it entertains."[64] Hurston's fieldwork sometimes functioned as the means by which she escaped intimate relationships that compromised her ability to work hard. Dissolving her relationship with Percival McGuire Punter, for instance, was among her many thoughts as she departed for the Caribbean. Like Herbert Sheen, Punter was standing between Hurston and her calling. She had not married Punter, but she was in love with him. "He was tall, dark brown, magnificently built, with a beautifully modeled back head ... I did not fall in love with him just for that," Hurston recounted. "He had a fine mind and that intrigued me. When a man keeps beating me to the draw mentally, he begins to get glamorous." According to Hurston, she had the psychological and emotional space for Punter *and* her work. "My work was one thing, and he was all the rest." But he was too demanding, "Nothing must be in my life but himself."[65]

According to Punter, Hurston was possessed by her work with an "almost priestly" devotion.[66] "We were alternately the happiest people in the world, and the most miserable," Hurston wistfully recalled. After a six-week stint down South with Elizabeth Barnicle and Alan Lomax, Hurston returned to New York to enfold into her joy-pain relationship with Punter. Although

Hurston may have been "hog-tied and branded," her work was an even more powerful attracting force: "A charge had been laid upon me and I must follow the call." With Herbert Sheen, her research contract with Mason gave her "a way out, without saying anything very much. Let nature take its course." With Percival Punter, the Guggenheim Fellowship "was my chance to release him, and fight myself free of my obsession."[67]

In Jamaica, she would not write Punter, fearing that their communication would undermine the distance she put between them. She wouldn't write him, but she would write about him. When she had finished poring over her feelings about Punter, she had written *Their Eyes Were Watching God*. In that novel, Hurston reminisces, "I tried to embalm all the tenderness of my passion for him.[68] The passion Hurston and Punter shared inspired the relationship between Janie, the main character of *Their Eyes*, and Tea Cake, the love of her life. After a loveless marriage to Logan Killicks and another marriage wherein the love died and was buried with her second husband Jody Starks, Janie met this "glance from God." Alone in the general store, "a tall man had come into the place," saying "Good evenin', Mis' Starks," with purple lips. He was Vergible Woods, called Tea Cake, and "sweet as all dat." He courted Janie with Coca-Cola, checkers, picnics, and fried fish. She was the light nobody could hold a candle to. He was twenty-eight, she was forty. He was dark-skinned, she was café au lait. He was a migrant worker, she was widowed and prominent. He was alive, and she wanted to live. Since "mourning oughtn't tuh last no longer 'n grief," Janie married Tea Cake less than a year after Jody's burial.[69] Like Hurston and Punter, the fictional couple spent equal time in heaven and hell, each passionate about and possessive over the other. Their love, however, no matter how intense and committed, was assailed by insecurities, uncertainties, and doubt, "the fiend from hell." Like Hurston and Punter, they fought. Each trying to beat down his or her own fear. And like them, they would love so hard and get so close, "you couldn't get a pin between" them.[70]

On the steamer to Jamaica, Hurston must have felt Percival Punter everywhere, like Janie whose "last-night memory" of Tea Cake was so palpable, "she could feel him and almost see him bucking around the room in the upper air."[71] Even as Hurston set her feet down in blooded tracks, she heard the words of her vow echoing through her mind: "I swore an oath to leave all pleasure and take the hard road of labor."[72] True to her oath, Hurston wrote to friends James Weldon and Grace Johnson, saying, "I am out here in this beautiful country and down at hard work."[73] As she traveled up steep hills and mountains and down valley trails into cockpits, Hurston found in Jamaica that the hard road of labor was not necessarily paved. Sometimes she would have to walk that road, as the mule provided for her transportation into the maroon village of Accompong, for instance, refused to carry her. And, sometimes on that road, which, more often than not was no road at all, she might even be faced with a charging wild boar. Desirous of some jerk pork, Hurston's request to her hosts resulted in a hunting party that ventured into the cockpit country of Accompong. "That is hard traveling even for us here who are accustomed to rocks and mountains," warns Colonel Rowe, the governing figure in the village. But that is where the wild hog was to be found; for the celebrated jerk pork of the maroons did not come from domestic pork. As a general rule women were not numbered among the hunting party, but Hurston looked forward to it—at least initially. "If I had had some sense, I would not have gone either, but you live and learn," she stated, after the fact. After a four-day march over terrain that "became more rocky and full of holes and jags and points and loose looking boulders," the party finally picked up signs of the boar. They separated into two factions. Escaping the first faction and in search of a hideaway, the animal headed up the trail in the direction of Hurston and the other half of the hunting party. "The men got ready to meet the charge. The boar with his huge, curving tusks, dripping with dogs' blood came charging down upon us. I had never pictured anything so huge, so fierce nor so fast. Everybody cleared the way."[74] Looking on from the protective cover of a large boulder, Hurston observed the hunters as they felled the boar. In the aftermath, the men ritualistically acknowledged each other's bravery, expressing gratitude "for dangers past," shaking hands and kissing one another.

During the dressing and preparation of the boar, and on the march home, as in the outset, the maroons told stories, sang songs, and talked. Hurston compared tales she heard in Jamaica with those found in the United States and in Haiti: "Brother Anansi, the Spider, that great cultural hero of West Africa who is personated in Haiti by Ti Malice and in the United States by Brer Rabbit."[75] As with the tales, she traced many of Jamaica's songs, puberty rites, and uses of medicinal plants to West African origin. Knowledge of Afro-Caribbean culture was helpful in better understanding the African American of the U.S. South. As Franz Boas noted in his preface to *Mules and Men*, "the strong African background in the West Indies" informed the historical character of the American Negro.[76] Some of the religious and spiritual practices Hurston observed and in which she participated, such as Jamaica's "Nine Night" ceremony, revealed African roots. Hurston concluded, "In reality it is old African ancestor worship in fragmentary form." Its purpose was to appease the dead so that the spirit of the deceased will not do ill among the living.[77] Hurston found Jamaica to be "a seething Africa under its British exterior."[78] She found in Haiti further compelling evidence of African heritage in the diaspora. Through her personal investigations, she confirmed Haitian Voodoo to be "a religion of creation and life," "the old, old mysticism of the world in African terms." Having utilized the anthropological method of immersion in studying Hoodoo practices in the U.S. South, Hurston likewise used this method in studying Voodoo. She "went Canzo." That is, she took the second step to the Voodoo priesthood. Through her initiation rites and attendance at various other ceremonies, Hurston learned the Voodoo pantheon, the symbolism of the major divinities or loa, their domain of influence, the manifestations of their possessions, the colors, songs, and flags with which they are associated, and their preferred offerings. She gained insight into the two "classes" of gods: (1) the Rada, "the 'good' gods," originating in Dahomey; and (2) the Petro, the gods that do good and evil and are said to be of Congo or Guinea origin.[79] She learned as well of the Secte Rouge or Secret Societies. Having heard the drums in the night, their sound and rhythm so different from those of the Rada ceremonies, Hurston prepared to investigate. Lucille, her maid and friend, advised her against it: "I am well content if you do not run to every drum that you hear" she expressed to Hurston. This drum with the offbeat that captured Hurston's attention was the drum of the Cochon Gris, a secret, cannibalistic society. Although outlawed and detested by all but its practitioners, the society managed to continue by representing themselves as Voodoo adepts.[80]

"Some things were good to know and some were not," Lucille chided Hurston. Despite warnings, even warnings against the possibility of death, Hurston persisted in probing the secrets of the Secte Rouge. She brought the same insistent curiosity to the practice of zombification. Having seen and photographed an actual zombie, "something never done before," she was "determined to get at the secret of Zombies." With the intention of putting the world right about Voodoo and about practices such as zombification an cannibalism, which had nothing at all to do with Voodoo, "a harmless pagan cult," Hurston justified her investigations: "But how can I say these things until I am very sure?"[81]

In October 1936, realizing the extent of her work, Hurston wrote Henry Allen Moe from Port-au-Prince, Haiti, requesting an application for a second Guggenheim Fellowship:

> I know that thousands of other people want a chance, but I want another one too. There is so much to write about in these waters. If I cease gathering material now and write, I will miss a great deal that I came for. If I continue to collect until March, I shall have no time to write.[82]

Even though she considered herself "an old hand" at collecting, Hurston was exhilarated by and present to her discoveries of the "gorgeous and exciting legends," rituals, and ceremonies of the Caribbean people. As a seasoned anthropologist, Hurston felt her own expansion: "I have grown in every direction in these six months," she told Moe.[83] She also felt her maturation as a writer and as a woman. Even as she contemplated a second Guggenheim Fellowship, she was making personal choices that defined who she chose to be. During seven weeks from November to December 1936, while in the field in Haiti, she would write *Their Eyes Were Watching God*.

After "twelve strenuous months," Hurston returned to New York in March 1937. In April, Hurston was awarded a second Guggenheim Fellowship to continue her work in the Caribbean. She was back in Haiti by May. In July she wrote Moe, "I have succeeded beyond my expectation." But there were repercussions. Hurston suffered what she called "A VIOLENT GASTRIC DISTURBANCE," and noted that "[i]t seems that some of my destinations and some of my accessions have been whispered into ears that heard." Hurston's work was curtailed somewhat. "I was one sick 'oman for awhile," she told Moe; "for a whole day and night, I thought I'd never make it." But after a couple of weeks, Hurston was able to get about on her own. She then sought protection with the American Consul at Port-au-Prince. After recovering from what she feared might be her imminent death, Hurston continued working on her field research and on the manuscript of *Tell My Horse*. As she put it, "No moss is growing on my back." Writing Moe in August, Hurston declared, "I am now in robust health again." She completed her work and set sail for the States on September 22, 1938, confident that "the book is in the bag."[84]

"PARLAY CHEVAL OU"

Hurston settled in Eatonville to polish her manuscript. There was enough material for three volumes, but her publisher wanted only one. *Bush* was an early title choice, but Hurston settled on *Tell My Horse*. Being reflective of the era in which it was published, the latter title carried more significance. *Tell My Horse* is a translation of the original Haitian Creole, "Parlay Cheval Ou." It is the saying of the loa Guede who possesses his "mounts" to make social commentary and criticism, to ridicule those who are vain and pretentious, and to jeer at those social classes that would despise him. Guede, Hurston explains, "is the deification of the common people of Haiti" and "is the one loa which is entirely Haitian." Mounted by this deity, the field hand, the market women, the domestics can launch stinging critiques of their "bosses," and attribute them to Guede: "Parlay Cheval Ou"—"Tell My Horse."[85] As an anthropologist, folklorist, and writer, Hurston amplified and interpreted the voice of the folk, "the Negro farthest down," the so-called common people.

President Franklin Delano Roosevelt and First Lady Eleanor Roosevelt saw the folk or the "common man" as an indispensable part of the American heritage and as a national hero. As America had begun to refashion itself in its own image distinct from England, America, like African America, would embrace the folk as an essential element in the creation of an American identity. That identity had, at its roots, the spirit of immigrant populations. It was an enduring spirit, the kind that was essential to surviving the effects of America's Great Depression. Through the various agencies associated with the FWP, the Roosevelts "brought to the attention of a confused and struggling people an awareness of their native culture."[86] As Simon Bonner explains,

> The Literature of the 1930s was devoted to the common man, the heroic figure of the Great Depression. Folklore, brought out in books, photographs, and painted murals by federally sponsored projects of the Works Progress Administration (WPA), showed the vitality of the nation.... Folk songs and folk arts no longer were a sign of backwardness, but was a source of pride in a forbearing American spirit. The nation saw in its native folklore a longstanding tradition that had carried on before the depression and would carry the country through it.[87]

The WPA's FWP had undertaken the writing and publication of an "American Guide," which was intended to "hold up a mirror to America." The guide was to chronicle the history of each American state and territory. In addition, three of the states, Florida, Louisiana, and Virginia had "Negro Units" that were designed to address the unemployment situation of black writers and to produce volumes that focused specifically on black life in those states. Learning that Hurston was residing in Florida, WPA representatives approached her about working as a consultant for the proposed book *The Florida Negro*. Hurston had just recently returned from the Caribbean and was hard at work on the *Tell My Horse* manuscript, so she declined the offer.[88]

With her Guggenheim funds waning, Hurston reconsidered the prospects of working with the WPA. The administrators of the FWP created "nonrelief" positions to attract skilled writers who would supervise literary projects and edit the copy of fieldworkers. Relief positions provided employment opportunities for "just about anyone who could literally write with pen and paper," and they paid half that of editorial and supervisory positions.[89] The editorial staff of Florida's FWP consisted mainly of individuals who had journalistic backgrounds writing for weeklies that were no longer publishing.[90]

Hurston, a renowned folklorist and writer, with two books in print and one pending publication, was qualified for a supervisory position. As Henry Alsberg, national director of the WPA's FWP, put it, "one person of writing and editorial ability...was worth fifty people without writing experience."[91] Whites in Florida who held white supremacist notions, however, maintained supervisory positions as whites-only set-asides. So, although preeminently qualified for an editorial-supervisory position, Hurston had to qualify for "relief." She had to prove her need of assistance, not unlike the majority of "welfare" recipients in today's society. Like present-day recipients, she had to allow herself and her home to be investigated by a "certification worker."[92] Some scholars, understandably, describe Hurston's experience of being "certified" as "humiliating" and believe joining the FWP was particularly "shameful" to Hurston. But as Boyd points out in *Wrapped in Rainbows*, a host of writers, both black and white, were in the employ of the FWP— Richard Wright, Ralph Ellison, Margaret Walker, Saul Bellow, Studs Terkel, and more. Besides, white WPA worker Stetson Kennedy pointed out that "sixteen million Americans were unemployed during the Depression era," and "[m]ost of the entire population, including former millionaires, were eligible" for relief.[93] In reality, what was humiliating was the entrenched insecurity and fear of many whites, masked by a bogey called Jim Crow. Working with the FWP, for Hurston, was no more shameful than being a maid—a lady's maid or a housemaid. It was a job. It paid a salary. At least, with the FWP, she was employed to do what she loved best—field research among black folk and writing.

On April 25, 1938, Hurston took the job of "junior interviewer" at $63.00 per month—$12.00 below whites at the same level and $84.00 less than entry-level editorial or supervisory employees. She did not bear the injustice silently. During a trip to Washington, D.C., to enter a group of singers into the National Folklore Festival, Hurston visited with national director Henry Alsberg. Alsberg saw in Hurston the skilled professional the agency needed. True to his ideals for the success of the FWP, Alsberg wrote to Carita Dogget Corse, director of the Florida FWP, stating that Hurston ought to be in charge of Florida's Negro unit and that she should assume the editing of *The Florida Negro*, with a salary of $150 per month.[94]

The prospect of Hurston joining the Florida FWP in a nonrelief, supervisory position alarmed the Florida editorial staff in Jacksonville. Corse did not want to defy the national office, but she also did not choose to be fair, preferring to maintain the Jim Crow status quo. Accordingly, blacks should never be seen as having parity with whites—even when, as with Zora Neale Hurston, the individual not only merited the position, but was head and shoulders above everyone in editorial-supervisory positions. In negotiating the politics of her dilemma, Corse made Hurston the titular "Negro Editor," but assigned her no editorial responsibility or power. And, although she would not increase Hurston's salary, she would attach an additional $75.00 for travel.[95] Whatever that course of action meant to Corse, the Florida office, and Jim Crow sympathizers, it allowed Hurston a more just salary, and as she worked unsupervised from her home she could continue to work independently with greater control of her time and activities—which was always her preferred modus operandi. Basically, Hurston continued in the position of a field interviewer. As such, she was required to submit 1,500 words on a weekly basis to the state office in Jacksonville. But Hurston "would go off and you wouldn't know where she was," whined Corse.[96] Although Corse and Florida FWP administrators could only conceive of Hurston as a junior field interviewer, Hurston behaved like the expert anthropologist and professional writer she was. She would periodically submit material to the Jacksonville office and then return to her other affairs, which included traveling to promote *Tell My Horse* (which had been published in October 1938), giving public lectures, producing folk concerts, and working on her *Moses, Man of the Mountain* manuscript.

In spite of their inability to acknowledge and properly value Hurston's achievements, Hurston made significant contributions to the floundering Florida branch of the FWP. Stetson Kennedy, director of the Negro unit and editor of *The Florida Negro*, "would receive a thick packet of fabulous folksongs, tales, and legends...each and everyone was priceless, and we hastened to sprinkle them through the *Florida Guide* manuscript for flavoring."[97] The manuscript was also "flavored" with an excerpt from *Their Eyes Were Watching God* and passages excerpted from Hurston's "Ocoee Riot" essay, which chronicled the 1920 lynching of a black citizen of the town of Ocoee and the terrorization of the town's Negro community. Although Hurston submitted considerable material to the state office for use in the *Florida Guide*, the editors elected not to use any essays in their entirety, but only to, as Kennedy stated, "sprinkle" sentences and passages from her work throughout the manuscript. Once the *Guide* was completed, the national office of the FWP requested that Hurston travel to Washington for the final editing of the manuscript. Each state office typically sent one or two representatives to the national office for the edit. Corse did not include Hurston among the editors from the Florida office. The national office sent for her, however, because "the more liberal national office supported broader inclusion of the multicultural point of view expressed in Hurston's folklore studies and town histories."[98]

Hurston also wrote several pieces specifically for *The Florida Negro*. By 1937, black FWP workers in Florida had compiled field notes and interviews that culminated in a 167-page draft manuscript of African American history in Florida. When she joined the project in 1938, the national office expected that Hurston would be editing the material and transforming it into publishable copy. The state office, however, continued to genuflect to the god of Jim Crow. Instead of having Hurston edit the material, she was assigned to write new chapters and expand on ones already written.

Included among the essays she wrote for the new chapters was "Go Gator and Muddy the Water." In this essay, Hurston described the organic processes of folklore and discussed the purpose of various forms of folklore, such as blues songs and ballads and trickster tales and hero tales. She wrote an essay on children's games and Negro mythical places, such as "Diddy-Wah-Diddy" and West Hell, and she gave an analysis of black religious traditions in "The Sanctified Church." In "Art and Such," Hurston explored black creativity and the racial politics that stifled it. After completing her assignments for the project, Hurston solicited publishers' interest, but to no avail. *The Florida Negro* manuscript was still in need of significant editing.[99]

By the summer of 1938, conservative politics had begun to undermine Roosevelt's New Deal efforts, particularly in relation to government-supported arts projects. The WPA's response was to generate public support of the FWP through public exhibitions, demonstrating the work and the achievements of the FWP. In this endeavor, Florida director Carita Corse looked to Hurston's skills as a dramatist. Corse asked Hurston to stage a performance of Florida folklore for the WPA's "National Exhibition of Skills" in Orlando.

The exhibition was held from January 16 to February 6, 1939. Hurston organized a local cast of singers, dancers, and musicians to produce a version of the "Fire Dance" finale of the folk concert "The Great Day," which always delighted audiences. Hurston staged two productions of the miniconcert—one held in January and one held in February.

In May 1938, the national office requested Hurston's services in the organization of field research expeditions. As the newly appointed director of the FWP folklore program, Ben Botkin created the Joint Committee on Folk Art, pulling from various representatives of the FWP's art and education branches. The Joint Committee undertook to audio record the folklore identified and documented by FWP fieldworkers in the Southeast. Botkin, knowledgeable of Hurston and familiar with her work, requested her help in outlining a plan for Florida and organizing and coordinating the proposed fieldwork. Along with the assignment came a salary increase that raised Hurston's monthly income to $79.80. In "A Proposed Recording Expedition into the Floridas," Hurston gave a cross-section of the state, identifying its various cultural communities and potential informants.

Upon completion of the proposal, Hurston was dispatched to Cross City. Functioning as an "advance scout," she prepared informants for the recording and photographing to be done by the other team members. Part of Hurston's work in Cross City also entailed study of the area's turpentine industry and collection of the life histories of the turpentine workers. Her essay, "Turpentine," describes a day at a turpentine camp from the vantage point of foreman John McFarlin. Overseer of the still's chippers, pullers, dippers, and choppers, McFarlin "rode the wood." It's lonesome work, he told Hurston, so there was no wealth of tales and songs to be had.[100]

From her many interviews, Hurston learned also that the 300 employees and their families lived under conditions akin to slavery. The white authorities in the camps raped women, exploited workers, and even beat workers to death. Appalled by the conditions and compelled to do something to help the workers, Hurston reported the cruelties to the white FWP fieldworkers who followed her to the camps. Nothing, however, was done. After leaving Cross City, Hurston is said to have reported "the terrible situation" to "Miss Catherine," part owner and manager of the Aycock and Lindsay Company that operated the camps. Still, nothing was done.[101]

Leaving Cross City with a heavy heart, Hurston's assistance was needed at the Clara White Mission in Jacksonville. There, she organized sessions of folktales, work songs, jook songs, blues, and spirituals to be recorded by FWP worker Herbert Halpert. Hurston contributed a number of songs herself to the recordings, some of which she collected in the South and in the Caribbean. In between songs, Hurston contextualized the songs and explained their significance. In the process, she also describes her methods of collecting folksongs:

> I just get in the crowd with the people if they singing and I listen as best I can and I start to joining in with a phrase or two and then, finally I get so I can sing a verse and then I keep on 'til I learn all…the verses. And then I sing them back to the people until they tell me that I can sing them just like them. And then I take part and I try it out on different people who already know the song until they are quite satisfied that I know it. And then I carry it in my memory.[102]

The Jacksonville recording sessions would be one of the last FWP projects with which Hurston was to be involved. Conservative politicians had garnered sufficient votes to institute a gradual termination of federal support for the arts as well as a general removal of workers from the WPA programs. The "eighteen-month rule," was implemented, terminating all workers with more than eighteen months' tenure with the agencies.[103]

The various programs and manuscripts generated under the FWP were transferred to state control. The materials gathered and manuscripts written by Hurston for the Florida FWP were filed and "largely forgotten."[104] Except for the "sprinkles" of her writing in the *Florida Guide*, Hurston's spectacular work with the WPA was lost. The dismantling of the FWP is apparently a major factor in this "loss."

But choices made by editors in the Florida office are another factor in the loss of Hurston's contributions. As state manuscripts were left to the discretion of the former FWP state offices, the Florida office decided to publish *The Florida Negro*. Assisted by Stetson Kennedy and Robert Cornwall, Carita Dogget Corse supervised a revision of the manuscript. In their revisions, the editors "deleted all of Hurston's writings from the final manuscript." They finally published the manuscript in 1993 as *The Florida Negro: A Federal Writers' Project Legacy*.[105]

Zora Neale Hurston was one of Florida's greatest "Negroes." She was committed to the goals and ideals of the FWP. She contributed extensive research to the agency's various projects. She was assigned to write and wrote a considerable number of essays for *The Florida Negro* manuscript. Although her contributions were expunged from the published volume, Toni Cade Bambara pulled several of Hurston's FWP essays from the decades-old files to complete a compilation of Hurston's folkloric and ethnographic works in *The Sanctified Church* (1981). *Go Gator and Muddy the Water: Writings by Zora Neale Hurston From the Federal Writers' Project*, edited by Pamela Bordelon, represents all of Hurston's known writings from that period.

In spite of the racist attitudes and acts of her FWP colleagues, Zora Neale Hurston "came out more than conquer." During her tenure with the FWP, she sharpened her expertise as an anthropological folklorist, gaining an even wider national reputation. She received an honorary doctor of letters degree from Morgan College. She promoted the publication of *Tell My Horse* while completing her *Moses* manuscript, and *Their Eyes Were Watching God* was being translated into Italian and otherwise "[attracting] attention on the continent." In Eatonville, at a monthly income of $154.80—the top salary for editorial positions was $160 per month—Hurston was living quite comfortably.[106] She maintained a house in Eatonville, kept a car, and took care of her nieces Wilhelmina and Winifred until they both married.

In the whirlwind of all she was doing, Hurston even found time for romance—and a second marriage. "Smooth brown," handsome, and twenty-three, Albert Price III was husband number two. On June 27, 1939, in a Fernandina courthouse, the couple wed. When they met, Price was also working with the FWP in the education department. Because married couples could not both be employed through the WPA, Price claims Hurston persuaded him to quit his job, given her salary was higher. Still a college student, Price assumed that Hurston would support the both of them. According to Price, Hurston assured him that "all she wanted was his SWEET SELF."[107]

In less time than it took her to write *Their Eyes Were Watching God*, Hurston left him. Hurston described Albert Price as a mama's boy, verbally abusive, and lazy. The couple had settled in Jacksonville where Price was from, but they never lived together more than a few days at a time. Price spent much of his time at his mother's home, where he expected Hurston to live. Just as Hurston had used her work as a strategy to separate from her first husband Herbert Sheen and from her lover Percival Punter, she used her second husband's refusal to work as a justification for separation. In her divorce suit, Hurston declared, "I was compelled to support myself."[108] Hurston arranged to join the faculty of the North Carolina College for Negroes in the fall. She resigned from her FWP position August 11, left her "boy-husband," and headed to Durham, North Carolina.

FOUR

"Coming Out More Than Conquer": Spirituality, Empowerment, Freedom, and Peace

Hurston began the fall of 1939 as a faculty member of the North Carolina College for Negroes (NCCN). The College president, Dr. James Shepherd hired her to organize a theater program and produce black folk plays. Even so, by the end of the year, curricular development in that direction "had not been planned out."

Thinking that the school may not have known what approach to take, Hurston offered a plan: "I suggest a course in playwriting, a course in play direction, a course in play production which would include, lighting, scenic designing, construction, costume designing, etc. These courses are not only basic and necessary, they are irreducible minimum if anything at all is to be accomplished."[1] Describing her endeavors as "rather interesting work," Hurston had committed herself to instituting a viable drama department and to producing authentic black folk plays. "We are going to try to make Negro plays out of Negro life in the Negro manner," she told her students.[2]

As with Bethune-Cookman College, factors conspired to undermine the development of a drama department at NCCN. Both of these middle-class college communities were confounded by Hurston's flamboyance and her independent spirit. In Durham, the rumor that Hurston was dating one of her students may have been a factor in the school's lack of support. Hurston mingled easily with the faculty and students of the University of North Carolina (UNC), a white segregated school in nearby Chapel Hill, which may have been disturbing to both blacks and whites.

Invitations to her celebrity friends to speak at the College and her efforts to involve UNC and the Carolina Players—its affiliated drama troupe—in the development of the theatrical program at NCCN suggests Hurston's sincerity in realizing the task she had accepted. As she wrote to Dr. Shepherd, "I set out to make a success of anything that I do."[3] Nonetheless, NCCN administrators did not encourage her success. Somewhat disillusioned by the turn of events, Hurston resigned as head of the drama department on March 1, 1940.

From her seat on the gatepost, Eatonville's daughter took the matter in stride. For as much as she desired to institute a Negro folk theater at NCCN, she was also quite interested in working with UNC professor Paul Green, writer of the 1927 Pulitzer prize-winning play *Abraham's Bosom*. She considered it her "good fortune to be included in [his] play writing class. I am proud of that," she wrote to her friend Edwin Osgood Grover. "I think that is one of the most pleasant things that has ever happened to me, and I think I'll benefit by it." Hurston anticipated her connections with Paul Green and "the crowd at Chapel Hill" to be "the door to a new phase" in her career.[4] Perhaps now, she, in collaboration with Paul Green, would launch the real Negro folk theater she had envisioned. "[I]n fact," she wrote enthusiastically to Green, "I see no reason why the firm of Green and Hurston should not take charge of the Negro playwriting business in America."

The dramatists had been discussing the possibility of writing "a very funny play." Hurston offered John de Conqueror—seasoned with character traits from John Henry, Marcus Garvey, and Father Devine, among others—as the play's protagonist.[5] It is likely that Hurston hoped her associations with Paul Green, UNC, and the Carolina Players would mirror her associations with Edwin Grover, Rollins College, and The Museum Theater in Fern Park. Clearly, Hurston saw the possibility of collaboration with Green as far more significant than remaining as head of the drama department at NCCN. Hurston wrote, "If you have decided to work on JOHN DE CONQUEROR, you do not need to concern yourself with the situation here at the school. I won't care what happens here or if nothing happens here so long as I do the bigger thing with you."[6]

But Green had not decided to work on the play with Hurston. He showed a dubious interest that prompted Hurston to write,

> I have the uncomfortable feeling that I have pestered you too much about this HIGH JOHN DE CONQUER. You have tried to feel it and you cant [sic], so I will take High John out of your lap and go off an[d] sit up with him awhile. As I said, I will write through the thing and let you see what I have done. If you feel like bothering with the thing again I will be very happy. If not, well then, you just don't feel that way.[7]

While engaged in preliminary work with Paul Green on the High John play, Hurston was also assisting sister anthropologist Jane Belo with research on the sanctified church. Belo had recorded episodes of trance experiences in Bali and wanted to compare her findings with the trance experiences among members of the sanctified churches in Beaufort, South Carolina. As Hurston assisted Belo with her project, she was also collecting material for other plays she had hoped to produce in collaboration with Green.

Of utmost importance to Hurston was the "GRAND music" she had heard. She feared, however, that she might not be the first to record it and make use of it. Belo returned to New York to marry Frank Tannebum, so Hurston carried on the research project alone. Belo was to send Hurston a recording machine to record the "GRAND music" that Hurston wanted. Instead, she informed Hurston that a film crew would be coming with equipment capable of simultaneous visual and audio recording. Hurston immediately wrote a letter to Paul Green urging him to "DO SOMETHING! We cant [sic] let all that swell music get away from us like that." She reminded him, "You said yourself that there ought to be lots of music in the play and music that had not become hackneyed and worn out." She told him to hurriedly dispatch someone with equipment to record some of the music. She was alarmed that the film crew included "two very enthusiastic Jews who wanted to take the spirituals for commercial purposes!"[8]

THE BIGGER THING

Over and above establishing a theater program and even over and above working with Paul Green, the "bigger thing" for Zora Neale Hurston was making Africana genius known to the world. Her faculty position at NCCN and, particularly, her collaborations with Paul Green appeared to be opportunities to do just that. Hurston knew that theatrical presentations of the creative genius of black folks created ritual spaces wherein the audience as well as the performers could touch their own divinity. She understood profoundly the value of cultural traditions and the importance of ritual performance. Through ritual, practitioners could become present to spirit, to essence, to consciousness. Expounding on the ideas of ethnologist Adolf Bastian, Joseph Campbell wrote, "You have to go through your own tradition—the local—to get to the transcendent...."[9] As an expert anthropologist, Zora Neale Hurston understood this truism and clearly expressed it in her essay on folklore, "Go Gator and Muddy the Water":

> In folklore, as in everything else that people create, the world is a great big old serving platter, and all the local places are like eating plates. Whatever is on the plate comes out of the platter, but each plate has a flavor of its own because the people take the universal stuff and season it to suit themselves on the plate. And this local flavor is what is known as originality.[10]

Therefore, the local tradition, which is expressive of a people's originality and genius, is their direct connection with the transcendent or the Universal, Divine Spirit.

From her youth, Hurston was able to distinguish transcendental and spiritual concepts. She was able to make a distinction between form and essence and matter and spirit. "There is an age," she remembered in *Dust Tracks*, "when children are fit company for spirits. Before they have absorbed too much of earthy things to be able to fly with the unseen things that soar." She lived as much in the world of imagination and dream as in the actual environs of Eatonville. The inner life she lived with Biblical heroes, Greco-Roman gods, sprites, and black folkloric fantasies unfitted her for a quotidian existence. "My soul was with the gods and my body in the village," she decried.[11] As an adult, Hurston came to see form and essence as one, because she recognized form as the ever-changing face of spirit.

Hurston's work as an anthropological folklorist was always a spiritual affair. Her work required her to keenly focus on cultural form while she investigated that to which the forms gave expression. Ultimately, with African American folklore, as with the lore of any folk, the forms gave expression to creativity, to cultural genius, to humanity, and to divinity. Hurston described her research as "formalized curiosity. It is poking and prying with a purpose. It is a seeking, that he who wishes may know the cosmic secrets of the world and they that dwell therein."[12] The study of folklore necessarily takes one back "to the beginnings of things." As Hurston wrote in "Go Gator and Muddy the Water," it was there, in the beginning, that the group had to interpret natural laws: "The group mind [used] a great part of its life span trying to ask infinity some questions about what is going on around its doorstep."[13] This doorstep, the folklore, is the local. It is the finite point through which the seeker moves toward the infinite, the transcendent, into an exploration of "cosmic secrets."

"[A]s early as I can remember," Hurston wrote in *Dust Tracks*, "I was questing and seeking." Filled with youthful curiosity and desire to know life's mysteries, she recalls, "I was always asking and making myself a crow in a pigeon's nest." Although "born with God in the house," she could get no satisfactory explanations about divinity, the universe, the world, life, or death. Answers adults gave "left a lack in my mind," she stated.[14] The patterns of their lives contradicted the wondrous glory of God and creation that was preached in the pulpit and "amen-ed" to in the pews. The revivals, the testifying, the prayers, and the preaching—including the sermons of her own father Reverend John Hurston—did not afford her any clarity on the cosmic questions she carried in her. She was enthralled by the ceremony and rituals of the Missionary Baptist Church, "[b]ut of the inner thing, I was right where I was when I first began to seek answers." When she was a student in primary school, Hurston knew that conformity was expected. So when asked whether she loved school, she said, "yes." As the daughter of a minister and Sunday school superintendent, she also thought better of defying the status quo of the church. She feared both reprimand and ostracism. "When I was asked if I loved God, I always said yes because I knew that that was the thing I was supposed to say. It was a guilty secret with me a long time."[15]

Hurston kept her bewilderment to herself. "The thing slept on in me until my college years without any real decision. I made the necessary motions and forgot to think." Courses in history and philosophy began to jog Hurston's memory. Her questions about "God's habits, His Heaven, His ways, and Means," surfaced again. In her study of the religions of the world, Hurston found that they all expressed a desire for empowerment: "I saw that even in his religion, man carried himself along. His worship of strength was there. God was made to look that way, too." She observed that "the great masses fear life and its consequences." Thus, the various religious traditions gave them a sense of security "in the face of great forces." Religion, then, represented an alliance between humanity and omnipotence. In her comparative research of religion and religious traditions, she found a consistency of ideological thought with varying details. "So having looked at the subject from many sides, studied beliefs by word of mouth and then as they fit into great rigid forms," she wrote in *Dust Tracks*, "I find I know a great deal about form, but little or nothing about the mysteries I sought as a child. As the ancient tent maker said, I have come out of the same door wherein I went."[16]

In his work *The Varieties of Religious Experience*, William James shared Hurston's insights:

> When we survey the whole field of religion, we find a great variety in the thoughts that have prevailed there; but the feelings on the one hand and the conduct on the other are almost always the same, for Stoic, Christian, and Buddhist saints are practically indistinguishable in their lives. The theories which Religion generates, being thus variable, are secondary; and if you wish to grasp her essence, you must look to the feelings and the conduct as being the more constant elements.[17]

As an anthropologist, Hurston focused on form and process or "conduct." As a seeker, her focus was on essence and "feelings." Through her folklore fieldwork, she had learned a lot about form, as she said; but it was essence, the unseen, that she longed to understand. Section eleven of the *Tao Teh Ching* eloquently illustrates Hurston's thought:

> Thirty spokes converge upon a single hub;
> It is on the hole in the center that the use of the cart hinges.
> We make a vessel from a lump of clay;
> It is the empty space within the vessel that makes it useful.
> We make doors and windows for a room;
> But it is these empty spaces that make the room livable.
> Thus, while the tangible has advantages,
> It is the intangible that makes it useful.[18]

Compelled by the preternatural, Zora Neale Hurston's anthropological investigations were always a meditation on the intangible, on spirit. In *Mules and Men*, Hurston described the lore as "that which the soul lives by." She prefaced the collection with a folktale. The following passage and excerpt from the tale is suggestive of Hurston's material and spiritual interests in the lore, and it is symbolic of the relation between the local and the transcendent, the tangible and intangible. "When I was rounding Lily Lake," she wrote,

> I was remembering how God had made the world and the elements and people. He made souls for people, but he didn't give them out because he said, "Folks ain't ready for souls yet. De clay ain't dry. It's de strongest thing Ah ever made. Don't aim to waste none thru loose cracks. And then men got to grow strong enough to stand it. De way things is now, if Ah give it out it would tear them shackly bodies to pieces. Bimeby, Ah give it out."[19]

God eventually gave humans "de soul-piece." Being the strongest thing God ever made, it stands to reason that one's soul requires conscious attention. Hurston's letters convey a watchful awareness of her feelings and spiritual state, as both were indicative of the condition of her soul. She would write to Langston Hughes, for instance, that although her work was going well, she was a "little depressed spiritually." In a later correspondence, she would tell him, "[Y]our last letter comforted my soul like dreamless sleep." When disappointed by some job possibility that did not materialize, she might write to Carl Van Vechten, "my feet got more tired and my spirits lower." Anticipating a reunion with a friend, she'd write, "I must talk with you to get back my soul." Her spirits could be up when she heard from friends Jane Belo and Frank Tannebum who shared Hurston's optimistic spirit and enthusiasm during "the War years."[20] And they could be devastated in the aftermath of the false moral charges she had to face. Hurston wrote her friend Fannie Hurst that "my soul is dead, and I care about nothing anymore." She thanked Hurst, for her "magnificence of spirit," as her friend was encouraging and supportive through the ordeal. "Your thrust of light reached me in my cave so dark and deep that it seems that all the suns of the universe cannot light it up.[21] As Hurston was tuned into her own "soul-piece," she vibrated with and was attuned to the souls of black folk, in particular, and the soul of America, in general.

Hurston's probing of the various expressive forms of the African American folk gave her insight into the "empty space" in the clay vessel, the unmanifest Source of the lore she collected and analyzed. As she proclaimed to Langston Hughes during the outset of her field research, "I am getting inside of Negro art and lore, I am beginning to see really...."[22] What Hurston saw was this tremendous human response to life. A will-to-freedom that defied a white supremacist system designed to destroy the spirit of black people. Nanny in *Their Eyes Were Watching God* tells Janie, "But nothin' can't stop you from wishin'. You can't beat nobody down so low till you can rob 'em of they will."[23] In "Crazy for this Democracy," Hurston bore witness to the mean-spiritedness of racism in American society that masqueraded in the guise of Jim Crow. "I have met it in the flesh," she wrote in *Dust Tracks*. And in "Crazy for this Democracy," she exposed the inimical spirit behind the mask of Jim Crow. The purpose of Jim Crow laws was to convince whites of their supposed superiority and to convince whites and blacks of the assumed inferiority of blacks. "By physical evidence, back seats in trains, back-doors of houses, exclusion from certain places and activities," adepts of the cult of white supremacy worked to "promote in the mind of the smallest white child the conviction of FIRST BY BIRTH.... Talent, capabilities, nothing has anything to do with the case. JUST FIRST BY BIRTH." Darker skinned folks were never to be perceived as equal.

> Seeing the daily humiliations of the darker people confirm the child in its superiority, so that it comes to feel it the arrangement of God. By the same means, the smallest dark child is to be convinced of its inferiority, so that it is to be convinced that competition is out of the question, and against all nature and God.[24]

Although Hurston would not enumerate or focus extensively on the racial incidents she encountered, all of her writings address racial bigotry and institutional racism—some very subtly and others quite directly. In "My Most Humiliating Jim Crow Experience," as in "Crazy for This Democracy," Hurston overtly addressed institutional racism. Ill with ailments of the digestive tract upon her return from fieldwork in the Bahamas, Hurston sought medical attention. Charlotte Mason had an appointment made for Hurston at the Brooklyn office of a specialist in internal medicine. Both the white receptionist and white doctor were nonplussed with the challenge of receiving a black Zora Neale Hurston. A nurse was directed to escort Hurston to "a private examination room." Hurston wrote that she didn't rate the room very highly. "Under any other circumstances, I would have sworn it was a closet where the soiled towels and uniforms were tossed until called for by the laundry. But," she noted, "there was a chair in there wedged in between the wall and the pile of soiled linen." The doctor came quickly and asked some questions in a manner that betrayed his disarranged mind. In a sweep, he "stuck a tube down my throat to extract some bile from my gall bladder, wrote a prescription and asked for twenty dollars as a fee." Hurston's first inclination when placed in the makeshift Jim Crow examination room was to briskly march out in high dudgeon. Her second inclination, which she followed, was to see how matters would unfold and to intensify the disquietude of doctor and associates. Afterward, "I got up, set my hat at a reckless angle and walked out, telling him that I would send him a check, which I never did. I went away feeling the pathos of Anglo-Saxon civilization."[25]

Hurston explained that

> the people who make a boast of racial, class, or national prejudices do so out of a sense of incapability to which they refuse to give voice. Instead they try to

be ingenious by limiting competition. They are racial card-sharks trying to rig the game so that they cannot lose. Trying to stack the deck.[26]

America's Peculiar Institution of slavery was a stacked deck. As was the institution of Jim Crow with its white "set-asides." As was its economic system of sharecropping and its unjust justice system and political schemes and terrorizing tactics designed to make null and void the American democratic promise of one person, one vote.

The deck was stacked, but Zora Neale Hurston chose to play the game: "I give the matter the corner of my eye and smile at the back-hand compliment."[27] Having been reared in the all-black, self-governed town of Eatonville, Hurston felt her own possibility as she shared the lived experience of black ingenuity. African Americans expressed a resilient spirit and an indomitable will to soar. Hurston recognized and documented this sensibility in the folklore she collected. The lore reflected strategies of survival, coping skills, and an intent to maintain spiritual integrity, that is, to continue ritualistic practices that kept the individual soul consciously connected to the Divine Spirit or Source. The culture heroes of black folklore embodied this indomitable spirit of black folk.

Hurston considered High John de Conquer to be one of the most significant of these heroic figures. High John's importance in the body of black folklore is articulated in one of Hurston's letters to Alain Locke wherein she urged Locke to write "a comprehensive work on HIGH JOHN DE CONQUER." This work would distinguish between High John, and the legendary John Henry. It would show High John to be the archetypal wish-fulfillment, trickster figure par excellence and a prototypical mythic figure. The work would also correlate High John with the "world-wide John concept." "Have you thought about the fact," she asked Locke, "that in every country there is a great John? John, Jack, Ja[c]ques... , Johannes, Juan, Giovanne? There must be some spiritual value assigned to the name of John." That the name could be "some secret symbol" was something to "speculate upon" she told Locke. Committed to publicizing the mythic folk figure of John, she sought to interest Alain Locke in High John as subject matter for a scholarly treatise. "If you are interested, I will work with you on it. You can do some reading on the European John business, and I will continue to set down what is in the mouths of people." What she heard from the mouths of people was that High John represented power and that those who carried about them a bit of the High John de Conquer root maintained a self-confidence and faith "that something better was coming." Hurston emphasized to Locke, that hundreds of thousands, if not millions, of Negroes in America carried the root, as well as a good many white folks. Those who carried it attested to its powers and considered it their "most valued possession." The point is that the John de Conquer root "MEANS SOMETHING TO THEM. I mean the people who carry it, are acknowledging some sort of divinity." She concluded from her research on High John and her speculations on the "world-wide John concept" that "there is a symbolic naming of a force universal that has more to it than appears on the surface."[28]

Hurston told Locke that she had published an essay on High John in the October 1943 issue of *American Mercury*, but that the essay was "a brief thing" that was "a mere scratch on the ... surface" of all that High John represented. She wanted to work with Locke to produce a more extensive work that would result in "something enduring for the world."[29] Working with Locke was not to be, but Hurston's publication does give us a profile of High John de Conquer, and her rendition of the tale gives some insight into her interpretation of John as a symbol of universal force.

In *Mules and Men*, Hurston described High John as the great human culture hero of African-American folklore who, with laughter "or in spite of laughter usually defeats Ole Massa, God and the Devil."[30] Her essay underscored the fact of John's humanity, but the narrative voice explained that John "was not a natural man." Like Jesus, the Christ of the New Testament, John was Divine Spirit made flesh. "First off, he was a whisper, a will to hope, a wish to find something worthy of laughter and song. Then the whisper put on flesh."[31]

In Hurston's essay, Ole Massa, God, and the Devil are highly symbolic characters in the mythology of High John de Conquer. God and the Devil represent transcendent spirit. For in the High John tale, as in other folktales, the Devil and God are equals. Neither is good or bad in the ordinary, conventional connotations of the terms. Ole Massa symbolizes the sphere of the mind and the mind's inherent dualistic nature and represents one polarity of the "master-slave" duality. High John symbolizes conscious thought or spiritual presence. Whereas God and the Devil reflect realms of spirit, John's character is symbolic of both the spiritual and mental (or physical) realms. His character, thus, is both human and divine, and represents the possibility of humans to transcend the duality of the mind and become one with Spirit. For when duality is transcended, one merges with *universal* force.

Just as Jesus brought the Word of God that promised the multitudes salvation and peace, John brought laughter and song to oppressed Africans that promised freedom and human dignity, personal power, and freedom. High John hailed from Africa, says the narrator.

> He came walking on the waves of sound. Then he took on flesh after he got here. The sea captains of ships knew that they brought slaves in their ships. They knew about those black bodies huddled down there in the middle passage, being hauled across the waters to helplessness. John de Conquer was walking the very winds that filled the sails of the ships. He followed over them like the albatross.[32]

Hurston profiled High John as the archetypal trickster figure of African American lore. Brer Rabbit and the "slave" John or Jack are but two faces of his many manifestations. His sign was a laugh and the drumbeat his "singing-symbol." Neither was audible to those who were "fixed to hear it." For, the heralding of High John "was an inside thing to live by."[33]

This laughter and rhythm also came to be characteristic attributes of the black folk. "The brother in black puts a laugh in every vacant place in his mind," Hurston wrote in *Mules and Men*. "His laugh had a hundred meanings. It may mean amusement, anger, grief, bewilderment, chagrin, curiosity, simple pleasure or any other of the known or undefined emotions." John's gifts of laughter and song made nighttime a joke "because daybreak was on the way."[34] As laughter dispels fear and anger, and as songs and stories of triumph tromp despair and restore hope, so, too, did black folk create tales and jokes, and riddles and stories, and songs that rearranged their minds to honor their being-ness in the world. High John was there.

Where the work was hardest and the lash cut the back, High John's presence was most pronounced. High John would see the violated and exploited through sorrow, and he would see them to freedom. On one such plantation, John deduced that the people needed a song, not just any song, but "a particular piece of singing." Because this song was nowhere about the place nor any place he knew, John declared that he and the bondaged multitudes must go in search of it. For those fearful of the wrath of Ole Massa, should they stray from the plantation, John told them, "Just leave your old work-tired bodies around for him to look at, and he'll never realize youse way off somewhere, going about your business." For those mindful of their attire, John encouraged them to look within. "Oh, you got plenty things to wear. Just reach inside yourselves and get out all those fine raiments you been toting around with you for the last longest." There were musical instruments inside there, too, which he told them to retrieve so they could enjoy music on their journey. Geared up, they left the plantation and experienced various adventures hither and yon, including places in heaven and hell. It was in heaven that Old Maker, pleased with the folk and their enjoyment of heaven and the shiny new instruments they were given to play, "made them a tune and put it in their mouths. It had no words. It was a tune that you could bend and shape in most any way you wanted to fit the words and feelings that you had. They learned it and began to sing."[35]

The rough holler of Ole Massa jerked the multitudes back to their circumstantial reality. Their spirits faltered at the reentry. But High John de Conquer was there to remind them of their ultimate reality. "Don't pay what he say no mind. You know where you got something finer than this plantation and anything it's got on it, put away." Then they remembered their "gift song," and knew from deep within that "[t]rouble don't last always."[36]

The High John essay reveals Hurston's philosophical belief that the internal world of mind and soul were as important, if not more important, than the external, physical world; it emphasized "the inner thing." One's ability to negotiate the dualities of the external world was directly related to one's ability to transcend those dualities in one's internal world. Throughout her autobiography, Hurston referred to her interior life. Whether she willfully drew her attention inward or was driven inward, she found her inner consciousness to be a place of peace, freedom, personal empowerment, and unlimited possibility. There, in her inner consciousness, was her black riding horse with white leather saddle and bridles. There, she spied horizons to which she would travel. There, she intuited the significance of black genius.

There, too, were daybreak and sunrise. Moses in *Moses, Man of the Mountain* epitomizes Hurston's belief in the power of the "inner thing." When Moses fled Egypt and the Pharaoh, he left behind all that made him Prince Moses. He was without his palace, his army, his family, his fortune—all those external things humans depend on for identity, power, and security. But Moses had a conception of self that spoke of a true personal power that was connected to an internal Source. He knew he was not defined by his things, his worldly trappings. As High John de Conquer coaxed the multitudes to reach inside themselves for what they needed to be self-realized, so Moses, too, bereft of the world of the aristocracy, turned his gaze inward to the world of infinite possibility.

High John was all about winning. His battle strategies spoke of the power of internal strength that was psychological and spiritual. "Hitting a straight lick with a crooked stick" was shrewd. "Winning the jack pot with no other stake but a laugh" was grace. When Zora Neale Hurston had a tête-à-tête with FWP National Director Henry Alsberg, she was throwing a crooked stick, the straight lick was higher pay and tacit respect. Her "jack pot" was the opportunity to live life on her own terms. In a Jim Crow and provincial American society that blinked "access denied" in neon lights—to blacks, to women, to Southerners, to particular social and economic groups—Zora Neale Hurston's ability to move across social and class lines to accomplish her objectives spoke to her inner drive and ability to "come out more than conquer."

"Conquer" is the black vernacular pronunciation of "conqueror." One might ask what does it mean to be more than a conqueror? To come out more than conqueror? What is there over and above winning? When we look more closely at the story of High John, we get more of a sense of what Lucy Hurston might have meant when she told John Hurston, "I'll be bound mine will come out more than conquer."[37]

As he toured and tenured on various plantations, High John de Conquer was never aggressive. In the guise of the wily rabbit or in the overalls of John or Jack, he tricks Ole Massa and is sometimes tricked by him. In all cases, the end is one of laughter—the equalizing force. Humor, story, song, and craft are the arms of choice. Although it is a "mighty battle" that is being waged, High John chooses to win "without outside-showing force." He chooses to win his war "from within." With subtle, life-affirming tactics, this approach allowed High John to win "in a permanent way, for he was winning with the soul of the black man whole and free. So he could use it afterwards." To win a war but lose your soul would be a costly victory. "For," the narrator writes "what shall it profit a man if he gain the whole world, and lose his own soul? You would have nothing but a cruel, vengeful, grasping monster come to power."[38] The High John essay makes it clear that what is being conquered are the illusions of dualistic thought patterns that breed fear and all the cowardly practices that fear engenders. As Hurston concerned herself with the bigger thing, that is, with Spirit, so, too, did she concern herself with the spiritual vitality of the folk.

THE SOURCE

Although deeply spiritual, Hurston was not religious. She identified with no denomination or named religious practice. As she responded to Henry Allen Moe while conducting research on Vodou[39] in Haiti, "No I have not been converted locally, tho I am not a Christian either."[40] From her probing and ongoing comparative analyses of the mysteries of Vodou, the Catholic and Protestant Churches, as well as Islam, Hinduism, Buddhism, and Taoism, among others, Hurston found that "there is no mystery beyond the mysterious Source of life."[41]

She saw that religions reflected the attempts of humankind to know this Source. She concluded that the tenets, doctrines, and articles of faith of each religion say more about the spirit of the group that created it than about the Source of life or the nature of God. William James addresses the consequent multiplicity of religions: "No two of us have identical difficulties, nor should we be expected to work out identical solutions. Each, from his peculiar angle of observation, takes in a certain sphere of fact and trouble, which each must deal with in a unique manner."[42] Given the subjective quality at the core of any religion, Hurston concluded that "God [was] made in man's own image," and that "Gods always behaved like the people who make them."[43]

Hurston's views on God and religion were consistent throughout her life. She questioned "the concept of God being that He is both omnipotent and omniscient, that He should want humans to know certain things and to be guided by these principles and reveal it to so few."[44] As a child, she found the explanations given to her about God and creation to be, at best, obscure and dissatisfactory: "My head was full of misty fumes of doubt."[45] Under the scrutiny of anthropological investigation, it became clear to her that religions constituted elaborate rules and rites that grew out of humankind's reverence for those aspects of nature that were perceived as vital or as otherwise empowering.

Her early letters from the field in the late 1920s show her no longer bewildered by the questions of her youth, but actively engaged in collecting, analyzing, and interpreting religious materials. Hesitant to formally propose views that might be perceived as heretical, she asks Franz Boas in an April 12, 1929, letter, "Is it safe for me to say that baptism is an extension of water worship as a part of pantheism just as the sacrament is an extension of cannibalism?"[46] The tentative, question-posing stance that characterized her letter to Boas on such questions gave way to a matter-of-fact, bold confidence in her April 30 letter to Langston on the same subject: "I am convinced that Christianity as practiced is an attenuated form of nature-worship. Let me explain," she wrote.

> The essentials are a belief in the Trinity, baptism, sacrament. Baptism is nothing more than water worship as has been done in one form or the other down thru the ages.... I find fire worship in Christianity too. What was the original purpose of the altar in all churches? For sacred fire and sacrifices BY FIRE.... The burnt offering is no longer made, but we keep the symbol in the candles, the alter and the term sacrifice. You know of course that the sacrament is a relic of cannibalism when men ate men not so much for food as to gain certain qualities the eaten man had.[47]

In a comparative observation, she curtly said, "Sympathetic magic pure and simple. They have a nerve to laugh at conjure. I shall ask is the Trinity, Fire, Water, and Earth? Who shall say me nay without making a purely emotional appeal."[48]

Hurston described religions as "organized creeds" that are "collections of words around a wish." As an adult, she declared in her 1942 publication of *Dust Tracks*, "I feel no need for such." "Life, as it is," she said, "does not frighten me, since I have made peace with the universe as I find it, and bow to its laws." Therefore, there was no need to pray for special favors over others. She would meet life head on and play "the rules of the game as laid down." She felt duly equipped to do so: "I accept the means at my disposal for working out my destiny. It seems to me that I have been given a mind and will-power for that purpose."[49]

In her later years, Hurston's thoughts in religious and spiritual matters remained constant. In a 1953 letter to first husband Herbert Sheen, Hurston gave him the benefit of her insights on his pending divorce from his second wife. She suggested that he ignore the Catholic church's ban and "go right ahead and get married if that is what you want." The priests rule by theory rather than practice, she reasoned, "and have no more intimate acquaintance with God than you have." Although she considered the Catholic church to be the greatest institution invented for human spiritual comfort, she stated, "I have never lost track of the fact that it is *human*."[50]

Hurston's faith was in transcendent reality or universal law: "To me there is LAW to which all things in the universe must conform. What the explanation of it is, I do not know, though I would like to know. We are confusing human social arrangements with divinity."[51] Religions presumed to know the answers to "cosmic secrets," but Hurston contended that they are unknown and unknowable. "It seems to me to be true that heavens are placed in the sky because it is the unreachable. The unreachable and therefore the unknowable always seem divine—hence, religion." Religion, however, "is simply not for me."[52]

Hurston studied, explored, and intimately investigated religious phenomena. Yet she never aligned herself with any religion. To do so, she felt, would somehow be limiting: "[W]hat need of denominations and creeds to deny the comfort of all my fellow men? The wide belt of the universe has no need for finger-rings." Nonetheless, Hurston observed that many of her "fellow men" desired affiliation with religious institutions. And "I would not," she wrote, "by word or deed, attempt to deprive another of the consolation it offers."[53]

Hurston respected those practices that were an integral part of her growing up and of those she had studied. In Hurston's hometown of Eatonville, there was a Methodist and a Baptist church. Just as one denomination stood alongside the other, so, too, did Christian ideology blend with traditional African spirituality. Although Hurston questioned the Judeo-Christian concept of God, she was enthralled by the dynamics of the services and ceremonies in the traditional black church. She was moved by the dramatic, communal action of the church and spellbound by the songs, prayers, and, especially, the sermons. She wrote admiringly of her father's "pagan poetry" and modeled the Reverend John Buddy Pearson, the protagonist in *Jonah's Gourd Vine,* on the life of her father.

THE INDESTRUCTIBLE STUFF OF THE UNIVERSE

Zora Neale Hurston's convictions about religion and spirituality are condensed in *Dust Tracks on a Road.* Hurston began writing the autobiography some time after leaving NCCN. After Hurston had completed her work with Belo, she spent some time in New York before she was invited by her friend, anthropologist Katharane Merson, to visit her in Altadena, California. While there, Hurston worked on completing a draft of her *Dust Tracks* manuscript.

In the meantime, she worked as a writer and technical adviser for Paramount Pictures at a salary of $100 per week. She unsuccessfully made efforts to interest the studio in producing movies based on her novels. Hurston's interest in Hollywood was not abiding. As she expressed to her friend Edwin Grover, "This job here at the studio is not the end of things for me. It is a means. My autobiography is due out in the spring."[54]

The *Dust Tracks* publication garnered Hurston the 1943 Anisfeld Award in Racial Relations and, with it, a $1,000 prize. Normally, the prize was awarded only to authors of scholarly books. But the 1942 awards committee elected to include creative works as a second competitive category, making Hurston's autobiography eligible for the award. Hurston wrote *Dust Tracks* during the World War II period. As other Hurston scholars have pointed out, beginning with Robert Hemenway, much of what Hurston wrote in relation to the war was excised, although the excised chapters have since been restored in appendixes to the narrative. Most contemporary black and some "progressive" white reviewers of *Dust Tracks* criticized it as a narrative that pandered to a white audience. It is a double irony that Hurston clearly expressed her criticism of American military campaigns in the excised chapters and that the Anisfeld Awards was also critical of American domestic and international politics. An article noting the award event vaguely referred to the intertwining problems of race relations and nationalism, which "might almost be said to be the theme of this war and one of the major problems of the peace." The article continued: "Nothing has more sharply emphasized the democratic problem which we inherited from slavery than the pressures of our present crisis and the obvious need of putting our own house in order before we talk too much of Americanism as a cultural and political success."[55] This last statement reflects the sentiments of Hurston's excised chapters. What Hurston shouted in the excised chapters, this brief article quietly stated—all was not well in America, and American politics jeopardized the democratic ideal at home and abroad.

Many readers of *Dust Tracks on a Road*, from the time of its publication until the present, have criticized the text. They interpret it as disingenuous and argue that Hurston did not "tell the truth"—neither about herself or about black life during that time period. As one recent critic wrote, "There is, despite its success in certain quarters, a strange distance in the book. Certainly the language is true and the dialogue authentic, but the author stands between the content and the reader. It is difficult, if not impossible, to find and touch the real Zora Neale Hurston."[56] The question might be asked, "What is the *real* Zora Neale Hurston?" Metaphysics tells us that those things we can touch and perceive about a person do not constitute the essence of that person. Who or what one *is* transcends individual physicality and history. Furthermore, the essence of all physical existence is consciousness. Hurston wrote in *Dust Tracks* that, as consciousness, she was "part and parcel of the world" and, therefore, indestructible, because matter "merely change[s] form."[57]

Hurston was telling her readers who she *really* was—she was more than a name, birth date, or address; more than her professional or social relations; and more than an accounting of her experiences. She was the indestructible stuff of the universe—spirit. Even so, *Dust Tracks* is not the fiction some critics make it out to be. Biographer Valerie Boyd noted, "Beyond the falsehoods she invents to support the deception about her birth year..., Zora does not tell many (if any) out-and-out lies about herself. Through omission, however, she presents a questionable and carefully constructed version of the truth." In her discussion, Boyd raises an astute question about genres, stating that *Dust Tracks* "is what readers today might view more as memoir than autobiography." The purpose of a memoir "is to capture not the letter of the life, but the spirit of it. And *Dust Tracks* does that exceedingly well."[58]

What Hurston gives the reader in her autobiographical narrative is the essence of herself. This is why she wrote in her 1943 letter to former colleague Hamilton Holt, "I did not want to write it at all, because it is too hard to reveal one's inner self, and still there is no use in writing that kind of book unless you do."[59] It is clear, then, that Hurston's intention in *Dust Tracks was* to give us her *real* self. In so doing, she was making an effort to put words to the unutterable. Yet, as Boyd stated, Hurston does succeed in communicating to us something of the spirit of her life. In her *Dust Tracks* narrative as well as in her anthropological essays and articles, Hurston gave expression to her interior, spiritual world. An examination of these works, as indicated in the passages above, reveals that black folk religious traditions had significant influences on her spiritual thought. Hurston wrote three essays on black folk religious traditions that were published in Nancy Cunard's *The Negro, An Anthology* in 1934: "Conversions and Visions," "Shouting," and "Spirituals and Neo-Spirituals." In these essays, Hurston analyzed various components of black folk religious expression. In the last essay, she explained "that the religious service is a conscious art expression. The artist is consciously creating—carefully choosing every syllable and every breath."[60] Hurston had the same appreciation of and respect for the religious practices of Vodou and Hoodoo. Her writings on the subject, in part, serve to dispel the misconceptions and distortions surrounding the practice. She stated that Hoodoo "is burning with a flame in America, with all the intensity of a suppressed religion." Hurston conjectured that there were thousands of adherents, but the true number would never be known "because the worship is bound in secrecy. It is not the accepted theology of the Nation and so believers conceal their faith."[61]

Hurston's investigations into Hoodoo took her into the dens of Hoodoo doctors throughout the South, particularly in New Orleans, Louisiana, and to the hounforts of houngans in Haiti. "New Orleans is now and has ever been the hoodoo capital of America," she wrote. "Great names in rites that vie with those of Hayti in deeds that keep alive the powers of Africa."[62] As with the black folk church, Vodou and Hoodoo were cultural institutions that continued some of the most significant and empowering aspects of traditional African society. Among them were oral tradition, community, and spirituality. The spoken word in traditional African society had a procreative force to name, to define, and to order the world. And the dynamics of African oral tradition fostered harmonious interrelations and community, because co-creativity is the very nature of antiphonal communication. Africana peoples found themselves uprooted from their African homelands and deposited in strange and inimical environments. The cultural traditions that gave birth to the humanity of African peoples would serve to empower Africans in the diaspora to survive, maintain, and recreate themselves as they resisted the attempts of Europeans and Euro-Americans to objectify and dehumanize them. The genius of oral tradition is its flexibility and adaptability. Thus, oral tradition equipped Africana peoples with the wherewithal to make their bid for freedom and peace. Like Moses standing at the Red Sea with little else but the clothes on his back, Africana peoples, stripped of their worldly goods even unto their loincloths, had nothing but what was within them. But what was within was a spirituality that contained worlds. Their words, inspired by their spirituality and infused by a life-affirming culture, fashioned new worlds everywhere they went. Hurston pointed out in

"Characteristics of Negro Expression" that "while he lives and moves in the midst of a white civilization, everything that he touches is re-interpreted for his own use. He has modified the language, mode of food preparation, practice of medicine, and most certainly the religion of his new country...."[63] In the pulpits and before the altars of Hoodoo doctors and houngans, Africana peoples empowered themselves and created worlds in their own image. Through song, prayer, sermon, and chant, they connected with one another, renewed themselves, and strengthened their collective spirit.

Hurston immersed herself in Hoodoo (and Vodou) as an anthropological investigator, but she was also a seeker. As an initiate of Marie LaVeau's nephew Luke Turner, and of other doctors as well, she would undergo the necessary preparations to earn the opportunity to "wear the crown of power," which would then allow her to "approach the Altar." Hurston's recounting of her initiation makes it clear that novitiates sought spiritual power. As she lay naked upon snake skins for three days, her "spirit went wherever spirits must go that seek answers never given to men as men."[64] After her spirit had sought the "Power-Giver" for sixty-nine hours, Hurston opened her eyes.

"Seeker, come," Turner called.

I made to rise and go to him. Another laid his hand upon me lightly, restraining me from rising.

"How must I come?" he asked in my behalf.

"You must come to the spirit across running water," Turner answered in a sort of chant.

So a tub was placed beside the bed. I was assisted to my feet and led to the tub. Two men poured water into the tub while I stepped into it and out again on the other side.

"She has crossed the dangerous stream in search of the spirit," the one who spoke for me, chanted.

"The spirit does not know her name. What is she called?"

"I see her conquering and accomplishing with the lightning and making her road with thunder. She shall be called the Rain-Bringer."[65]

Dressed with the symbol of lightning painted down her back, a pair of eyes painted on her cheeks, and the sun on her forehead, she was seated before the altar. With "the crown of power in his hand," Turner then stood behind her and said, "Spirit! I ask you to take her. Do you hear me, Spirit? Will you take her? Spirit, I want you to take her, she is worthy!" Hurston wrote, "he lifted the veil from my face and let it fall behind my head and crowned me with power."[66]

Hurston was Turner's apprentice for five months. In Hurston's letters to Hughes describing her fieldwork, she expressed exhilaration and delight. "I am getting on in the conjure splendidly." She continued, "[w]ait till you see my conjure material. Oh, Langston, my 'crowning' ceremonies were thrilling!"[67] What the letters don't evince is the extent to which Hurston was serious about her study and experiences and to what extent she was moved by the beauty and power of Hoodoo. Turner wanted Hurston to work in partnership with him and, eventually, assume the business. For not only did he judge her a good doctor and "the last doctor he would make," but also Turner anticipated his death. "It has been a great sorrow to me that I could not say yes," Hurston regretted.[68] What Hurston was saying no to was more than a business partnership. As a Hoodoo adept in the lineage of Marie LaVeau, Hurston was saying no to becoming a Vodou Queen, and by virtue of that position, she was also saying no to becoming an activist leader. In making Hurston his partner, Turner would have been transmitting to Hurston the "Heritage of Power."

In her work titled *Heritage of Power*, Susheel Bibbs gives the reader a biographical sketch of Mary Ellen Pleasant, a nineteenth-century activist who was mentored by and worked with Marie LaVeau. In outlining Pleasant's background, Bibbs also informs the reader that Marie LaVeau was a social and political activist who drew on her power as Vodou Queen to protect the vulnerable, heal the ailing, free the enslaved (she was an abolitionist), and bring calm to the chaos that had become New Orleans in the aftermath of the Louisiana Purchase. Her deeds were the obligations of Vodou Priests. LaVeau's ability to fulfill the duties of her office was widely recognized. Luke Turner informed Hurston that people came "from the ends of America" seeking LaVeau's aid. Even Queen Victoria sought the hand of Queen Marie LaVeau.[69] LaVeau scholar Ina Fandrich wrote, "it is precisely the beauty, strength and wisdom of LaVeau's African cultural capital that enabled her to be who she was and what she stood for."[70] Alexander was one of LaVeau's first teachers. He "felt the power" in her and encouraged her study of Vodou. Turner, likewise convinced of Hurston's desire to know and to learn, took her as his student.[71] Hurston joked with Hughes that she would someday wear the crown of Marie LaVeau. She could have.

Yet, for as much as Hurston was a seeker, she was also a social scientist and a writer and had many more horizons before her. Later, having acquired two Guggenheim Fellowships that allowed her to travel to Haiti, Hurston immersed herself in the religious rites of Vodou as well. Although she did not become a mambo or Vodou priestess, she "went Canzo," which is to say she was initiated into the second stage of preparation for the priesthood. Hurston does not describe her preparations as she did when preparing for the priesthood under Turner, nor does she expound on the significance of this phase of the initiation. This excerpt from Luisah Teisha's poem, "Congo Square," which pays "homage to Marie LaVeau," suggests the import of the rite:

> Piled high, wood is burning,
> Black cauldron filled with oil
> The faithful step forth bravely,
> While the charlatans recoil.
> Now is the magic moment.
> The test of truth is here.
> Only the devoted plunge their hands
> In the pot of oil without fear.[72]

Hurston's account of her experiences and observations in *Tell My Horse* casts light on the religion of Vodou. To some extent, she addresses the negative perceptions many people have about this spiritual tradition and practice. Misconceptions and distortions generated by ill-informed, prejudiced social scientists and print and mass media producers, who were steeped in notions of the primitive and the exotic, partly explain the shroud over Vodou. In addition to "bad press," the demonization of Vodou is directly related to Western fear of its power.

The Haitian Revolution of 1791 that defied and defeated the Napoleonic powers of France has been traced directly to Vodou. According to James Ferguson,

> [a]s the representatives of the Amis des Noirs and the Club Massiac argued in the National Assembly, and as whites struggled to contain mulatto militancy, the black slaves finally made their move. On August 22, 1791, a secret ceremony presided over by a Vodou priest, Boukman, brought together slave leaders from the sugar plantations surrounding Saint Domingue's main town, Cap Français. The meeting was the signal for the insurrection to begin, and within days, the rich plain in the north of the colony was devastated by fire and bloodshed.[73]

Before and after the Revolution, many Haitians escaped the devastation of the island by going to New Orleans. Among their numbers were Vodou priests and practitioners. Haitian adherents of Vodou blended in with those in New Orleans, creating a formidable culture of power. Marie LaVeau would, in time, become the most revered, renown, and effective executor of this power:

> Inside she shelters runaways,
> Takes poor girls off the street.
> She purifies and teaches them,
> In a manner most discreet....
>
> Their children will be born there,
> The old and sick will heal.
> Her gumbo, sent to those condemned,
> Gives death a peaceful meal.
>
> And when the slaves revolted
> Against their wretched lot,
> Mam'zelle Marie is found to be
> The mistress of the plot.[74]

THE MATRIX OF HER FICTION

Hurston infused her writings with the empowering aspects of traditional African and African American culture. As she incorporates the lore of the folk into her novels she gives the reader insight into the dynamics of black folk communities, the spiritual traditions that sustain them, and the oral traditions through which the members of the community express themselves. Some critics have suggested that the main value of Hurston's *Dust Tracks* is that it discloses "the matrix of her fiction." They state that the key to understanding Hurston's life is to be found in her fiction and folklore work, not her autobiography. Although these statements are debatable, it is so that Hurston's writings, particularly her novels, give insight into Hurston's worldview. In her first novel, *Jonah's Gourd Vine*, for instance, the text is imbued with an oral quality that engages the inner ear as well as the eye. Her characters speak in the black vernacular and the dialogue is phonetic, capturing the nuances that approximate the characters' speech. She integrated into the narrative traditional oral expressive forms, such as sermons, prayers, song, and proverbial expression, through which her characters reveal their personalities and express their humanity. Central to the novel is John Buddy Pearson who marries the sweetheart of his youth, Lucy Ann Potts. John declares to Lucy "Ah loves you and you alone." Yet, John indulges in extramarital affairs. He swears that each time is the last time and begs Lucy's forgiveness and God's tolerance. John resorts to the power of prayer to reconcile his own mind and convince Lucy of his sincerity, and he begins to pray in church. The deacons of Madedony appraised John's efforts and concluded that he had "uh good strainin' voice," and resolved to "make 'im pray uh lot." The deacons observed,

> John never made a balk at a prayer. Some new figure, some new praise-giving name for God, every time he knelt in church. He rolled his African drum up to the altar, and called his Congo Gods by Christian names. One night at the altar-call, he cried out his barbaric poetry to his "Wonder-working" God so effectively that three converts came thru [sic] religion under the sound of his voice.[75]

John Buddy Pearson was endowed with the power of the Word. "Dat boy is called tuh preach and don't now it," the deacons deduced.[76]

John was to find out soon though. Escaping criminal charges for assaulting his brother-in-law Bud Potts and escaping the "patter rollers" who were "sick and tiahed uh de way [John was] keerin on," John boarded a train to Sanford, Florida. There, he became a part of the railroad camp and the church life of the town. Back at the camp, to entertain and awe the workers, John would mimic the pastors he heard. "Pity you ain't preachin' yo'self," said an impressed camp worker named Blue. There was a "Meth'dis" preacher in Eatonville one of his co-workers wanted him "tuh mark." So John Pearson found himself in an all-Negro town that had "uh mayor and corporation." Having taken in the church service, John had taken in the town, too. "Ahm comin' back tuh dis place. Uh man kin be sumpin' heah 'thout folks tramplin' all over yuh. Ah wants mah wife and chillun heah." John's sexual entanglements with women in Sanford and at the camp undermined his resolve to move to Eatonville "on next pay-day." By the time John moved to Eatonville and sent for his family, it was "might nigh uh year." Happy to be rejoined with her husband, nonetheless, Lucy was not happy with the material conditions of their living. Lucy urged John to "get a home of our own" and to "git somethin' tuh do 'sides takin' orders offa other folks. Ah 'bominates dat," she frowned. Just as she urged John to "jump at de sun," she inculcated in her children their ability "tuh be bell cows theyselves." In a town where there were "no other kind uh folks actin' top-superior over 'em," they'd have the spunk to jump, too.[77]

The Pearson family prospered. As John's hands built physical houses for the newcomers to Orange County, his words built spiritual mansions for those seeking shelter in the house of God. "De words dat sets de church on fire comes tuh me jus' so," he shared with Lucy, excitedly. "Ah reckon de angels must tell 'em tuh me." So when John rose to tell the congregation that "God done called me tuh preach," nobody was surprised. As pastor of a church in Ocoee, then at Zion Hope in Sanford—with a membership exceeding 300 and growing—the Reverend John Pearson could dump "a heavy pocketbook" in Lucy's lap. Lucy was more than pleased with the much-improved material conditions of their living, but she could hardly reconcile herself to the spiritual condition of their lives. The mayor of Eatonville, moderator of the state Baptist Association, and pastor of Zion Hope, John was away from his wife and seven children—often by the necessity of his various occupations, but not infrequently by choice. Unwilling to endure the tension of caring for his infant daughter Isis, ill from typhoid and at death's door, John left Lucy at their child's bedside and escaped to Tampa. Hattie Tyson found the Reverend there and offered him the comfort of a bed and her embracing arms.[78]

Hattie Tyson was one of many women with whom John had affairs and referred to as "dem trashy women." John's inability to control what he called "de brute beast" in him, resulted in his jeopardizing his position in the community and in the pulpit. More than once, Lucy coached John Pearson back into the good graces of his membership. Even so, being "in de majority," as Lucy put it, John's repentant disposition lasted as long as dew drops in the brilliant sun. "A do ez Ah please," he says blatantly to a heartsick Lucy. Like the chinch-worm that cut down Jonah's gourd vine, John's infidelities cut Lucy's spirit until "[t]he vital Lucy was gone."[79]

The narrative plot suggests that, in addition to John's sexual unfaithfulness, there was another factor that accounted for Lucy's failing spirits. Although John had managed to stay away from Hattie nearly two months, Hattie would not be denied. Feeling her womanly wiles insufficient to regain the Reverend's attention, she sought to strengthen her hand by contracting the services of An' Dangie Dewoe, a "two-headed" doctor. After giving Hattie certain instructions to carry out, she assured Hattie that, being the powerful conjure doctor that she was, Hattie was "bound to come out more 'n conquer." She added, "Jes you pay me what Ah ast and 'tain't nothin' built up dat Ah can't tear down." To which Hattie responded, "Ah know you got de power." Hattie took her leave as An' Dangie continued her preparations to destroy Lucy and John's relationship. Lighting her inverted candles, she chanted, "Now fight! Fight and fuss 'til you part." Then, adorned with "war powder" and with the "cat bone in her mouth," she lay in a "red coffin facing the altar and went into the spirit."[80]

If John Pearson "was glad in his sadness" over the departed Lucy Ann Pearson, Hattie was ecstatic. "He was free." And Hattie could have him. In three months' time they married. But Hattie's carrying of the John de Conquer root that was braided in her hair and her continual visits to An' Dangie Dewoe, and then to another doctor named War Pete, could not mitigate the seven years of conflict that characterized Hattie and John's marriage, nor its eventual court-decreed termination. Hattie filed suit and John pled guilty as charged, even though Hattie accused him of all that he had done and much that he had not done. "Ah did it all," he swore. In the wake of his marriage to Hattie, John was removed as moderator of the state Baptist Association. Zion Hope would have let him go, except there was no one who could preach the Word like John. Deacon Harris conspired to find someone who could. Reverend Cozy was his name, and Harris maneuvered him into Zion Hope's pulpit, confident that he would be the end of Reverend Pearson, Deacon Harris's nemesis. But the congregation was unimpressed.

> "How y'all lak de sermon tuhnight?"
> "Sermon?" Sister Boger made an indecent sound with her lips, "dat wan't no sermon. Dat wuz uh lecture."
> "Dats all whut it wuz," Sister Watson agreed and switched on off.[81]

Nonetheless, John Pearson was losing the support that bore him up in the church and in the community. During the divorce proceedings, some of the members of his church, including those he thought to be good friends, testified against him. Without the support of the community, John lost his spirit to continue as pastor. When next he preached, the theme of his sermon was "the wounds of Jesus." The text: "'What are these wounds in thine hand?' He shall answer, 'Those are they with which I was wounded in the house of my friends.' Zach. 13:6." As John Pearson's sermon grew from the conversational opening, to the stating of the text, then to the crescendo chanting of the preaching of the Word, the Reverend Pearson took his congregation up to the heights of heaven where "God stood on the apex of His power," down to "de chasm of hell / Where de fire's never quenched" and "de grave / Where de worm never dies," and out to "the rim bones of nothing." From the creation of man, to Jesus' plan to "go his bond before [God's] mighty throne"; then to "de supper table" where Jesus cried out,

> My Soul is exceedingly sorrowful unto death, ha!,
> For this night, ha!
> One of you shall betray me, ha!
> It were not a Roman officer, ha!
> It were not a centurion

But one of you
Who I have chosen my bosom friend
That sops in the dish with me shall betray me.

The Reverend Pearson then cried out,

I want to draw a parable.
I see Jesus
Leaving heben with all of His grandeur
Dis-robin' Hisself of His matchless honor
Yielding up de scepter of revolvin' worlds
Clothing Hisself in de garment of humanity
Coming into de world to rescue His friends.
Two thousand years have went by on their rusty ankles
But with the eye of faith, I can see Him
Look down from His high towers of elevation
I can hear Him when He walks about the golden streets
I can hear 'em ring under His footsteps
Sol me-e-e, Sol do
Sol me-e-e, Sol do
I can see Him step upon the rim bones of nothing
Crying I am de way
De truth and de light
Ah![82]

They could see it, too. They could hear it, too. For that moment, Reverend Pearson's congregation was one with creation and the Creator. He uplifted and inspired them. His words moved them through dimensions of space and time, and empowered them to see the unseen, bear witness to a past that was thousands of years old, reach the unreachable, and know the unknown. They could play with the heavenly stars and brag kinship with the sun and moon. Through his words, he could bring them face to face with God. They could then look upon God and be whole. Every Sunday, John Pearson re-created the world for his congregations. Less and less could he do so for himself. Reverend John Pearson walked away from Zion Hope that Sunday afternoon. With so many in his church against him, he preferred to step down, saying, "Ah don't b'lieve Ahm fitted tuh preach de gospel—unless de world is wrong."[83]

Once John is no longer covered by the mantle of his ministry, he falls in further disfavor with the church and the community. But even with a fresh start in Plant City, Florida, with Sister Sally Lovelace, John is challenged by his tendency to engage in extramarital affairs. Though married to Sally and prosperous as he ever was, John succumbs to the spirit of the flesh. Anxious with guilt, John determined to tarry no longer and make his way home in the blue and silver Cadillac that Sally bought him as a wedding and one-year anniversary present. "He drove on but half-seeing the railroad from looking inward," he was struck by an oncoming train.[84]

John's ability to preach the Word facilitated his movement from share-cropper in Notasulga, Alabama, to a propertied civic leader in Eatonville and Sanford, Florida. His friend Sam Mosley claimed that "anybody kin preach. Hard work and hot sun done called uh many one?" But getting into a pulpit is one thing, as Reverend Cozy found out, staying there is another. In her May 8, 1934, letter to James Weldon Johnson, Hurston discussed with Johnson one of the reviews of *Jonah's Gourd Vine*. "I never saw such a lack of knowledge about us," Huston wrote. The *New York Times* reviewer found the pagan poesy of her character Reverend John Pearson to be incredulous:

> He does not know that merely being a good man is not enough to hold a Negro preacher in an important charge. He must be an artist. He must be both a poet and an actor of a very high order, and then he must have the voice and figure.[85]

His or her poetry and artistry is a means by which the minister connects the congregation to its vital Source, just as the Source inspires the minister. As John told his members, "When Ah speak tuh yuh from dis pulpit, dat ain't me talkin', dat's de voice uh God speakin' thru me. When de voice is thew. Ah jus' uhnother one uh God's crumblin' clods."[86]

THE LIGHT AT DAYBREAK

In her works, Hurston gives voice to the folk and dramatizes the oral traditions that have served to inspire their humanity and collective identity. Within their own culture, black folk could express their full humanity. They were saints and sinners and everything in between. But as they engaged Euro-American culture, that humanity would be significantly narrowed and diminished in the eyes of their white beholders. This was John Pearson's reasoning, and this is why he called no witnesses and denied no charges. His friend Hambo wanted so much to "tell 'bout de mens Ah've knowed Hattie tuh have" and "'bout all dat conjure and all dem roots she been workin' on you." Pearson explains,

> And dat's how come Ah didn't have 'em tuh call yuh. Ah didn't want de white folks tuh hear 'bout nothing' lak dat. Dey knows too much 'bout us as it is, but dey some things dey ain't tuh know. Dey's some strings on our harp fuh us tuh play on and sing all tuh ourselves. Dey thinks wese all ignorant as it is, and dey thinks wese all alike, and dat dey knows us inside and out, but you know better. Dey wouldn't make no great 'miration if you had uh tole 'em Hattie had all dem mens. Dey spectin' dat. Dey wouldn't zarn 'tween uh woman lak Hattie and one lak Lucy, uh yo' wife befo' she died. Dey thinks all colored folks is de same dat way. De only difference dey makes is 'tween uh nigger dat works hard and don't sass 'em, and one dat don't. Otherwise wese all de same. Dass how come Ah got up and said, "Yeah, Ah done it," 'cause dey b'lieved it anyhow, but dey b'lieved de same thing 'bout all de rest.[87]

John Pearson articulates the ongoing spiritual battle that Africana peoples face in a society that has not ceased making judgments based on racial prejudices and stereotypes. Just as black folk traditions were vehicles of collective identity and empowerment, they also were vehicles of individual identity, self-realization, and personal empowerment. In *Their Eyes Were Watching God*, the protagonist Janie Mae Crawford experiences her personal empowerment to the extent that she can speak for herself. In the beginning of the novel, Janie's sense of self is inchoate, unformed. She cannot even recognize her own image in a photograph taken with other neighbor children. As she grows older, she feels the urge to explore life's mysteries. Under the pear tree in her grandmother Nanny's backyard, she was entranced. The life that quickened the tree, pushing glistening buds and tender, virgin-blooms out of "barren brown stems" awakened the life force in her. "It had called her to come and gaze on a mystery." The alto-chanting bees that pollinated the blooms excited the entire tree, from root to stem, to the very delight of every blossom. "So this was a marriage!" thought Janie. "She had been summoned to a revelation." These singing bees sang "of the beginning of the world!" The holy union of bee and bloom was creation's flute song whispering the refrain of the mystery of life. It was a miniature grand pageant of the orgasmic dance of life. It compelled her to seek and know her inner mystery, and her own song, and her own story. Everywhere she looked over her grandmother's garden, she saw another variation of the melodious refrain, heard another key or another tone, and whiffed another fragrance. Hurston wrote, "She was seeking confirmation of the voice and the vision, and everywhere she found and acknowledged answers. A personal answer for all other creations except herself."[88]

Like High John de Conquer in search of a song, Janie was in search of herself. Who was she and what magic would ignite her blooming? "She had glossy leaves and bursting buds and she wanted to struggle with life but it seemed to elude her." Echoing the observations of High John, "Nothing on the place nor in her grandma's house answered her." Just as High John had to leave the plantation in search of a "particular kind of singing," Janie "searched as much of the world as she could from the top of the front steps and then went on down to the front gate and leaned over to gaze up and down the road. Looking, waiting, breathing short with impatience. Waiting for the world to be made."[89]

Janie would learn that what she sought was not outside herself. Her journey "up and down the road" would eventually bring her back "home" to the consciousness that was awakened under the pear trees. But at sixteen, she knew none of this, and neither did Nanny. Seeing Janie leaning over the front gate, being "lacerated" by a kiss from "breath-and-britches" Johnny Taylor, Nanny decided it was time to have Janie married to Logan Killicks, as had been one of her plans for Janie's life. Killicks "spoke to me 'bout you long time ago," Nanny revealed to Janie. But Nanny kept silent "'cause dat wasn't de way Ah placed you. Ah wanted yuh to school out and pick from a higher bush and a sweeter berry."[90] Janie tried to speak up for herself and about the vision she had for her life, but,

Janie didn't know how to tell Nanny that. She merely hunched over and pouted at the floor.

"Janie."

"Yes, ma'am."

"You answer me when Ah speak. Don't you set dere poutin' wid me after all Ah done went through for you!"

She slapped the girl's face violently, and forced her head back so that their eyes met in struggle.[91]

This was not the struggle she anticipated. Janie wanted to "struggle with life," her life. But she found that she would have to struggle with those who thought they knew better what she should do with her life and where her place in life should be. *They* would be the author of her life's story. Nobody cared *who* she was or what story she had burning inside her. It never occurred to them to ask and she didn't know how to say. Logan Killicks firmly believed Janie's life was best used behind a mule, plowing his fields.

Six months into their marriage, he had stopped talking to her "in rhymes" and started talking in terms of work: "If Ah kin haul de wood heah and chop it fuh yuh, look lak you oughta be able tuh tote it inside." His "fust wife" would "sling chips lak uh man," so why not Janie? He couldn't convince her of that, but he thought he could yoke her to a mule. Killicks owned sixty acres of land and he intended for Janie to help him cultivate those acres: "Taters is goin' tuh be taters in de fall. Bringin' big prices. Ah aims tuh run two plows, and dis man Ah'm talkin' 'bout is got uh mule all gentled up so even uh woman kin handle 'im."[92]

Logan searched Janie's face to see how she took things. In bed one night after his return, Janie tried to talk to her husband about their marriage and her discontent, but Logan pretended sleepiness and aggravation.

"'S'posin' Ah wuz to run off and leave yuh sometime," she asked Logan. This was Logan's "held-in fear." Often the human response to fear is anger— instead of honesty. Anger is what Logan expressed.

After giving his wife a reading that judged her (and her mother and grandmother) as sexually promiscuous, unworthy, ungrateful, and incapable of taking care of herself, Killicks gruffly snapped, "Ah'm sleepy. Ah don't aim to worry mah gut into a fiddle-string wid no s'posin'."[93]

The next morning, when Janie resisted Logan's command to help him "move dis manure pile befo' de sun gits hot," Logan flew hot and informed Janie on just what her place was—which was in the house initially but quickly was becoming "wherever Ah need yuh."

Janie's response met with a silencing threat: "Don't you change too many words wid me dis mawn'in, Janie, do Ah'll take and change ends wid yuh! ... Ah'll take holt uh dat ax and come in dere and kill yuh! You better dry up in dere!"[94]

Folks had a role for Janie to play in their lives, as though she was just what they needed to realize themselves, their dreams and goals. Logan claimed he was doing Janie a favor by marrying her, feeding her, and allowing her to take pleasure in his sixty acres. Not only was Janie not impressed with Logan's acreage, but she was totally uninterested in plowing them: "Ah could throw ten acres of it over de fence every day and never look back to see where it fell," she told her grandmother.[95]

Nanny, too, had a story, and she had determined what role Janie was to play in it. Nanny claimed she had Janie marry Logan Killicks so that Janie might have "protection." Maybe so. But the forced wedding was also Nanny's way of punishing Janie for interrupting and frustrating her narrative. She wanted Janie to complete her story, to give outward expression to Nanny's inside feelings about the world and about life: "Ah wanted to preach a great sermon about colored women sittin' on high," she told Janie.[96]

The circumstances of Nanny's life dictated otherwise. So Nanny was heartened by the notion that her daughter Leafy, Janie's mother, "would expound what Ah felt." Disappointed in that hope, Nanny determined that she would "save de text" for Janie. Nanny mistakenly believed that she could achieve *self*-expression and *self*-realization through another. She mistakenly believed that *her* dream "of whut a woman oughta be and to do" would, *should*, also be her daughter's dream *and* her granddaughter's dream.[97] When it appeared to Nanny that Janie, too, would not be the outward expression of her inner thoughts, Nanny slapped her face.

Janie couldn't put words to her own feelings, let alone her grandmother's. And when she did find her tongue to speak up for herself with Logan, he threatened to kill her. Like Logan, Eatonville Mayor "Jody" Starks talked "in rhymes" and had a story about where he had been and where he was going and how Janie fit into it: "Ah wants to make a wife outa you."[98]

Janie knew that Jody "did not represent sun-up and pollen and blooming trees, but he spoke for far horizon," so Janie Mae took a chance.[99] She was to learn, however, that the holy union she envisioned would also not be realized with Joe Starks. Such a union required a joining of equals. But Jody never conceived of Janie as an equal. He never conceived of women as equals. He never conceived of anything female as equal, sensible, or capable.

"Somebody gotta think for women, chillun, chickens, and cows," commented Jody. He did not see Janie as wholly human, as a full, complex character. To Jody, Janie was one-dimensional, "a pretty doll-baby," who was "made to sit on de front porch and rock and fan [her]self." As mayor of Eatonville and proprietor of the city's general store, Jody was able to supply Janie with a front porch and a two-story house to go with "de front porch." Jody was realizing his vision of "whut a woman was" and his vision of being "a big ruler of things with her reaping the benefits."[100] Janie had a role to play as Mrs. Mayor Starks, but Jody refused her any role in the development of the town over which he officiated nor did he allow her to participate in the real life of the town. Whether the town's folk were engaged in business or ballyhooing, Joe Starks sought to keep his wife separate from the "common lot."

When Tony Taylor ceremoniously requested "uh few words uh encouragement" on the occasion of Jody's "election" as mayor, Jody cut in: "Thank yuh fuh yo' compliments, but mah wife don't know nothin' bout no speech-makin'. Ah never married her for nothin' lak dat. She's uh woman and her place is in de home." But the same night, he figured her place was in "de store." His responsibilities multiplied as town mayor, so he decided Janie "kin look after things" in his absences.[101]

Amid the scrub oaks outside of Logan's farm, where Janie and Jody plotted their elopement, Jody promised, "You come go wid me. Den all de rest of yo' natural life you kin live lak you oughta." But Janie felt that the life they were living as Mr. and Mrs. Mayor was unnatural, superficial:

> "Well, honey, how yuh lak bein' Mrs. Mayor?"
>
> "It's all right Ah reckon, but don't yuh think it keeps us in uh kinda strain?"
>
> "Strain? You mean de cookin' and waitin' on folks?"
>
> "Naw, Jody, it jus' looks lak it keeps us in some way we ain't natural wid one 'nother. You'se always off talkin' and fixin' things, and Ah feels lak Ah'm jus' markin' time. Hope it soon gits over."
>
> "Over, Janie? I god, Ah ain't even started good. Ah told you in de very first beginnin' dat Ah aimed tuh be uh big voice. You oughta be glad, 'cause dat makes uh big woman outa you."
>
> A feeling of coldness and fear took hold of her. She felt far away from things and lonely.[102]

Jody's big voice subsumed Janie's personal authoritative voice, effectively silencing Janie's thoughts, wishes, dreams, and feelings. The unnaturalness between them bloomed into thorns and needles and sharp edges. Jody's impatience and frustration blossomed into looks and words that ridiculed and belittled Janie. But criticizing her was losing whatever satisfaction Jody had derived from it. Seven years into the marriage, he slapped her. The dinner she prepared was not quite right. When the ringing in her ears subsided, she went inside herself and saw that the image she had of Jody had fallen and was shattered. Looking beyond the shards, she saw years of repressed dreams and thoughts and feelings that she never shared with Jody and, now, she knew she never would.

She was saving up feelings for some man she had never seen. She had an inside and an outside now, and suddenly she knew how not to mix them.[103]

Like John Buddy and Lucy, Janie and Jody had all the material comforts they desired. Also like them, the spirit of their relationship suffered. John Buddy and Jody both wanted their wives' submission, but neither was successful in attaining it. So both attempted to undermine their wives' personal power of self-expression by silencing them in one way or another—by not allowing them to speak, by threatening them, and by physically abusing them. In spite of Jody's domineering ways, Janie would, from time to time, verbally defend herself. She even defended other women. She would try to tell her side of a story as she also tried to join her voice into the conversation of voices in the store. After hearing an earful of insults and jokes at the expense of some of the wives in the town, Janie blatantly stated to the men-folks in the store,

> "Sometimes God gits familiar wid us womenfolks too and talks His inside business. He told me how surprised He was 'bout y'all turning out so smart after Him makin' yuh different; and how surprised y'all is goin' tuh be if you ever find out you don't know half as much 'bout us as you think you do. It's so easy to make yo'self out God Almighty when you ain't got nothin' tuh strain against but women and chickens."
>
> "You gettin' too moufy, Janie," Starks told her.

Joe and the other men dismissed her voice, giving no validation to what she was saying, as though she had said nothing at all. Then Joe Starks commanded her to fetch the checkerboard so the men could continue their fun.[104]

Over the next ten years, Janie's face had drawn itself into a mask that marked her physical presence in life. But she had emotionally and spiritually withdrawn. Her fighting spirit that once fueled her desire to struggle with life seemed subdued. As her voice was suppressed, so, too, was her spirit. Janie thought that the fight had "gone from her soul."[105]

She found out differently when she stood in the middle of the general store, going toe-to-toe with Jody in a signifying ritual of insult that would prove injurious to both parties. Any perceived fault in Janie had become an opportunity for Jody to ridicule her. The way in which she cut a piece of tobacco for a customer one day became just such an opportunity:

> "I god amighty! A woman stay round uh store till she get old as Methusalem and still can't cut a little thing like a plug of tobacco! Don't stand dere rollin' yo' pop eyes at me wid yo' rump hangin' nearly to yo' knees!"

Janie's retort initiated a sally of insults between the two that came to an end when Janie delivered the verbal blow that would, for the first time, silence Joe's big voice:

> "Naw, Ah ain't no young gal no mo' but den Ah ain't no old woman neither. Ah reckon Ah looks mah age too. But Ah'm uh woman every inch of me, and Ah know it. Dat's uh whole lot more'n you kin say. You big-bellies round here and put out a lot of brag, but 'tain't nothin' to it but yo' big voice. Humph! Talkin' 'bout me lookin' old! When you pull down yo' britches, you look lak de change uh life."
>
> Joe Starks didn't know the words for all this, but he knew the feeling. So he struck Janie with all his might and drove her from the store.[106]

Jody's banishment of Janie from the store is reminiscent of God's driving Adam and Eve from the Garden of Eden. They had eaten of the tree of knowledge, of good and evil, and so they had begun to see things, really. The store was Joe Stark's Eden. As he had said to Tony Taylor,

> Ah got tuh have a place tuh be at when folks come tuh buy land. And furthermo' everything is got tuh have uh center and uh heart tuh it, and uh town

ain't no different from nowhere else. It would be natural fuh de store tuh be meetin' place fuh de town.[107]

As Joe Starks made the store the heart and center of the town, He made himself the center of the town's life. Prefacing his speech with "I god," he commanded, demanded, judged, damned, or pardoned all under the sound of his voice. But Janie stood in the middle of the store that day and usurped Jody's seat of power. Henceforward, the town had another story to tell about Mayor Joe Starks. They had begun to see things, really, too. "They'd look with envy at the things and pity the man that owned them. Good-for-nothings like Dave and Lum and Jim wouldn't change place with him. For what can excuse a man in the eyes of other men for lack of strength?"[108]

In their battle of words, Janie had won. Joe's big voice had been humbled. And as he grew silent, so also did his spirit and will diminish. The wedge between Jody and Janie grew bigger as Joe fell ill and accused Janie of "fixin'" him. The kidney disease to which Joe refused to attend weakened his physical vitality until he had no more. Janie felt the weight of oppression lift in the absence of a husband who had long sat "in de rulin' chair." She decided, "This freedom feeling was fine."[109] While reflecting on her twenty years of life with Jody and the years before, she recalled her awakening and her yearning for life:

> She had been getting ready for her great journey to the horizon in search of *people*; it was important to all the world that she should find them and they find her. But she had been whipped like a cur dog, and run off down a back road after *things*.[110]

Nine months after Jody's death, Janie had not taken one step on her journey to the horizon. She was still "clerking for Joe." But the world found her where she was and Tea Cake walked into her life. He stepped into the store, courted her, and, in spite of some doubt and trepidation, she married Verigible "Tea Cake" Woods. He was like none of the men she had known. "He looked like the love thoughts of women. He could be a bee to a blossom—a pear tree blossom in the spring."[111]

He was all that to Janie, and so with Tea Cake she journeyed to new horizons and met people. After they married, she and Tea Cake went on "de muck" and moved "down in de Everglades round Clewiston and Belle Glade where dey raise all dat cane and stringbeans and tomatuhs. Folk don't do nothing' down dere but make money and fun and foolishness."[112] It was their Eden, and it was where Janie could find out about "the beginnings of things" and learn a "maiden language" to tell the tale of it. Janie became a part of the transient community on the muck. Tea Cake would pick his "box" or start a hand of cards and folks would gather about. There would be singing, joking, and storytelling.

On the muck, Janie "could listen and laugh and even talk some herself if she wanted to. She got so she could tell big stories herself from listening to the rest."[113] Unlike Jody, who tried to keep Janie alienated from the

Eatonville folk and out of the conversation and fun they enjoyed, Tea Cake encouraged her. Janie worked alongside Tea Cake in the field as well. He didn't need her out there as an extension of himself to pick more or bigger bushels. Tea Cake explained that he was losing both time and money running back to the quarters so often because he felt so lonesome without her. As she told Phoeby before she married Tea Cake, "Dis ain't no business proposition, and no race after property and titles. Dis is uh love game."[114]

This was the marriage she envisioned. They had the same feelings about life, and they found joy in each other's presence. This was the union to which she wanted to give herself. This was the man for whom she had been saving her feelings. For two years they laughed and loved and fought. Although their life dance would end unceremoniously, they voiced no regrets, just gratitude and appreciation.

"If you kin see de light at daybreak," Janie told Tea Cake, "You don't keer if you die at dusk."[115] Janie, Tea Cake, and other workers were trapped on the muck in the midst of a hurricane. Bitten by a rabid dog, Tea Cake would eventually become a casualty of the storm. Janie Mae was forced to shoot the delirious Tea Cake to save her own life. As irony would have it, the two lovers stood opposite each other. Tea Cake, in a state of delirium, pointed a pistol at Janie. Janie, in a critical dilemma, hoisted a shotgun in self-defense. Tea Cake's shot missed. But the love between Tea Cake and Janie made his death a lie. Even in his physical absence, Janie felt his presence and found comfort therein. "He could never be dead until she herself had finished feeling and thinking."[116]

THE POWER OF THE SPOKEN WORD

Hurston's novels are testaments to the power of the spoken word and the genius of the oral tradition in black folk culture. In *Jonah's Gourd Vine*, Hurston highlighted the transformative power of the spoken word through the oral form of the traditional folk sermon. In *Their Eyes Were Watching God*, Hurston highlighted the tradition of storytelling. As High John de Conquer searched for his song, Janie Mae Crawford searched for her story.

Touring heaven and hell and points in between, High John found "the particular piece of singing" the folks needed to renew and realize themselves. Janie found the story—her-story—that empowered her to project her own voice, to be whole and self-expressed. She now had a story to tell. She shared her tale with her friend Phoeby, and gave Phoeby leave to tell it to the others. After she had come from burying the dead, she sat on her back porch in Eatonville, joined by Phoeby and ate the welcome-home meal Phoeby brought her. Her friend had been "a delegate to de big 'sociation of life," and Phoeby was eager to hear all about it. Janie spoke of the muck, three husbands, a grandmother who "mis-loved" her, and a mother toward whom she felt indifferent. She spoke of her struggle with life, which was her determination to find out what the sound of her own voice was like. She spoke of the glory of a love so genuine and so bright that "her soul crawled out from its hiding place."[117] She spoke of stormy times with Tea Cake—her jealousies, his fears, the life they led, and the death he died. She spoke of life because she had lived some and had something to say and Phoeby listened.

"Ah done growed ten feet higher from jus' listenin' tuh you, Janie," Phoeby said in awe. "Ah ain't satisfied wid mahself no mo'. Ah means tuh make Sam take me fishin' wid him after this."

As the congregation at Zion Hope could climb the heavens to the throne of God upon the words of Reverend John Pearson, so Phoeby could vicariously walk to the horizon, and standing on the edge of Janie's story, peer beyond it to imagine her own possibilities.

THE INSIDE SEARCH

Introspection is key to personal empowerment, thus the "inside search" encourages self-awareness and nurtures consciousness. Hurston's ideas about self-introspection and consciousness were influenced by the philosophical ideas of Benedict de Spinoza and Friedrich Nietzsche and the spiritual ideas of Eastern thought. She integrates self-knowledge and consciousness as key components of the individual and collective journey inward and onward to the horizon—to one's destiny. Defined as an aspect of thought that points to the transcendent, consciousness is the vital connection between the individual soul and divine spirit, universal oneness, or God.[118]

Zora Neale Hurston declared, "I am a conscious being." This was Hurston's way of saying, "I have a mind of my own." Hurston not only was critical of the ideas, beliefs, and opinion of others, but also scrutinized her own thoughts.

Joseph Campbell explains that in the yogic tradition of India, "we attempt to yoke our consciousness to the source of consciousness." This is achieved by "the intentional stopping of the spontaneous activity of the mind substance."[119] It is necessary to slow the mind down. Self-introspection is one means of assisting this process.

Hurston's characters exhibit various modes of entering into a contemplative state of mind, and they have varying degrees of success in connecting with spirit. To the extent that they are successful in being "yoked" or connected with spirit, they experience their personal power and a sense of freedom and peace.

From the beginning of Janie's story to the end, and points in between, Janie is self-aware and introspective. As she begins to share her life's story with her friend Phoeby, "she went on thinking back to her young years.... She thought awhile and decided that her conscious life had commenced at Nanny's gate." When Nanny saw Janie let Johnny Taylor lean over the gatepost and kiss her, Janie had partaken of the proverbial fruit of the tree and had awakened to the pulse of life in and around her. It had become Janie's habit, her practice, to lie under the blossoming pear tree and contemplate the mystery of life. She spent most of the day under the tree and "had been spending every minute that she could steal from her chores under that tree for the last three days." She stretched out on her back beneath the tree as child, but she got up as a woman who knew her own mind. She wanted "to struggle with life," to find out the meaning of what she had witnessed with bee and bloom and frothing blossom. She was intoxicated with the wonder of life. Its perfume permeated her being: The rose of the world was breathing out smell. It followed her through all of her waking moments and caressed her in her sleep. It connected itself with vaguely felt matters that had struck her outside observation and buried themselves in her flesh. Now they emerged and quested about her consciousness.[120] The bliss of union, of oneness, had been revealed to her, and she wanted to touch it.

Janie could not articulate this vision to her grandmother. Even if she could have, it is likely that Nanny would have been even more alarmed. She kept counsel with herself, though, and grew in wisdom as the communion between her soul and spirit strengthened through her continuous introspection. "She knew things that nobody had ever told her," like the words of trees and wind and the whispered good wishes of seeds drifting to earth: "Ah hope you fall on soft ground."[121]

With Logan Killicks, Janie found that marriage did not make love. Instead of experiencing the bliss that would yoke her to Universal Spirit, she found that Logan only wanted to yoke her to a mule. Talking into the darkness with Phoeby, Janie recalled the many times she retreated within herself until she finally put up a protective barrier that separated her inner and outer selves. Even then, so much of Janie's interior life was conscious of Jody, diminishing her connection to herself and to her Source. On his deathbed, she reviled Jody for this: "Mah own mind had tuh be squeezed and crowded out tuh make room for yours in me."[122]

In spite of twenty years with a man who demanded obedience, Janie Mae Crawford never bowed. In her moments of introspection during their marriage, she would remind herself of her true destiny, even as she existed in circumstances that would deny her that. But as Nanny had said to her, "nobody can't stop you from wishin', ... and nobody can beat you down so low that they rob you of your will." Janie would lay awake in bed at night after "asking lonesomeness some questions" and learned more about herself and what she desired, her likes and dislikes.[123]

With no outside force to crush her thought and ambition, she took a chance with gambling, happy, sensual Tea Cake. The judgment of the town, though, was not in Tea Cake's favor, and they sent Phoeby to tell Janie that. But Janie's years of inner reflection started a low-burning fire that transformed her girlish wishes to the will of a woman. So Phoeby found in Janie someone who was not so easily swayed by the opinions of others: "Well, if yo' mind is already made up, 'tain't nothin' nobody kin do." Janie had lived life other folks' way. "Now Ah means tuh live mine," she told Phoeby.[124] As Janie's will grew stronger from her clarity of thought and conscious reconnection with life, she felt herself empowered with the courage to be her own woman and to journey to the horizon.

> It's a known fact, Phoeby, you got tuh go there tuh know there. Yo' papa and yo' mama and nobody else can't tell yuh and show yuh. Two things everybody's got tuh do fuh theyselves. They got tuh go tuh God, and they got tuh find out about livin' fuh theyselves.[125]

In the silence that filled the spaces where words had been, Janie sat in the quiet presence of Tea Cake and was at peace. Janie "pulled in the horizon like a great fish-net.... So much life in its meshes! She called her soul to come and see."[126]

Quiet self-introspection was Janie's path to divinity. Prayer was John Pearson's path. Just as Joe Starks worshipped the works of his own hands, John Pearson loved the sound of his own voice and bragged of his oratorical gifts to his friends Sam Moseley and Mayor Clarke and others. Sam Moseley teased him, "Well, John done got tuh be uh preacher."[127] John had "the voice and figure" and the discerning wisdom of Lucy Ann. Therefore, John was successful, and despite his scandalous ways, Macedony would retain him as their minister. John could deliver the Word, but he couldn't deliver himself from a guilty mind.

Successful on the outside, he was continually agitated on the inside. Being seen as a "woman-made" man and unable to reconcile the spirit of the Word with the spirit of the flesh kept John from feeling whole and at peace. The power he felt in the pulpit did not translate to feeling empowered in his personal life. Although John was in the business of soul saving, he had little interest in soul searching. Through his prayers, he attempted to appease his guilt-ridden mind. He desired to slow down the thoughts that upbraided and berated him, but he thought little about changing the behavioral patterns that led to his haunting thoughts.

This voice that could bring converts through religion did precious little for John's own personal salvation. Rather than face himself, John chose escape. Escape may have been useful for some things, but John applied it as a formula to solve all his difficulties. When he wasn't running from his life, he was denying the deeds that made his life difficult. For example, John would rather silence Lucy than be confronted with his infidelities:

> "Youse livin' dirty and Ahm goin' tuh tell you 'bout it. Me and mah chillen got some rights. Big talk ain't changin' whut you doin'. You can't clean yo'self wid yo' tongue lak uh cat."
>
> There was a resounding smack. Lucy covered her face with her hand, and John drew back in a sort of horror, and instantly strove to remove the brand from his soul by words, "Ah tole yuh tuh hush." He found himself shaking as he backed towards the door.[128]

As Lucy made a futile effort, on her deathbed, to get John to see that "ignorance is de hawse dat wisdom rides," so too did Janie's confrontation of Jody on his deathbed prove futile: "Ah knowed you wasn't gointuh lissen tuh me. You changes everything but nothin' don't change you—not even death."[129] Neither man would look inward. Neither would take responsibility for their actions and their suffering. Jody blamed Janie and conjure. John Buddy blamed "dem trashy women," his wife Lucy whom he conceived of as "uh hold-back," Hattie Tyson and her conjuration, and the world itself. When John stepped down from the pulpit of Macedony Baptist, he told his friend Hambo, "Ah don't b'lieve Ahm fitted tuh preach de gospel—unless de world is wrong. Yuh see dey's ready fuh uh preacher tuh be uh man uhmongst men, but dey ain't ready yet fuh 'im tuh be uh man uhmongst women."[130]

But it was John who didn't see. "He's a Battle-Axe in de Time Uh Trouble" was the hymn that John raised in the Covenant meeting preceding his declaration of receiving and answering the Call. John was in a battle, but he wasn't winning with his soul "whole and free." He had plenty "outside showing force," whether with his words, his physical stature by which some men were intimidated, or his large hands with which he slapped Lucy and beat Hattie. What John did not see was that the battle was within, not without.

When John prayed, "He rolled his African drum up to the altar, and called his Congo Gods by Christian names," a telling element in John's story is revealed.[131] In the Vodou pantheon of divinities, as Hurston pointed out in *Tell My Horse* and Susheel Bibbs stated in the *Heritage of Power*, there are two major classifications of gods: The Rada or Arada gods of Dahomey who constitute the deities "known also as the original spirits" of the Vodou faith and who are "regarded as 'cool,' benevolent, or helpful." The Kongo (or Petro/Petwo) gods of the Kongo people are warrior gods that are characteristically defensive, and retaliatory and "are regarded as aggressive, unpredictable, or 'hot.'"[132]

John Buddy Pearson's actions and his defensive postures in relation to those actions reflect a warring spirit. Instead of a self-introspection that might have given him an understanding of himself and his life, and thus a greater self-control, John's tendency was to vanquish all opposition to the image he had of himself. Instead of taking responsibility for his life, his prayers—a kind of spiritual lobotomy—were pleas to free him from personal responsibility. One of John's first prayers beseeched God to find what sin that might lurk in his heart and to "pluck it out and cast it intuh de sea uh fuhgitfulness whar it'll never rise tuh condemn me in de judgment."[133]

Pearson was aware of his lack of reflection and was bold in his will to continue mindlessly in his actions: "Ah ain't got no remembrance. Don't keer if Ah laugh, don't keer if Ah cry, when de sun, wid his blood red eye, go intuh his house at night, he takes all mah rememberance wid 'im.... Ah ain't got no mind."[134]

Janie Mae Crawford had an "inside and an outside." So did John. Whereas Janie was conscious of both, John relieved himself of the responsibility of being conscious about anything. He believed that he was *just* a "crumblin' clod." By the time John appeared ready to recognize that he was a conscious being, too, and that his actions affected others, he was literally at the cross-roads of his life. He seemed ready to take the journey inward. John's fate is an ironic one as well: his intent inward gaze rendered him unconscious to his outward surrounding and the engineer's whistle.

THE SPIRIT OF FREEDOM

The "High John de Conquer" tale speaks to the spirit of freedom. As the plot of the tale indicates, even if one is not physically free, one can be men-tally free. And mental freedom is conceived as a prerequisite to both physical freedom and peace. When one recognizes the dualistic and oppositional nature of thought, and allows the mind to reach a still point, one can tran-scend thought to spirit and thus to a greater wisdom. Just as conscious thought can bring the individual to the point of transcendence and possibil-ity, reactive thought can imprison and limit the individual.

In "The Race Cannot Become Great Until It Recognizes Its Talent," Zora Neale Hurston made the pronouncement that "the world's most powerful force is intellect. The only reality is thought."[135] In the writing of *Jonah's Gourd Vine*, Hurston discussed the pressure to bow to the dominate dis-course of the day which dictated that the younger writers and artists express the ideology of the New Negro—as conceived by the pundits of the Black Intel-ligentsia. Integral to that ideology was the race debate and the notion that artis-tic expression should be propagandistic and, thereby, expose white racism.

Hurston stated, however, "[w]hat I wanted to tell was a story about a man," not the race problem. "My interest lies in what makes a man or a woman do such-and-so, regardless of his color," she explained.[136] As an anthropologist, Hurston was simply and profoundly interested in human nature. In her novels, she utilized plot, dialogue, and narration to reveal and analyze the mental processes and motivations of her characters. In exploring John Pearson's interior life and inner machinations, Hurston demonstrated how a lack of consciousness can undermine an individual's very life. Just as John Pearson numbed the activity of thought in his mind, Arvay Henson in *Seraph on the Suwanee* was consumed by her thoughts.

Arvay was married to a Jody Starks–like go-getter and self-made man. Industrious, far-sighted, and full of possibility, Jim Meserve had plans for his life and his wife. "I'm going to marry you first and last," he told Arvay, with-out even a pretense of desiring to know her feelings or wishes. Arvay, doubt-ful of Jim's sincerity and mindful of her own vague plans, countered Jim's announcement: "I been keeping off to give my life to missionary work.... I'd have to take time to make up my mind." Like Joe Starks, however, Jim never considered that women had any minds at all, except as they might be uti-lized in taking orders from men:

Oh, I mean it sure as you're born, and so far as making up your mind is concerned, that matters a difference. Women folks don't have no mind to make up nohow. They wasn't made for that. Lady folks were just made to laugh and act loving and kind and have a good man to do for them all he's able, and have him as many boy-children as he figgers he'd like to have, and make him so happy that he's willing to work and fetch in every dad-blamed thing that his wife thinks she would like to have. That's what women are made for.[137]

Arvay was too full of wonder that Jim had interest in her at all to consider what he was offering and under what conditions. Arvay was to have no voice. She was to have no will. She was to have no dreams—at least none of her own. Given Arvay Henson's sense of herself as worthless and sinful, she did not feel as though she deserved to speak, to have a voice, anyway. She had no critical mind with which to analyze Jim's statements or ask questions. She was too spellbound by the fact that this handsome, laughing, "first-class" fellow would deign to marry her.

Arvay was never clear about what she wanted from life except that she desired her brother-in-law, the Reverend Carl Middleton. Arvay saw Carl as a love-interest and was sure the Reverend felt the same about her. Carl's frequent visits to the Henson home, where Arvay and Carl would discuss music selections for the church service, would constitute their courtship. "The pastor leaning over her shoulder while she sat at the organ, little touches of his hand seemingly by accident, softness in his voice, and telling her that she was an exceptional young girl," made Arvay feel important, warm, and secure.[138] For once in her life, she was special and someone wanted her.

Just as a young tree standing in the shade of a taller tree never grows into its full height nor stretches its limbs to the sky, so Arvay stood in the shadow of her older sister, feeling small and unloved. Insignificant. Carl Middleton's attention was a light in her dim thoughts. "Arvay shone inside at Middleton's very presence. She fell in love, and began to live a sweet and secret life inside herself."[139]

While Arvay was "shy and almost wordless" and sure Carl Middleton was out of her reach, her sister Larraine was outspoken and, moreover, wore long dresses and could "keep company." Arvay's reactionary thinking about the marriage of her sister to the Reverend Carl confirmed Arvay's conception of herself as worthless, assured her she could not trust her own feelings, and generated in her a paranoia that befuddled anyone who attempted to get close to her. Would-be suitors were spurned or discouraged by Arvay's "fits and spasms" or seizures:

They had no way of knowing that Arvay was timid from feeling unsafe inside. Nor had anyone, not even her parents, the answer to Arvay's reaction to people. They did not suspect that the general preference for Larraine, Arvay's more robust and aggressive sister, had done something to Arvay's soul across the years. They could not know, because Arvay had never told anyone how she felt and why.[140]

When Larraine married Carl, Arvay withdrew from the world and grew in her Christian faith. Because she could not give "her whole heart and life" to Carl, she resolved to give them to God. Her religious fervor led her to renounce men and announce to the members of Day Spring Baptist Church her intention "to take the Word to the heathens" in Africa, China, and India.[141] In actuality, Arvay's desire to escape into missionary life was her attempt to flee the thoughts of her own confused mind.

Like Reverend Pearson, Arvay was tormented by guilt. For the five years that Carl Middleton had been married to her sister, Arvay had silently lusted for him. Her inability to control her feelings and thought or her irresistible urge to spy on Carl and Larraine during intercourse left her feeling debased and morally depraved. Instead of tending to her own "sins," and feelings of emptiness, she felt compelled to save the "heathens" from theirs.

Arvay never made any effort to go in search of her "heathens." Her feelings of inferiority and moral turpitude resulted in a conviction that she was undeserving of any joy in life. So when Jim Meserve declared his intentions, she cowed and seemed to be oblivious to his rough treatment of her.

Having been persuaded by his employee and "pet-Negro" Joe Kelsey that he must be forceful, Jim rapes Arvay before he marries her: "Most women folks will love you plenty if you take and see to it that they do. Make 'em knuckle under. From the very first jump, get the bridle in they mouth and ride 'em hard and stop 'em short. They's all alike, Boss. Take 'em and break 'em." Although Arvay vacuously states, "All Ah know is that I been raped," she does not protest Jim's actions or tell her folks.[142]

She immediately feels that she has been "taken for a fool" and assumes Jim's intentions to leave her debauched and in a worse situation than before. After all, Arvay thought, she was white, but poor and common. When Jim professed that he loved her "a million times more" and was still intent on marrying her, she was taken aback. "No need for you to go proaging clean around the world no more looking for no heathens to save," he told her. "No more missionarying around for you. You done caught your heathen, baby. You got me all by yourself. And I'm here to tell you that you done brought him through religion and absolutely converted his soul."[143]

Arvay thought her marriage to Jim was a sign and symbol: "Her secret sin was forgiven and her soul set free!"[144] But even as Arvay felt forgiven by God, she felt condemned by Jim. Arvay's low opinions of herself were legion, and they poisoned her relations with virtually every one in her circle of life, which grew to be smaller and smaller. Arvay felt insignificant as the younger daughter, inadequate as a wife, unfit as a mother, and inferior as a white woman. Jim Meserve's brash and domineering ways and Arvay's insecurity and the displaced anger stemming from her own negative sense of self resulted in a tumultuous union.

When Jim suggested that their mentally ill son Earl be institutionalized, Arvay's depression, guilt, and resentment of Jim gathered like a storm. Jim attributed Earl's illness to Arvay's family lineage, and Arvay felt condemned by the accusation. Jim's suggestion was Arvay's opportunity to finally speak her peace to Jim about the matter:

> I know that you been had it in you to say all the time. I been looking for you to puke it up long time ago. What you stay with me for, I don't know, because I know so well that you don't think I got no sense, and my folks don't amount to a hill of beans in your sight. You come from some big high muck-de-mucks, and we ain't nothing but piney-woods Crackers and poor white trash. Even niggers is better than we is, according to your kind....[145]

After many battles of wit and will between the two, the couple eventually separated. Jim removed himself to *The Arvay Henson*, one of the shrimping vessels he owned, and Arvay toyed with the idea of returning to her home-town, Sawley. She was too insecure in her relationship with Jim to go off on her own volition, but when she received the telegram of her mother's illness, she saw her return to Sawley as God's will:

> God worked in mysterious ways His wonders to perform.... God was taking a hand in her troubles. He was directing her ways. The answer was plain. He meant for her to go back home. This was His way of showing her what to do. The Bible said, "Everything after its own kind," and her kind was up there in the piney woods around Sawley.

Whereas she had once loathed herself and her family as "piney-woods crackers," through her inflected lens of superiority, she now made a virtue of poverty and ignorance and quickened her steps to go back to her beginnings. Arvay interpreted the telegram as a sign: "God was showing favor to His handmaiden?"[146]

In returning to her home and her mother, Arvay had come full circle. She took stock of the rundown condition of her homestead and the emaciated body of her mother Maria, and she began to understand something about the poverty of spirit that characterized her family. As Arvay listened to Maria on her deathbed, she learned of the mean-spiritedness of her sister 'Raine, her husband Carl, and their three children. Carl hadn't been pastor of Day Spring Baptist for some while and seldom held a job. They were all dependent on the monies Arvay and Jim sent Maria every month. Of herself, Maria said to her younger daughter, "I know that I don't amount to much. I'm just one of the nothing kind of human things stumblin' around 'mongst the toes of God." Though Maria felt her self insignificant, she would be grateful to have a funeral ceremony befitting someone of importance. With Arvay's promise for such a funeral, Maria died.[147]

'Raine and her family had taken and stolen from Maria since her husband Brock died. And then they waited for her death, watching like "turkey buzzards" for a meal. But Maria left the land and the rat-infested house to Arvay. Having granted her mother's wishes, Arvay returned to the Henson home-stead. She walked through the rooms heavy with want and listened to the scurrying of rats between the walls. The house had a distemper, she decided.

The depressed spirit of her family members became part of the house, and the house had "a soul of its own now." It was an infectious environment that had caught people in it and "twisted the limbs of their minds." She might have left the house to 'Raine, but she had seen the same impoverished spirit in their eyes. She placed burning rags and trash in and around the house and set it ablaze. At a safe distance from the house, under the mulberry tree in the backyard, Arvay watched and thought:

> Looking at the conflagration, exultation swept over her followed by a peaceful calm. It was the first time in her life that she was conscious of feeling that way. She had always felt like an imperfect ball restlessly bumping and rolling and rolling and bumping. Now she felt that she had come to a dead and absolute rest.[148]

Arvay had finally reached a still point.

The competitive feelings of inferiority and superiority and all the reactive thoughts, emotions, and actions to which they gave birth were the psychic kindling that fueled the fire.

> The dry old house burned furiously, and as Arvay watched the roaring and ascending flames, she picked herself over inside and recognized why she felt as she did now. She was no longer divided in her mind. The tearing and ripping and useless rending was finished and done. She made a peace and was in harmony with her life.

As the smoke cleared, her mind cleared. She "knew her own way now and could see things as they were." She had an inner strength. "I'll do all in my power to take care of things my ownself. No need of wearing God out."[149]

Sitting before the fire, her thoughts stilled, Arvay could now move beyond the dualism of her childhood. She was now at the border of transcendence and open to a wisdom, a higher knowing, and an understanding. Whereas before she was bogged down in reactive patterns to external phenomena, now she could see her own trap and the source of it. She saw it in her sister 'Raine and her family, and she had compassion for them. In her solitude, she rediscovered that all she wanted to do and to be was to nurture and to mother.

Jim wanted her and needed her mothering, but he didn't know how to ask for it, so he demanded it. She would not submit to Jim, but she would surrender. And even her surrender was not to Jim, but to her inner calling to nurture and to mother. Out of her separation from Jim and her time of self-introspection, Arvay gained clarity of vision and felt empowered to realize her vision. With confidence, she would return to Jim Meserve. Even if it were too late for her relationship with Jim, she now knew her way. Later, from Jim's cabin on The Arvay Henson, Arvay watched the sun rise above the horizon, making a new day. She had come to a new consciousness.

> All that happened to her, good or bad was a part of her own self and had come out of her. Within her own flesh were many mysteries. She lifted her left hand before her eyes and studied it in every detail with wonder. With wonder and

deep awe like Moses before his burning bush. What all, Arvay asked herself, was buried and hidden in human flesh? You toted it around with you all your life time, but you couldn't know. If you just could know, it would be all the religion that anybody needed. And what was in you was bound to come out and stand.[150]

THE TWO-SIDED SWORD

Their Eyes Were Watching God may be Zora Neale Hurston's popular masterpiece, but *Moses, Man of the Mountain*, her underread second masterpiece, is equally important. Whereas *Their Eyes* focuses on the journey of the individual, *Moses* is a paradigm of the journey for the individual and the collective. In terms of her published works, *Moses, Man of the Mountain* is Hurston's fullest realization of her ideas and philosophy on spirituality, empowerment, freedom, and peace.

Dispossessed of his kingdom and crown, Moses embarks on his path to self-realization. His personal journey unfolds in tandem with the journey of the Hebrews from their exodus out of Egypt to the Promised Land of Canaan. The novel is allegorical. Moses represents ideal black leadership and the Hebrews represent the phenomenon of cultural transformation, mirroring the evolution of Africans into African Americans. The journey to the Promised Land is the saga of the African American struggle from slavery to freedom.

Through characterization, dialogue, plot, symbol, and narration, Hurston again presents oral tradition, community, and spirituality as empowering elements of black folk culture. Those elements become fully integrated and reach their fruition in the character of Moses, whom Hurston billed as the greatest Hoodoo man to ever live.

As leader of the Israelites, Moses has a daunting task. In addition to leading them out of bondage, he must fashion them into an autonomous people, a nation that is capable of protecting its freedom and determining its destiny. For the work at hand, Hurston empowered Moses with a strong hand. The Judeo-Christian legend of Moses is already one that speaks to power and freedom. In this legend, Moses is perceived as the servant of God who is empowered by God to do God's bidding. In the legends of Moses that originate in Africa and the East, Moses is perceived as a god himself. As a divine being, he is already endowed with the power to go to God on Israel's behalf. In Hurston's introduction to *Moses, Man of the Mountain*, she wrote,

Anyone could bring down laws that had been handed to them. But who can talk with God face to face? Who has the power to command God to go to a peak of a mountain and there demand of Him laws with which to govern a nation? What other man has ever seen with his eyes even the back part of God's glory? Who else has ever commanded the wind and the hail? The light and darkness? That calls for power, and that is what Africa sees in Moses to worship. For he is worshipped as a god.[151]

Hurston's 1934 publication of *Jonah's Gourd Vine* introduced Moses as a folk hero who is enriched with the powers of traditional African spirituality. Like High John de Conquer, Moses hails from Africa. As High John surfaces to assist the oppressed, so, too, does Moses. "Wherever the children of Africa have been scattered by slavery, there is the acceptance of Moses as the fountain of mystic powers." But, Hurston informed us, Moses' power "does not flow from the Ten Commandments. It is his rod of power, the terror he showed before all Israel and to Pharaoh, and THAT MIGHTY HAND."[152]

In *Jonah's*, Hattie Tyson Pearson and Deacon Harris feel themselves to be victims of John Pearson's actions, and both feel helpless to do anything about him. But Harris tells Hattie, "They is help if you know how to git it. Some folks kin hit a straight lick with uh crooked stick. They's sich uh thing ez two-headed men." Hattie feigns innocence about such matters. "You b'lieve in all dat ole stuff 'bout hoodoo and sich lak, Brer Harris?" watching Harris with wary eyes. "Yeah, Ah do, Mrs. Rev'und. Ah done seen things done. Why hit's in de Bible, Sister!" Deacon Harris explains,

> Look at Moses. He's de greatest hoodoo man dat god ever made. He went 'way from Pharaoh's palace and stayed in de desert nigh on to forty years and learnt how tuh call God by all his secret names and dat's how he got all dat power. He knowed he couldn't bring off all dem people lessen he had power unekal tuh man! How you reckon he brought on all dem plagues if he didn't had nothin' but human power? And then agin his wife wuz Ethiopian. Ah bet she learnt 'im whut he knowed. Ya, indeed, Sister Pearson. De Bible is de best con-jure book in de world.[153]

Through Harris's dialogue, Hurston vested Moses with the humanity and divinity she also gave to High John de Conquer. In her short story "Fire and Cloud," also published in 1934, Hurston configured Moses as a godlike heroic figure who sees past the resentment of those he leads to the possibility that they have. Moses sits at the top of Mount Nebo reflecting on his journey and the journey of the Hebrews. He is ready to return to Median, and he has done all he can to raise the Hebrews to a conscious awareness of themselves as a great people. So they stand poised at the Jordan River, with their destiny in sight.

Harris's belief in conjure as an empowering force is based on his interpretation of the biblical Moses legend and on his personal observations. As he said, "Ah done seen things done." Zora Neale Hurston, too, had heard of and seen things done. Researching the Moses legend for her novel was part of Hurston's Guggenheim proposal. In Haiti, she heard that Damballah, the supreme deity among the Rada gods, was identified as Moses, and the serpent was his symbol of power as well as his rod of power. "This worship of Moses," Hurston wrote, "recalls the hard-to-explain fact that wherever the Negro is found, there are traditional tales of Moses and his supernatural powers that are not in the Bible, nor can they be found in the written life of Moses." As the most powerful Rada deity, Damballah/Moses "never does 'bad' work," Hurston is told. "If you make a ceremony to any of the other gods and ask favors, they must come to Damballah to get the permission and the power to do it. Papa Damballah is the *great source*."[154]

In Accompong, Jamaica, Hurston had "seen" the magic of a local medicine man. She had expressed to Medicine Man the wish of silencing the tree frogs that, in anticipation of rain, "were keeping up a fearful din." Medicine Man responded to her wish:

> He stood up and turned his face toward the mountain peak opposite and made a quick motion with one hand and seemed to inhale deeply from the waist up. He held his pose stiffly for a moment, then relaxed. The millions of frogs in the trees on that uninhabited peak opposite us ceased chirping as suddenly as a flash.

There was "sudden silence." Medicine Man assured her that they would not sing again until he allowed them. After passing a certain destination and whistling, they would begin again, he told her. Hurston listened eagerly for the whistle. Upon hearing it, "like an orchestra under the conductor's baton, the frog symphony broke out."[155]

Medicine Man in the hills of Accompong, like Moses in the wilderness, like all Vodou doctors, had learned the secrets of nature. Hurston's biblical knowledge and her investigations into black spiritual traditions shaped and informed the character of Moses in *Moses, Man of the Mountain*. In the novel, Moses' power is inspired by black folk traditions and is clearly the result of his own inner journey. As the story unfolds, Miriam, the daughter of Amram and Jochebed tells the lie that Moses is her brother. The lie generates suspicion that Moses is not of royal heritage. Those in the palace—specifically, Moses' uncle Ta-Phar and the priesthood, who are jealous of Moses and wish to see him removed from power—use Moses' compassion for the exploited and suffering Hebrews as evidence that he is an imposter and a traitor. After Moses kills an Egyptian overseer in defense of a Hebrew, the Pharaoh plots to seize him. Moses learns of the plot from his steward and plans his escape. He confides to his steward his decision to go westward into the desert. Everything follows the sun, Moses reasoned, and he wanted to just think. "I feel something I have never been conscious of before," he told his steward, "and I must find out from within myself what to do about it."[156]

Moses had become conscious of the duality of political power. He was commander-in-chief of the Egyptian army and had won many battles for Egypt and expanded Egypt's land and rule. He contributed greatly to Egypt's immense wealth and fame, but now Egypt murmured against him.

> I feel the cursing thought of the law and power. I had always felt the beneficence of law and power and never stopped to consider that it had any other side. It is a sword with two edges. Never mind whether it is directed against me honestly or not. That has nothing to do with its power to injure me.[157]

As Moses traveled toward the desert, he pondered this notion of power. Observing his natural surroundings of moonlight and fowls and sky, he recalled all the questions he wanted to ask Nature. Curious as a child, Moses would pose his questions to the adults around him. Only Mentu, the stable-man, could oblige Moses with answers. "He had answers in the form of sto-ries for nearly every question that Moses asked and he told stories unasked because they just came to him to tell." These included stories of the creator and creation and creatures created. "When you are older," Mentu promised, "I will tell you how it is that men can understand the language of the birds and the animals and the plants."[158]

Motivated by Mentu's stories, the young Moses studied the works of the palace priests and kept asking questions—much to their annoyance. Hearing Mentu speak of the Book of Thoth and the deathless snake that guards it, Moses demanded that Mentu tell him more. "To tell you the truth, I don't know anything about it," Mentu responded. "All I know is what I have heard." He explained:

> The cry of it is that there is a book which Thoth himself wrote with his own hand which, if you read it, will bring you to the gods. When you read only two pages in this book you will enchant the heavens, the earth, the abyss, the mountain, and the sea. You will know what the birds of the air and the creep-ing things are saying. You will know the search of the deep because the power is there to bring them to you. And when you read the second page, you can go into the world of ghosts and come back to the shape you were on earth. You will see the sun shining in the sky, with all the gods, and the full moon.[159]

Knowledge of the Book of Thoth was transmitted to Mentu from the previous generations: "It was told by the father of the father of my father to the father of my father and the father of my father has told it to my father," said Mentu.[160]

The stories Mentu tells and the means by which Mentu receives knowl-edge of the Book of Thoth reflect Hurston's sense of the significance of community and of the oral tradition and its empowering attributes. The sto-ries fire Moses' imagination, and the legend becomes an integral part of Moses' journey and a major source of his powers, as he eventually returns to Egypt to the river Koptos and finds the Book of Thoth. Moving through the darkness, nearing the shore of the Red Sea, Moses recalled his earlier conscious thoughts of the two-sided sword of political power. He had been on both sides of it and was determined that there was something more to life than what he had experienced and witnessed so far. As a soldier, he had led many battles and chopped down his share of men, Moses asserted. "But I doubt that any life I have ever taken benefited anybody. The property I took from conquered countries didn't make anybody rich. It just whetted their appetites for more."[161]

Moses anticipated something beyond the existence he lived as a pawn for the forces of greed. "The man who interprets Nature is always held in great honor," Moses concluded. "I am going to live and talk with Nature and know her secrets. Then I will be powerful, no matter where I may be." Although one of Pharaoh's best military strategists, Moses resolved that "his sword should cease to think for him." He would study Nature and all her nuances.[162]

> He realized now how Mentu had aroused his thought, and that once you wake up thought in a man, you can never put it to sleep again. He saw that he had merely been suppressing himself during his military period. That was over and gone. Everybody has some special road of thought along which they travel when they are alone to themselves. And his road of thought is what makes every man what he is.[163]

Moses' road of thought led him to a path of self-realization and uncommon power. Mentu was Moses' mentor. "Mentor" is from the Greek "mentor," the guide and adviser of Odysseus' son Telemachus. Its base meaning is "remember, think, counsel." Aware that he was nearing death, Mentu counseled Moses with one last bit of advice:

> "[D]on't forget what I told you about the monkeys and the snakes. It might be true you know. The old folks often know things you can't find in a book."
> "Oh, I won't forget. I won't forget anything that you have ever taught me, the sayings, and the proverbs and all. They have helped me a lot."
> "You are right to listen to proverbs. They are short sayings made out of long experience. Goodbye, son."[164]

Moses recalled all this as he stood at the Red Sea in search of a vessel to take him across. He learned from an old codger of a strait he could walk across during low tide. So he did. He crossed over, and on the other side, he sat on a rock and thought, and "conferred with the Never Untrue, which is a common way of speaking people call Experience."[165]

Moses sat down a disinherited and despised contender for the throne of Egypt. He stood up into a heritage of power. When Arvay Henson in *Seraph on the Suwanee* returned home, she told Jim Meserve that she had within her all she needed to handle his case. Moses, with his own curiosity and the mentoring of Mentu, already had within him all he needed to handle the Pharaoh's case and the case of the Israelites. What Moses had learned under Mentu would be augmented by his father-in-law Jethro, who mentored him about plants and their properties and other aspects of the natural world.

Once in the desert, Moses made his way to Midian where he met Jethro and fell in love with Zipporah. Moses desired only to be a good husband and son-in-law and sit on Mount Horeb and ask Nature questions. He became complacent about his mission to return to Egypt to the river Koptos in search of the Book of Thoth. But Jethro's words to Moses were like Moses' own voice echoing in the chambers of his memory: "Oh you were out of dreams for the moment, but the great dreamer, the great leader was there. You have a great soul and something down in Egypt waked it up. And you can't wake up thoughts in men and put them back to sleep again."[166]

Moses had a calling, Jethro explained to him. The god of the mountain had called Moses to free the Israelites and bring them to the god of Mount Horeb. "He could do it easy, with the power he's got," Jethro said to Zipporah. "The man is just running over with spirit." Moses persisted in saying he was done with missionary work, but as Jethro predicted, "The backside of that mountain may get too hot to hold him yet."[167] One of Moses' many thoughts was to know Nature and her secrets. This road led him to Mentu, then Jethro, and eventually to the Book of Thoth. And what he learned from the god of the mountain kept him on the road to what he was—a leader.

In *Moses, Man of the Mountain*, Hurston distinguished between being a leader and a ruler. As Moses discovered, rulers were simply vehicles of formal power. They were interested in their own personal gain and were obliged to the state and were functionaries in the affairs of the state. They had no freedom. Leaders accepted their responsibilities, and undertook them with an independent spirit. Leaders gave up things. They were responsive to the needs of the people and practiced patience and compassion.

Moses had many occasions to question his decision to lead the children of Israel. He had gone into Egypt and led the Hebrews out with a high hand. Then he struggled with them from can't to Canaan. They wanted freedom, but they didn't want to fight for it. They wanted liberty, but they preferred to be told what to do. They wanted independence, but they longed for the "flesh-pots" of Egypt. They wanted peace, but they were motivated by "ambitions of littleness." They wanted leadership, but they resented being led. They were still dominated by a slave mentality. Moses concluded that those whose thoughts bespoke a slavish mind could not enter the Promised Land: "I can make something out of their children, but not out to them. They have the essence of greatness in them and I shall fight them and fight myself and the world and even God for them. They shall not refuse their destiny."[168]

"My People, My People," was Moses' cry. But Moses saw through them to their possibility. When Moses escaped the Egyptian empire he had helped to build, disillusioned by the treachery he had experienced, he had imagined something better. "He was wishing for a country he had never seen. He was seeing visions of a nation he had never heard of where there would be more equality of opportunity and less difference between top and bottom."[169]

That nation was Israel. He had struggled with Israel, defied and defended her, and refused to allow her to betray her destiny as a great and noble nation. Moses "loved freedom and justice with a fierce love," and envisioned Israel as a free people in a just society. He refused the "kingly crown" Israel fashioned for him from the molten gold of crowns of conquered kings. He reminded them of the precious gift that freedom is: "It ain't something permanent like rocks and hills. It's like manna; you just got to keep on gathering it fresh every day. If you don't one day you're going to find you ain't got none no more." He advised them against being so willing to have someone rule over them: "You done got free of Pharaoh and the Egyptian oppressors, be careful you don't raise up none among yourselves."[170]

Poised at the Jordan River, Israel was ready to cross over. Moses surmised that they were not completely free inside. They had not learned all of what he had tried to teach and show them, but they had gained courage and a soul. They had commandments, self-governing laws so that Israel would know peace and justice. These laws "had something of the essence of divinity expressed in order. They had the chart and compass of behavior. They need not stumble into blind ways and injure themselves. This was bigger than Israel itself." God had called Moses and Moses had answered. Israel gazed into its own destiny.

> Moses felt happy over that. His dreams had in no way been completely fulfilled. He had meant to make a perfect people, free and just, noble and strong, that should be a light for all the world and for time and eternity. And he wasn't sure he had succeeded. He had found out that no man may make another free. Freedom was something internal. The outside signs were just signs and symbols of the man inside. All you could do was to give the opportunity for freedom and the man himself must make his own emancipation.[171]

Moses wanted Israel to come out more than conquer. He wanted them to win their battles, not only externally, but also internally. He wanted them to win with their soul whole and free. Knowing he had done all in his power to give the Hebrews their opportunity to strive with life, Moses was at peace.

FIVE

Who Was Herod and
What Made Him Great?

O ne of the last letters Zora Neale Hurston wrote was addressed to
Harper Brothers publishing house. Her letter asked whether they
would publish her biographical account of King Herod I. The letter
was written in longhand and it was brief.

> This is to query you if you would have any interest in the book I am laboring
> upon at present—a life of Herod the Great. One reason I approach you is
> because you will realize that any publisher who offers a life of Herod as it
> really was, and naturally different from the groundless legends which have
> been built up around his name has to have courage.[1]

As the address 1734 School Court indicates, Hurston was living in her
Fort Pierce, Florida, home at the time. Dated January 16, 1959, the letter
was written after her first bout with hypertensive heart disease. She was
sixty-eight years of age. Written almost a year before the date of her death
on January 28, 1960, it is the last letter she would write to a publisher.

The letter underscores two characteristic orientations of the life of Zora
Neale Hurston and is indicative of two more. First, the letter emphasizes
Hurston's perception of herself as a writer who has another story to tell.
It emphasizes her belief in the power of the written word to capture
the imagination as well as to influence thought. The written word, though
thrice removed from experience, was a very powerful source of received

knowledge. It had the power to record history, and it had the power to set the record straight—of course, from the writer's point of view.

It was her point of view about Herod that she wanted Harper to consider. Her view was not the popular view; thus, she warned Harper that courage would be required of any publisher. Hurston was perplexed by the historical account of Herod as a cultural iconoclast and anti-Christ. Her years of reading about and examining the life of Herod led her to investigate the history of his era, the first century B.C.E., giving particular attention to the evolution of the culture of the Jews from their crossing the River Jordan into Canaan to the birth of Christ Jesus. "Herod the Great" is very much a kind of sequel to *Moses, Man of the Mountain*. As Hurston wrote in the introduction, "the evolution of Jewish culture and thought from the time of Moses to the fall of Jerusalem to Titus in 70 A.D. had been neglected. Therefore, it appears that the Jews had and have no life except in the Bible. Like a pressed flower between the leaves of a book."[2]

The January 16, 1959, letter to Harper Brothers was her last query on behalf of the "Herod the Great" manuscript. The first query letter to a publisher was written to Burroughs Mitchell of Scribner's Publishing in July or August 1951. But Hurston had been thinking about Herod at least as early as 1942 as indicated by her allusion to Herod in *Dust Tracks on a Road*.

In the formerly excised chapter, "Seeing the World As It Is," Hurston explored the idea of justice and concluded that justice in the absolute "is not to be found, as human beings are not made so it will happen." Therefore, justice is always twisted by "the selfish hand." As she stood on the "watchwall," peering into time, everywhere she looked she saw that righteousness and justice were determined by the viewpoint of the beholder. Even in the Bible, the "Book of Books," she noted that this was so. "The Old Testament is devoted to what was right and just from the viewpoint of the Ancient Hebrews. All of their enemies were twenty-two carat evil." No matter how unjust the Canaanites might view the aggression of the Hebrews, the Hebrews' manifest destiny of the "promised land" justified it all. As the Hebrews vilified their enemies, they were vilified in turn: Those who ushered in the doctrine of Christianity made an enemy of the Orthodox Jew. "To this day, the names of Pharisee and Sadducee are synonymous with hypocrite and crook to ninety-nine and a half percent of the Christian world." In the eyes of their detractors, "[t]hose Jews who would not accept Christianity look very bad in the New Testament."[3]

According to Hurston's biography, Herod I was neither of the Jewish priesthood nor was he of Jewish lineage. Nonetheless, he reigned as King of Judah from 40 to 4 B.C.E. He, too, was cast in negative character in historical texts, including the text of the New Testament. In tongue-and-cheek fashion, Hurston questioned the credibility of the biblical record.

> Then there is the slaughter of the innocents by Herod. One thing strikes me curious about that slaughter. The unconverted Jews never seemed to have missed their babies. So Herod must have carefully selected babies from families

who forty years later were going to turn Christian. He probably did not realize what a bad example he was setting for the new religionists. He could not have known that centuries later Christians would themselves slaughter more innocents in one night than his soldiers ever saw.[4]

Hurston formally studied world religions, but she developed a negative view of Herod from the religious teachings of her youth—from both Sunday school lessons and pulpit sermons. "I tumbled right into the Missionary Baptist Church," Hurston wrote in *Dust Tracks*.[5] So she was familiar with the Christian version of King Herod.

She quite likely heard her father Reverend John Hurston preach the Christmas morning sermon. He likely took his text from the second chapter of the book of Matthew, and he likely took his time in reading the verses therein. Then in picture-making detail, he described for his congregation the Magi, the Three Wise Men from afar, who told Herod of the prophecy that foretold the birth of Christ. As his cadence quickened, the Reverend Hurston then likely began, in earnest, to preach Herod's words, as he sat on his throne, saying unto the Magi, "When ye have found *him*, bring me word again, that I may come and worship him also." But the wise men were wise, indeed, he likely explained; they knew that Herod intended to kill the child. So with warning from the Magi, Mary and Joseph escaped to Egypt to bring forth Jesus in the manger of a lowly stable. The Reverend Hurston then, with punctuating histrionics, likely told how Herod, in his frustration and fear of being overthrown by this foretold authentic "King of the Jews," commanded his soldiers to slay "all the children that were in Bethlehem, and in all the coasts thereof, from two years old and under, according to the time which he had diligently inquired of the wise men."[6] Reverend Hurston no doubt then preached with incredulity of the terrible, misguided, and undone Herod, and in the next breath, preached with tidings of good joy of the miraculous preservation of the life of the Christ. For most Christians then, the miracle of the Christ is inextricably linked to the terrible and murderous Herod.

Zora Neale Hurston heard this portrayal of King Herod from many pulpits. And as a student of the Bible from her youth, she read the account of Herod in the Gospel according to Matthew:

> Now when Jesus was born in Bethlehem of Judaea in the days of Herod the king, behold, there came wise men from the east to Jerusalem, Saying, Where is he that is born King of the Jews? For we have seen his star in the east, and are come to worship him.[7]

In her autobiography, Hurston spoke of her proclivity to question everything. Particularly, in the chapter titled "Religion," she questioned what others had to say about God, the Holy Bible, creation, death, and salvation. In her biography of Herod I, Hurston questioned the Judeo-Christian historical depiction of the life of Herod and challenges the New Testament account of Herod.

Perhaps it was during her collegiate years at Barnard when she studied the history of the great religions of the world that she formally studied the Bible and biblical history. She had learned that not only were the gospels written more than a century after the death of Jesus, but also that they were written by individuals who were not contemporaries of Jesus. She shared her insights with friend Mary Holland: "The synoptic Gospels, Matthew, Mark and Luke were all written so long after His death that legend crept in, so that even they differ on events of the life of Christ. Nobody can be sure of even their authorship."[8]

Hurston's probing of the cultural history of the Jewish people as it relates to the reign of Herod I points to the second orientation of Hurston's life: She was a consummate social scientist, and her social scientist mind-set worked integrally with her writer's heart. Just as Hurston never abandoned her art, she never abandoned science, or perhaps it is truer to say that they never abandoned her. Hurston used the spyglass of anthropology to probe the cosmic secrets of humanity. What cosmic secrets was she looking for in the life of Herod I? In the introductory pages of her work on Herod I, Hurston posed questions about the beliefs, customs, and mores of the Jews, because they—and everyone else in the southwest Asia of Herod's time—were politically, economically, and culturally influenced by the Persian Empire and by the Roman Empire, which, itself, had been heavily influenced by the Greeks. As she investigated the legends of Moses, which led her to question the biblical accounting of Moses' Hebrew birth and the source of Moses' power, Hurston likewise challenged the "groundless legends" surrounding Herod.

The January 16, 1959, letter of inquiry demonstrates that Hurston was still absorbed by the life of Herod. Not only did she have a story, but she was indefatigable in her efforts to have her story published. At age sixty-eight she was still alive *and* well because work, for Zora Neale Hurston, was its own reward. In *Dust Tracks*, Hurston wrote,

> I don't know any more about the future than you do. I hope that it will be full of work, because I have come to know by experience that work is the nearest thing to happiness that I can find. No matter what else I have among the things that humans want, I go to pieces in a short while if I do not work.[9]

An October 2, 1953, letter to Burroughs Mitchell describes Hurston's enthusiasm for her research on Herod: "Under the spell of a great obsession." She had written several chapters of the manuscript and wanted Mitchell's nod before continuing. "So, it is my wish to submit Herod for your inspection, and hope intensely for your approval."[10] She believed that, in spite of history's condemnation of King Herod, a book on someone of his force of person and personality and his compelling historical importance would appeal to readers and to film audiences alike.

She contemplated collaborating with Orson Welles, should the work be produced as a movie, and wondered whether Cecil B. de Mille might be gotten to play the part of Herod. She later solicited, but did not obtain, an introduction to and commentary on the work from Sir Winston Churchill.[11] Hurston noted that other contemporary writers and scholars had interest in Herod as an important historical figure and as a literary subject. She included in her correspondence with Mitchell a supporting letter to that effect. Hurston had been interested in writing a book on Herod for years, she conveyed to Mitchell. But she "hung back on offering him" because the masses of people had been convinced that he was guilty of the "massacre of the innocents," that he "murder[ed] all the babies in the hope of catching the infant Jesus in the dragnet." Based on her extensive and comprehensive research, Hurston dismissed the claims against Herod and sketched Mitchell a profile of his "magnificent character."[12]

Her explanation for not sketching this profile before, as articulated to Mitchell, recalls her fears regarding the writing of her first novel *Jonah's Gourd Vine*. Although her serious interest in the life of Herod I had been longstanding, the force of the dominant discourse around him gave her cause to question the writing of a book that would sharply contradict the official and sanctioned view of Herod. Both in relation to *Jonah's* and to "Herod the Great," Hurston felt anxious about writing from a perspective that was contrary to popular opinion—specifically in relation to race, on the one hand, and religion, on the other.

A September 12, 1945, letter to her dear friend Carl Van Vechten disclosed that the story she was "burning to write," was one that would be "highly controversial." This story, however, was not specifically about Herod. It was generally about the historical struggle of the Jewish people wherein Herod figured only tangentially. After a lengthy, detailed outlay of the story she proposed, Hurston invited a response from Van Vechten and his wife Fania Marinoff.

> I want you and Fania to tell me if you think it should be written. I have no doubts about the story possibilities. The stuff is there! It is the biggest story in the world.... If you think it should be done, (and I trust your judgment) I am going ahead. I know that it will make thousands mad, but "Let there be light!"[13]

Whatever the response of the Van Vechtens, Hurston found the courage within to write to her own truth. Some scholars claim that by the time she wrote "Herod the Great" Hurston "had lost touch with her audiences and with what they—and her publisher—wanted her to write."[14] Although it is true that Hurston—any writer—had to consider her audience and publisher, Hurston's work always defied the one or the other. Her refusal to write within the prescribed conventions of her time was one factor in the literary judgments against her and her work.

She was supposed to write about the "race problem," but she wrote about the human problem. She was supposed to represent the Black Intelligentsia, but she spoke for and wrote in the voice of the folk. She was supposed to write about "the Negro," but she also wrote about Anglo-Americans, Jews, and ancient Greeks and Romans. She was supposed to be provincial and chauvinistic, but she had broader views on the world. She wrote less for the public and the publishers than she wrote for herself and for posterity. She was always about "the bigger thing."

In Herod, Hurston saw someone who also aspired to the bigger thing—a prominent attribute of an idealist. For Zora Neale Hurston, vision and the courage to realize the vision were characteristic of a great soul. This combination—of vision and courage—was ideal. Herod, like Moses, was representative of Hurston's ideal individual. The idealism that informs his characterization points to the third orientation of Hurston's life, as she was an idealist, too. In "Looking Things Over," Hurston wrote,

> Being an idealist, I too wish that the world was better than I am. Like all the rest of my fellow men, I don't want to live around people with no more principles than I have. My inner fineness is continually outraged at finding that the world is a whole family of Hurstons.[15]

One major tenet of idealism is that humans experience external phenomena through mental perception: The mind perceives, translates, and interprets what is external to it, but what is external to it is a construction of the mind. This construction becomes objective reality. These ideas are inherent in Hurston's declaration that "thought is the only reality."[16] Thus, truth is subjective and dependent on the particular vision of the perceiver. To the extent that one is conscious of this epistemological dynamic or this aspect of knowing, one might also have the wisdom to consider other and varying points of view.

"Herod the Great" constitutes another point of view. "We speak of the man or woman in the work," wrote Harold Bloom, "we might better speak of the work in the person. And yet we scarcely know how to discuss the influence of a work upon its author, or of the mind upon itself."[17] Hurston labored over the Herod manuscript for fourteen years or more. She spent "a good six years" researching her subject matter. She likely completed her first draft between 1945 and 1951, and she revised the manuscript for Scribner's a number of times over the years.

On June 13, 1955, from Eau Gallie, Florida, she wrote to Mary Holland, "I am more than two-thirds done with the final writing, and hope and pray that Scribner's will be pleased with it." On June 20, 1955, she wrote to Mrs. Martin, Mitchell's assistant, "I sent the Mss of Herod The Great to Mr. Burroughs Mitchell by Express on June 3, but have not had a card saying it arrived as yet."[18] Hurston anticipated Scribner's rejection of the manuscript.

"I seek your advice on a very serious matter," she wrote to editor and author Max Eastman on August 2, 1955.

> Nearly ten years ago I fell in love with the story of the life of Herod the Great. I have done enormous research on it, and now it is almost all written. I think that Scribner's is a little timid about it on account of the possible opposition of the Catholic Church. Bishop Fulton Sheen advised me to do "as a good

Catholic" which means that I must do the man an injustice in order not to disturb the established Feast of the Innocents.[19]

Accustomed to explaining her standpoint on Herod and the Jewish people, she acquainted Eastman with her position and purpose then asked, "Now, would you dare to do the book if you were in my place." Fairly certain of her facts, she wondered had she "gone wrong anywhere in spirit so far." She requested that, if he would dare to write such a book, might he look over the manuscript.[20]

Hurston's August 12, 1955, letter acknowledged Burroughs Mitchell's decision against publishing "Herod the Great." "Naturally, I am sorry that you found HEROD THE GREAT disappointing, but do not feel concerned about the refusal upon me. I am my old self and can take it easily." Hurston was not daunted by Scribner's refusal. "Perhaps it is because I have such faith in the material and now my conviction that I can handle it. All is well."[21]

She continued to revise "Herod" and to seek a publisher. In September 1958, she wrote a letter of inquiry to the David McKay publishing company, but did not receive a favorable response.[22] For nearly fifteen years (c. 1945–1959), from the Roof Garden Hotel in Belle Glade, Florida, to the rustic cabin in Eau Gallie (which she refurbished and in which she had written *Mules and Men*), to the little house near Patrick Air Force Base at Cocoa Beach, to the trailer-house on Meritt Island, and then to 1734 School Court in Fort Pierce, Florida, where she wrote the letter to Harper's, Hurston labored over "Herod the Great."

Hurston wrote as much during the 1950s as she did in earlier years. Even as she wrote other book manuscripts and journalistic articles during this time, "Herod the Great" was her abiding passion. She continued to research Herod's life and the era in which he lived, and she continued to revise the manuscript. During this period, Robert Hemenway noted that Hurston "wrote constantly and without much success."[23] Yet, as Carla Kaplan points out, "When Hurston believed in her material as she did with both the Golden Bench of God and Herod the Great, she was capable of taking tremendous personal risk."[24]

Actually, Hurston had been "taking tremendous personal risk" all her life—whether she was being insistent on expressing her desire for a black pony with a white leather saddle, or persistent in creating and telling "lies," or courageous about traveling alone through Florida swamps and work camps or up the hills and down in the vales of Jamaica and Haiti. Proclaiming herself a social scientist and a writer was risk enough for a black woman of Hurston's day. Even into the 1970s, Alice Walker reminds us that to assume the identity of black woman *and* writer was cause for trepidation:

> Having committed myself to Zora's work, loving it, in fact, I became curious to see what others had written about her. This was, for the young, impressionable, barely begun writer I was, a mistake. After reading the misleading, deliberately belittling, inaccurate, and generally irresponsible attacks on her work and her life by almost everyone, I became for a time paralyzed with confusion

and fear. For if a woman who had given so much of obvious value to all of us (and at such risks: to health, reputation, sanity) could be so casually pilloried and consigned to a sneering oblivion, what chance would someone else—for example, myself—have? I was aware that I had much less gumption than Zora.[25]

Yet, Hurston faced the challenges to her multiple identities with such aplomb that we are amazed at her ability to do so and at her stalwart resilience in the face of challenge. As Toni Cade Bambara expressed it, "she never missed a beat." In truth, Hurston could not do otherwise. Zora Neale Hurston followed her bliss. She lived a life that honored her passion, not her purse. How is one to interpret this grand passion that often left her penniless—even during the time when most people her age were retiring? In an undated fragment of a letter, apparently enclosed with material that was to be archived, Hurston wrote, "to add to the store of human knowledge and permanent literature. So don't bother about me. You could never understand me. Cordially yours. Dr. Zora Neale Hurston, Lit.D."[26]

The fragment suggests that Hurston understood herself to be a contributor to the bank of human knowledge through the deposit of her literary works. It also suggests that as she is unknowable in any fixed sense, so also is humankind unknowable. Thus, the need to continually probe, search, explore, and question persists. As she, in essence, cannot be definitively understood, humankind also defies easy and definite knowing and therefore is always poised on the precipice of possibility. "High John de Conquer," *Moses*, and "Herod the Great" are primary examples of this possibility.

A FAMILY OF HURSTONS

Idealists believe in the possibility of the archetypal idea, pattern, form, or standard. But there is the awareness among them that, in the everyday existence of human beings, humanity rarely experiences the ideal. Humankind, as Hurston described it, is a family of Hurstons. Yet, the possibility of attaining, creating, achieving, or experiencing the ideal is what motivates the pursuit of the idealist. In her writings, particularly in her fiction, Hurston sketched portraits of ideal individuals and she explored the possibility of ideal relationships—with the self, between humans and nature, between individuals (friends, lovers, spouses, parents and children, for example), between the individual and society, and between societies or nations.

From her first published short story "John Redding Goes to Sea," to her last unpublished manuscript "Herod the Great," this idealism is evident. *Moses, Man of the Mountain* is a key example of Hurston's use of ideal figures in stories that explore complex relationships. In her novel, Moses, the ideal individual, subsequently becomes the ideal leader. His charge is to create an ideal nation: Israel.

Hurston's notion of the ideal is complex, because it reaches beyond simplistic concepts of good and bad and perfect and imperfect. The ideal human is not without flaws. The ideal society is not utopian. Integral to Hurston's idealism are the Eastern concepts of yin and yang: the idea that perceived negative and positive forces are relative and complementary and are in constant flux. Neither is essentially "good" or "bad" and both are impersonal, temporary qualities of energy, consciousness, force, or nature. As Hurston avowed, "I know that destruction and construction are but two faces of Dame Nature and that it is nothing to her if I choose to make personal tragedy out of her unbreakable laws."[27]

Humans are challenged with negotiating these shifting forces, finding balance, and transcending the dualism, which allows one to experience peace and freedom. For the vast majority of humankind, this balance or transcendence is neither constant nor permanent. A vigilant consciousness is required. When Moses refused the crown offered to him by the newly emancipated Hebrews, he warned them against their easy readiness to have someone rule them and impressed on them the need to be vigilant in safeguarding their freedom. "This freedom is a funny thing," he told them. "It ain't something permanent like rocks and hills. It's like manna, you just got to keep on gathering it fresh every day. If you don't, one day you're going to find you ain't got none no more."[28]

Although not completely successful in having Israel understand freedom from his profound perspective, Moses was satisfied that he had given Israel "the strife of freedom."[29] Israel now had the opportunity to participate in life on its own terms. Freed from Pharaoh and Egyptian oppressors, the Israeli people were empowered to engage in and negotiate the everyday, fluctuating matters of their living. Unlike the Western Christian notion of "happily ever after," wherein some ideal state is reached that will be constant or static and permanent, the Eastern notions of yin and yang recognize the dynamic quality of life, the conscious negotiation that Hurston described as "the strife of life."

The strife of life is experienced by young Janie in *Their Eyes Were Watching God* as she anticipates her desired engagement in the world beyond Nanny's front gate. She felt herself in bloom like the pear tree. "She had glossy leaves and bursting buds and she wanted to struggle with life, but it seemed to elude her."[30] Eventually, she found her complement in Tea Cake Woods. Their struggle was the negotiation of their fluctuating desires, fears, and passions.

Strife is a key element in understanding relationships, especially connubial relationships in Hurston's oeuvre. For within her writings, marriage never guarantees a static happily-ever-after fairy-tale life. Peace and freedom require constant and conscious negotiation.

Idealism is not to be found in acquiring some perfect, self-perpetuating, permanent state. It is to be had in the glory of meeting ever-changing life head on with conscious awareness. "Like all mortals," Hurston wrote in *Dust Tracks*,

I have been shaped by the chisel in the hand of Chance—bulged out here by a sense of victory, shrunken there by the press of failure and the knowledge of unworthiness. But it has been given to me to strive with life, and to conquer the fear of death.[31]

And so, she states, "I am in the struggle with the sword in my hands, and I don't intend to run until you run me."[32] The ideal individual assumes the responsibility for her own life, even in less than ideal circumstances. As long as one has sword in hand, one continues and pursues the ideal. "The sword," in relation to Hurston's life, can be interpreted as a metaphor for "the pen."

With each successive work, Hurston pursued her ideal representation of individual and societal possibility. Hurston dedicated *Moses, Man of the Mountain* to her friend Edwin Grover and shared with him her assessment of the book. Although she hoped Grover would be pleased with her effort, she was doubtful of her success:

> I have the feeling of disappointment about it. I don't think that I achieved all that I set out to do. I thought that in this book I would achieve my ideal, but it seems that I have not reached it yet but I shall keep trying as I know you want me too.[33]

In theme and character, "Herod the Great" was Hurston's continued effort in achieving her ideal. How does a writer capture greatness? How does she make palpable the abstract notion of "the bigger thing." The fear "that greatness may be unable to renew itself," said Harold Bloom, "is the ultimate anxiety of influence." In other words, one may fear that "one's inspiration may be larger than one's own powers of realization."[34] Hurston was inspired by the hero and the heroic deed—from her youth, as she listened to stories of African American folk heroes and read stories of Greco-Roman myth and legend, to adulthood, as her anthropological investigations expanded her knowledge and deepened her appreciation of the heroic.

The works of an author who is inspired by "idealized forerunners" characteristically evince an anxiety of influence. Moreover, in the process of capturing or reflecting the genius and greatness of the idealized predecessors, the author creates works that reveal her or his own genius. Hurston's writings, particularly in regard to Moses and Herod, readily reflect her sources of inspiration. She was enthralled by these "idealized forerunners," their heroic stature and genius, and was compelled to create *Moses, Man of the Mountain* and "Herod the Great," literary works that are expressive of Zora Neale Hurston's fourth orientation: her genius. Bloom wrote that "there are common characteristics to genius, since vivid individuality of speculation, spirituality, and creativity must rely upon originality, audacity, and self-reliance."[35] Hurston was audacious in her heroic conception of King Herod. She certainly had to be self-reliant given the seemingly universal condemnation of this man. Original in thought, she had to be bold in spirit as she created a work that defied history. She had to be hearty in her perseverance as she continually sought publication after each publisher's letter of decline. She saw genius gleaming from the eyes of Herod, this "Lion of Judah." She perceived value in his story, and she believed in her ability to tell it. In her pursuit of this ideal, we see genius at work.

HURSTON'S GREAT OBSESSION

Initially, Hurston wrote, "like other Christian (?) ignoramuses," she had been "taught of the evil ways of Jews" and had conceived of Herod as "a mean little butcher."[36] But upon reading that there was no basis for the legends about him, she began her quest: Who was King Herod, really? Hurston began her search with Nicholas of Damascus, Herod's "official biographer." The greater part of his work, "The Commentaries of Herod the Great," was lost to history. So, too, was a second source, that written by biographer Strabo of Cappadocia. The main extant source of biographical material on Herod is that of first-century Jewish historian Flavius Josephus (c. 37–c. 100 C.E.). But Hurston adjudged Josephus's work as "a poisoned source." He stated that he followed closely the works of the previous biographers, but his portrayal of Herod I, according to Hurston, was a biased, prejudiced, and revisionist account.[37] Hurston read Flavius Josephus and the depiction of King Herod in the New Testament's Gospel of Matthew against writers of early Egyptian and Roman histories and such biblical scholars as Titus Livius, Eusebius ("the father of Church history") Plutarch, and Benedict de Spinoza.[38]

Hurston's research and writings suggest that Josephus's account of Herod I agrees with other accounts only on the point of Herod's kingship. On virtually every other point of his life, leadership, and political career, Josephus and the Book of Matthew stand in sharp contrast against other writers. Although his death date has been disputed, Hurston contended that Herod was born in 72 B.C.E. and died in 4 B.C.E.[39] He was the second son of Antipater the Idumean and Cypros of Petra in Nabatea. Whether his father Antipater was of Jewish ancestry or of the lineage of Idumeans who converted to Judaism under the rule of Maccabean John Hyrcanus is also disputed. Hurston made clear in her introductory material that Herod I was a self-professed Jew and he numbered among the "progressive" or Hellenized Jews. Flavius Josephus was an Orthodox Jew. In his writings, Hurston noted that Josephus repeatedly stated that "he was a Pharisee, anti-Greek learned, of the first of the twenty-four courses of the priesthood," and descendant of Jonathon of the Maccabees, founder of the Asamonean dynasty, which was succeeded by the Herodin dynasty established by Herod's father. Flavius Josephus's indictments against King Herod were that Herod was "of low birth," a usurper of the throne of Judea, and a "Romanized Jew" who was "of the Greeks." Josephus accused Herod of being a "wicked" king who led "his nation to sin," and in so doing, created a schism among the Jews. Josephus's allegiance to the priesthood, his lineage within the Maccabee family that lost power, and his orthodox disposition render his biographical writings on Herod suspect, Hurston warned. "He announces that he will tell the truth concerning Herod, and he does, but after he has related a particularly splendid act of Herod's or his close relations, he will follow with his own interpretation of Herod's motive or motives, which will tend to cancel out the fine act." Given that Josephus was born about forty years after Herod's death, Hurston found it incredulous that Josephus could presume to have known Herod's unexpressed motives.[40]

Regarding Herod's birth, Hurston informed the reader that Herod was of royal lineage. Not only was his mother a princess, but his father's family was of ducal status and had been so for so long that there is no mention of a lower social standing alluded to in history. Far from being a usurper, Hurston wrote that Herod's kingship filled the void left by the Asamonean leaders who fell into disfavor with the Jewish people and with Rome. Herod *was* a Hellenized Jew. The elite families of Herod's day spoke Greek as their mother tongue and attended Greek schools. Herod, himself, Hurston wrote, was educated at the Greek university at Damascus. Like other Hellenized Jews, Herod was familiar with Greek art, literature, and philosophy. In this, he was not an anomaly. Most of Lower Asia and a great portion of the Jewish population had been influenced by Greco-Roman culture. Many had assumed the language and manners of the Greeks and had absorbed aspects of the religion and philosophy of Persia and India.[41]

As Hurston wrote, during their Babylonian captivity under King Nebuchadnezzar, the Hebrew language had been lost to most of the Jewish people, saving some among the priesthood, so they spoke the Aramaic language of Persia. The more than three centuries of Greek presence and domination in Asia, which intensified with Alexander the Great's crossing of the Hellespont in 326 B.C.E., had a significant impact on the Jewish people. In relating these factors, Hurston emphasized the point of the evolution of Jewish thought and culture. To assume that the Jewish people of Herod's day were "no different from the tribes who received the Law at Sinai," she intimated, is to willfully ignore history and the natural processes of acculturation, which are essential to an appreciation of history that would allow for an honest understanding of King Herod I.[42]

Hurston described Flavius Josephus's partisan interpretation of Herod I as "'legitimistic' spite." In other sources she researched, Hurston found what she considered to be more objective, therefore, more reliable data. These sources spoke of Herod I as the ideal individual and ruler. "Herod of the Sun-Like Splendor," "Herod the Over-bold," "Herod, the Beloved of God," are among the recorded descriptives. The negatives that highlight Josephus's work are contradicted by the superlatives in other sources: "the handsomest man of his time," loyal and trusted friend, unsurpassed athlete and "first soldier," "first administrator," and builder of marvelous temples.[43]

Hurston's investigations led her to conclude that Herod was a "singular character" whose personal life was of such intense drama that it justified her writing the biography. "It climbs to the very summit of triumph, and plumbs the depths of tragedy."[44] Moreover, his personal life unfolds within one of the most pregnant eras of human history—first-century B.C.E., which Hurston configures as "the century of decision." It was the era of "Julius and Augustus Caesar, Marc Antony, Cicero, Cato, Brutus, Cataline, Cleopatra, who found Herod alluring enough to attempt to seduce him…Cassius, Crassus, the death of the Roman Republic and the Birth of the Roman Empire."[45] It was the century when the age-old conflict between East and West manifested itself in the hostilities between Parthia and Rome: Parthia declared "Asia for Asiatics" and Rome was intent on conquering the then-known world and realizing the Pax Romana. As Rome's client-king in Judah, Herod stood between these two worlds.

This was Herod, but what made him *"Great"*? Chapter One of Hurston's life of Herod the Great opens with Antipater, Herod's father, standing before an assembly in the temple of Zorabel. He faced the gathering, with the Great Sanhedrin to his back. The seventy members of the priesthood formed the traditional semicircle, with the high priest John Hyrcanus seated in their midst. Antipater stood at the lectern, for the first time, as the Procurator of Judea, newly appointed by Julius Caesar, emperor of the Roman Empire. Internecine struggles among the Asamoneans, the ruling family of Judea, had led to a civil war. One faction of the embattled family drew the hostilities of Rome, incurring the wrath of Rome and resulting in the loss of Judea's independence. Swayed by his friendship with Antipater, Caesar declared Judea a client-state, rather than a subject of the Roman Empire. Having more confidence in the administrative skill and military valor of Antipater over that of Hyrcanus, who was considered "feeble-minded" and who had been dethroned by his brother Aristobulus, Caesar empowered Antipater to assume governorship of the Jewish provinces. As Antipater related the state of affairs to those assembled, he also announced that his eldest son Phasaelus was to be governor of Jerusalem and his second son Herod was to be governor of Galilee. Herod was twenty-five.[46]

As governor of Galilee, Herod vowed to "put down all disorder and restore security and prosperity." This task entailed subduing Hezekiah, the notorious bandit leader who, in the absence of any effective governance in Judea, robbed, raped, murdered, and generally terrorized the people of Galilee and parts of Syria. The people referred to him as "the human monster." Although some among the assembly thought it curious and foolish that Antipater would send his younger and most beloved son to sure death, others wanted such a turn of events. In spite of the contributions Antipater made to the stability and progress of the Jewish people, most of the priesthood and others of like mind preferred to be rid of Antipater and his sons. Eleazer contended that "his administering the civil authority is a violation of our laws. That Idumean is not of the priestly line." This law was contested by Pollio, one of the "progressives" among the priests, and it was agreed that the leadership of Hyrcanus and the priesthood was questionable and even undesirable at present, but the majority still resented Antipater and his sons and wagered against Herod's success: "Ten shekels that Hezekiah destroys Herod within a month!" was the first bid.[47]

Hurston wrote that, unlike the majority of the priesthood, many of Judea's citizens, particularly the youth, were pleased with Antipater's leadership and were charmed and exalted by his sons, especially Herod. As Herod and his troops prepared to march out of the city toward Galilee, they shouted: "Hail, Herod the Magnificent!" "Herod the Defender!" "Herod Nicator!" The crowd cheered, and Herod acknowledged them. "He waved his right hand in salute to the people, flashed his brilliant smile, drew his jewel-hilted sword and waved it above his head as he announced in a loud and convincing voice that the Lion of Judah sought his prey." The people went mad and cheered louder. "That was their Herod." "Nicator" was also the name of Herod's Arabian stallion. Nicator meant Conqueror. "We ride now toward our destiny," Herod had whispered to Nicator as they assumed position at the front of the cavalry. And so they did.[48]

Herod and his contingent routed the army of bandits and hanged Hezekiah's dead body "at the crossroads at Cana." Sextus Caesar, cousin of Julius Caesar and governor of Syria lauded Herod as "the Conqueror of Hezekiah." News of Herod's victory traveled far and fast. This battle would foreshadow Herod's future military, administrative, and political career. As his accomplishments engendered the goodwill of some of the people, the same deeds engendered the enmity of others. This was the destiny into which Herod road. The Sanhedrin saw in Herod's victory an opportunity for his defeat. Those of the Sanhedrin who desired to restore theocratic rule conspired with Hyrcanus to have Herod tried for the unlawful murder of Hezekiah. "[I]f the Sanhedrin condemns him for killing [Hezekiah] without bringing him to trial for his crimes before the seventy, we will not only rid ourselves of Herod, but cause his great victory to be looked upon as a crime."[49]

To the incredulity of the nation and to Rome, a summons went out from Hyrcanus that Herod was to stand trial for murder. Rome regarded the move as an act of revolt against the Empire. Antipater, preferring to avoid civil war, made no move. Herod, on the other hand, had been schooled well and was a good pupil. He recalled the teachings of Demosthenes, which had been inculcated in him by his father: "What is the chief part of a statesman? Action! And the next? Action! What next again? Action! It fascinates and binds hand and foot those weak in judgment or weak in courage, which constitutes the majority."[50]

Herod took action. He marched into Jerusalem, flanked by trusted soldiers. Then he marched into the assembly of his accusers. With loyal soldiers to his back, he confronted Hyrcanus and the semicircle of priests. With his feet clad in gold-leather sandals, his torso draped in royal purple, bedecked with chains and armlets of gold, and his gold-hilted sword at his waist, Herod did not appear to be a criminal supplicant. The criminally accused were traditionally attired in tattered black raiment. Bowed and submissive, they prostrated themselves and pleaded for mercy. But it was Herod who stood before them, strong and fully present, with penetrating eyes that found and searched the eyes of every member of the priesthood. Because of fascination or weakness or both, none could speak. Hyrcanus, himself, fainted. Yet none would move to assist the high priest. Their silence spoke loudly and indicated the lack of courage of the majority to speak publicly what had been whispered privately. Receiving no response to his wordless statements, Herod then spoke: "My generous nature permits you to escape my wrath this time, but if ever again you interrupt my duties as governor of Galilee to ride to Jerusalem to answer your foolish and old-womanish charge, you shall feel the weight of my sword."[51] With his soldiers trailing his steps, Herod left. In the space of his absence, the Sanhedrin began to move as though thawing from a hard freeze. They found their tongues and their limbs and became animated with speech and movement. Sameas, student of Pollio, spoke:

> O Hyrcanus and my assessors, hear this. The future master of Lower Asia stood before us this day. He exhibited his superiority over us by the disdain with which he treated this body. He recognized that the power had shifted to other hands, a fact which you refuse to admit…. Of this I am persuaded, that one stood before us this day who shall be the master of this nation in no long time.[52]

As Sameas predicted, Herod's leadership and influence quickly expanded. In recognition of Herod's military skill, as indicated in his report of the battle against Hezekiah, Sextus Caesar promoted Herod to the office of general. Caesar praised Herod's "exceptional abilities as an administrator as well as a soldier. I am so impressed," he told Herod, "that I have already dictated a letter to Rome on it and notified my distinguished cousin and the Roman senate that I have advanced you to commander of the armed forces of Celesyria." The location of Celesyria was crucial to those forces contending for the "mastery of Asia." Its location made it a gateway into Asia. Advancing Herod to commander was a stratagem in securing control of this gateway for Rome and in extending the Roman Empire in Asia. As Caesar explained to Herod, "There lies Arabia and Egypt to our south. Who holds Celesyria holds the key to the south. *It must be held for Rome.*"[53]

Because of his military and administrative genius and his "unshakeable fidelity to Rome at the repeated risk of his fortune and life," Herod was later proclaimed King of Judea by Marc Antony, Octavius (Augustus) Caesar, and the Roman Senate.[54] Under Herod's reign, Judea enjoyed "security and peace and such wealth as the nation ha[d] never seen before in all its history." Even as Herod secured stability in Judea, he continued to conduct military campaigns to protect and extend Roman rule in Lower Asia. His own rule was extended to all of west Asia, and Augustus Caesar awarded him with the designation "Herod Magnus, Herod the Great."[55]

These are among the accomplishments that made Herod "*Great.*" But what made Herod's life Hurston's "great obsession"? Beyond his intensely dramatic personal life and flamboyant political career, Hurston saw Herod as an icon of the first century. Whereas Josephus describes Herod as a wicked usurper who caused his nation to sin, Hurston wrote that Herod "merely supported, as King, what was already being done."[56] What was afoot was change—and Herod stood for change. From the days of the Restoration leaders Zorabel,

Ezra, and Nehemiah, the Jewish priesthood was painfully aware that Jewish culture had undergone a radical evolution. They sought to eradicate the cultural influences of the Persians and the Greeks by "fix[ing] the laws of Moses and the way of life upon the people." In so doing, the priests edited the literature of the Hebrews and created a canon that became the Old Testament. "The decision was made as to [w]hat was to be regarded as sacred and of divine authority, inspired scriptures, and what was to be excluded from this category."[57] Even as the priesthood worked to counter external influences, the philosophies of Persia, India, and Greece had already penetrated the hearts and minds of the Jewish people. With the same ardor that the Greeks and Romans desired to spread their culture, the Orthodox Jews resisted it. The Maccabees of Modin revolted against the Seleucid Greeks, for example, and worked to extirpate all apostates among them. The slogan of the Orthodox priesthood was "Beware of the Greeks and Satan."[58] Herod was conceived of and vilified as a combination of both. Like the Romans and the Greeks before them, the Orthodox priesthood, too, was battling for the hearts and minds of its people.

As King of the Jews and a citizen of Rome, Herod was truly at the center of this political and ideological warfare. A progressive Jew who fought for the welfare of all Judea, his sympathies for Greco-Roman and Eastern cultures were also clear, and thus he continuously battled with the Chasidim. Herod's volatile life is the aperture through which Hurston has the reader peer into a world in flux. As she interprets it, this era was about more than the acquisition of territories and the subjugation of populations. It was about something imminently more profound: It was about establishing "empires of the mind." Aristotle had articulated the idea that nothing binds men more than common manners. This idea inspired Alexander the Great in his mission to Hellenize the then-known world. Where the Greeks left off, the Romans continued:

> Thus, the mighty and prolonged conflict for the mastery of Asia which began at Troy...was now taken up again in the first century with Rome the champion of the West, and Parthia the defender of the East. As at present in the world, the mightiest nation of the West, the United States, and the East, Soviet Russia, face each other for the minds of men and the mastery of the world.[59]

Aristotle's idea, which gave expression to a human cultural phenomenon, was implicitly understood by others as well, including the Jewish priesthood. Hurston pointed out that this was exactly the historical problem in relation to Herod.

Herod was a converted Jew and fought to defend and secure Judea, but he was also Rome's representative in Lower Asia and "of the Greeks." He imbibed Greco-Roman culture and debated Greek and Eastern philosophy. The three major philosophical Jewish sects of that time reflected Greek thought: "the Pharisees were 'kin' to the Stoics; the Sadducees were of the persuasion of the Greek pragmatists"; and the Essenes, the newest of the three, were influenced by Epicurean thought.[60] Central to Epicurean philosophy was the idea of free will, that is, the belief that the gods did not concern themselves with humans, and the notion that death was not to be feared. As Hurston restated in the introduction, "The aim of philosophy [was] to free men from fear, and more than anything else, from the fear of gods. The gods are not to be feared; death cannot be felt, the good can be won; all that we dread can be conquered." Hurston wrote that the Essenes had been greatly influenced by India's doctrine of Logos. She indicates that one means by which this doctrine came to the Jews was through the Greeks. Quoting Megasthenese, Seleucid's ambassador in India, "There is among the Brahmans, a sect of philosophers who hold that God is The Word, by which is meant, not articulate speech, but the discourse of reason—the second personality of God—that which is charged or entrusted with creation."[61]

Herod was particularly drawn to the philosophy of the Essenes, the sect with which Jesus was affiliated. In Hurston's biographical narrative, it is to the monastery of the Essenes that Herod repairs for rest and rehabilitation after the death of his beloved Mariamne. Judas, a healer and seer among the Essenes was also a friend to Antipater, Herod's father. Witnessing Herod's "distress of soul" and sense of guilt over the death of his wife, the monk invited Herod, who had been staying with a friend in Samaria, to the monastery:

> But peace is not in Samaria, nor yet in Judea, my son. Arise this very hour and be off to the community of the Essenes which [is] situated in the Desert of Quietude east of the Jordan and submit yourself to the ministrations of the Brethren there. I have sent word that you are coming to them.[62]

Herod remained with the Essenes for the duration of a month before returning to Jerusalem. "It was from this experience that the influence of the Essenes was to cling to Herod until the end of his life."[63]

Perhaps the most compelling aspect of this ideological drama for Hurston was that the very individual who was a major factor in the growth of the movement that came to be called Christianity was also vilified by Christians.

> Herod lent his aid to the movement out of which Christianity evolved. Thus it is ironical that he should be the boogerman of our religion. When you review the tenets of the Essenes, that third philosophical sect in Palestine, you will find that everything Christ did or said, according to the Four Gospels was straight from it.[64]

Herod's strong affiliation with the Essenes was cause for complaint from Flavius Josephus who stated that Herod "paid the Essenes a reverence greater than their mortal nature required." As Hurston wrote, "Herod trampled upon the Pharisees and the corrupt Sanhedrin mercilessly.... The Sanhedrin lost prestige under Herod and the Essenes gaine[d], thereby forming a matrix for the growth of Christianity." Thusly, Herod "had a great influence in preparing the way for Him."[65]

AN APPRECIATION OF PERSONALITY

Hurston's delineation and literary presentation of the dates, events, and circumstances of Herod's life, to a certain extent, is academic. But this "great obsession," this undying passion Hurston had with publishing her research on the life of King Herod the Great speaks to something beyond the academic, something beyond setting the record straight. "If genius is a mystery of the capacious consciousness," Harold Bloom wrote, "what is least mysterious about it is an intimate connection with personality rather than with character.... When we know enough about the biography of a particular genius, then we understand what is meant by the personality of Goethe or Byron or Freud or Oscar Wilde." Bloom pondered, "biographical inwardness" leads to appreciation of personality.[66] As Hurston probed the life of Herod the Great, she encountered a personality very much like her own, one who experienced personal situations that were comparable to her own. Among the personal qualities she saw in Herod and with which she identified were an expansive soul, fidelity, strength, innocence, and resilience. These qualities are consistently highlighted throughout all of Hurston's writings on Herod, including the letters and introductory proposals as well as the various longhand and typed manuscripts.

Hurston wrote in one version of the introduction to "Herod the Great" that "Herod appears to be singled out by some deity and especially endowed to attract the zig-zag lightning of fate."[67] In Hurston's autobiographical, folklore, and fictional writing, lightning is associated with divine power. A red and yellow lightning bolt is the symbol Luke Turner painted down Hurston's back during her Vodou initiation ritual. She was to conquer and accomplish with lightning, as she made her road with thunder. The lightning symbol was to be her sign forever.[68] Hurston's character Moses, too, is associated with this symbol. Atop Mount Nebo, Moses contemplates Israel camped below at the foot of the mountain. Fulfilling his mission, he had delivered the Hebrews into the promise of their God Yahweh. His rod lifted, Mount Nebo trembled as the moon, the seven suns, and the firmament itself reflected Moses' greatness. "He stood in the bosom of the thunder and the zig-zag lightning above him joined the muttering thunder."[69] Just as Yahweh had singled out Moses, "some deity" had singled out Herod. Whereas Moses' extraordinary charge was to free the Hebrews and lead them from Egypt to the Jordan River, Herod's charge was to govern the Hebrews in the various lands in which they had settled after crossing Jordan. According to the narrative, Herod's successful reign, which extended thirty-seven years, was due, in large part, to his great soul. He cared for and defended his citizenry—even against Rome—and the people loved him for it. "They loved Herod, threw garlands at him when he appeared in the streets," Hurston wrote. Through halted language, Flavius Josephus admitted Herod's "glorious deeds" and generosity of spirit. Josephus wrote, "The people loved Herod, but it was only because of his splendid appearance...and because he took such good care of them."[70]

Hurston illustrated Herod's magnanimous spirit in a scene wherein circumstances in Judea and surrounding provinces resulted in famine. A throng of anxious and hungry people crowded "before the palace to protest their condition and to denounce the king for it." Herod refused to "drive them away by force" as he was advised to do.

> "No, invite them into the kitchen and allow them to share what we have," Herod said calmly. [First] the people came in a belligerent mood, but when they had been fed exactly as the king, their attitude softened, because the Jewish people being unalterably democratic, when they saw that their king did not exalt himself above them, they were more patient.[71]

In spite of their extraordinary abilities and vast consciousness, or, more likely, because of it, Hurston's ideal characters are very human in that they are emotionally vulnerable. They honor intimacy, both within friendships and within romantic and connubial relationships. Friendships, however, seem to be the most sacred kind of relationships to Zora Neale Hurston. Readers familiar with Hurston's own biography are aware of her friendship with Langston Hughes, its promising possibilities, and its eventual demise. It was a loss that she felt deeply. Many years after the dissolution of their relationship, she shared with friend Arna Bontemps her disappointment. Bontemps disclosed Hurston's sentiments to Hughes: "She said that the cross of her life is the fact that there has been a gulf between you and her. She said she wakes up at night crying about it even yet."[72] Friendship was precious. Friendship was something she had met in the flesh, too:

> Personally, I know what it means. I have never been as good a friend as I meant to be. I keep seeing new heights and depths of possibilities which ought to be reached, only to be frustrated by the press of life which is no friend to grace. I have my loyalties and my unselfish acts to my credit, but I feel the lack of perfection in them, and it leaves a hunger in me.
>
> But I have received unaccountable friendships that are satisfying. Such as I am, I am a precious gift, as the unlettered Negro would say it. Stripped to my skin, that is just what I am. Without the juice of friendship, I would not be even what I seem to be.[73]

"Two Women in Particular," chapter thirteen in *Dust Tracks*, is an ode to friendship. The two women in particular are Fanny Hurst and Ethel Waters. The erstwhile excised version of this chapter, "The Inside Light—Being a Salute to Friendship," is a virtual roll call of friends. Some were friends for a time. Others were lifetime friends who endured from her years at Howard or Barnard, to the Harlem Renaissance, the Great Depression, and the World Wars, through the heinous morals charges, and unto her illness and death. Herbert Sheen, Dorothy West, Fannie Hurst, Carl Van Vechten, Arna Bontemps, and Richard Bruce Nugent number among the many. Hurston was inclined to think of friendship as the sine qua non of life: "It seems to me that trying to live without friends, is like milking a bear to get cream for your morning coffee. It is a whole lot of trouble, and then not worth much after you get it."[74]

In her biography of Herod, that same feeling about friendship is present. Hurston perceived in Herod, and in his father Antipater as well, the realization of the possible heights and depths of friendship. As Antipater was known as the steadfast friend of John Hyrcanus—despite the latter's betrayal of him—Herod was admired and respected for his faithfulness as a friend. Herod's most celebrated friendship was with Marc Antony. Early on, both having desires for political advancement, they made a pact:

> Antony stood and extended his right hand, and Herod leaped to his feet and firmly grasped the hand of the Roman.
> "Signed and sealed in our own blood, O Antony. Each to the death for the interest of the other."
> Thus began a friendship which was to become famous in the world of that time, and was to have immense influence on the careers of both men.[75]

Antony marveled at Herod's "unexcelled fidelity" in friendship. Herod explained that this quality in him was to be attributed to his father for whom fidelity in friendship was a religion: "The relations of friends," Antipater declared, "is the most sacred in the world. There is nothing in Heaven, in the waters beneath, nor upon the lands so holy as the bonds of friendship."[76]

In all his relations, Herod showed a remarkable faithfulness. If there were a fault in Hurston's otherwise ideal portrayal of Herod in this regard, it was to be found in his judgment in romantic and marital relations. Although she applauded Herod's integrity in such relationships, she questioned the wisdom of his unquestioning loyalty. Hurston characterized Herod's marriages as exceedingly tedious and problematic. And, in the case of his renowned marriage to Mariamne, for whom Herod had an excessive and obsessive love, the marriage even proved to be dangerous. Influenced by her mother Alexandra to conspire against Herod, Mariamne emotionally distanced herself from Herod and became a pawn in Alexandra's power play. Herod blamed himself for the turn of affairs:

> You have taken pains to have me understand that you do not love me. Very well I accept your conclusion and match it with equal indifference to you in the future, for I realize that I have brought it upon myself by my excessive love and worship of you, to my own injury, for a man in love cannot be true to his own interests. It is impossible to love and be wise, for no man ever thinks as much of himself as he does of the one he loves, his weakness is not only plain to others but to the one he loves. And it has been proven repeatedly everywhere that if the love he offers is not felt to an equal degree by the object of his love, he is rewarded by a secret contempt. In every love affair there is either reciprocation or contempt. And my love for you has been rewarded by contempt. And out of your own mouth I hear that my love is rewarded by your hatred.[77]

In his solitude, Herod questioned his judgment in allowing Alexandra to remain within the palace, knowing her will, as a member of the Asamonean line, to regain the throne. Why hadn't he had her executed "like any other seditious malefactor?" he queried. "Because," the response reverberated in the stillness of his mind, "Alexandra was the mother of Mariamne, and love had made a coward of him."[78]

In Hurston's own life, love and romance would always yield to work and far horizons. She enjoyed romantic relations, but Hurston perceived affairs of the heart as enervating impediments to a dynamic and free life. This perspective is apparent in her portrayal of Herod's romantic and marital relations. At the monastery of the Essenes, the monk who received Herod after Mariamne's death counseled him thusly:

> "Cease to torture your soul over the death of a woman who had a great capacity for pride and ambition, but little for love, Son," the director told him. "Never did Mariamne really love you, but at first she was content with the extreme pleasure which she obtained from your magnificent body, for she was by nature, addicted to the lust of the body. You have lost nothing but an evil obstruction to your abilities. Your finest hour is yet to come."[79]

And so it did. Herod emerged from his depression like sunrise. He returned to Jerusalem and immersed himself in the affairs of office with renewed vigor. He dressed himself in splendor, and in anticipation of hosting Augustus Caesar, he employed thousands to have Jerusalem and all roads leading to it as splendid in appearance as he. Herod then turned to the erection of a temple in Samaria, which was famous for its "perfect beauty." He built monuments that commemorated past victories and that gave life to old dreams. One such dream was "a city of polished white-marble climbing the long gentle incline from the Jewel blue Mediterranean." His most challenging and auspicious endeavor was the rebuilding of the temple at Jerusalem, which "for perfection of architectural lines and rich endowment, became one of the show-places of the world."[80]

Herod's ability to overcome *his* obsession and return to his calling spoke to his true strength and personal power. For Hurston, strength—true strength—was complemented by clarity of thought and purpose and the courage to pursue the ideal. In rebuilding the temple, for instance, there were those who doubted the possibility of constructing the sacred edifice and doing so according to its proper measurements. Some, including many of the priesthood, "feared that the existing temple would be torn down, and the king then find that he could not replace it. The undertaking appeared too vast to their minds and impossible of accomplishment."[81]

Herod prefaced the announcement of his building plans by recalling to the memory of the people his previous works. Then, with the courage of his own conviction and strength of purpose, Herod prevailed.[82]

Hurston admired Herod's physical vitality and was smitten by Herod's handsome qualities and his "beauty-worshipping soul." She was moved by accounts of his integrity and sense of loyalty. She was impressed by his abilities, creativity, idealism, and productivity. But what may have endeared Herod to Hurston most was her sense of his innocence. The notion of an innocent Herod egregiously contradicts Herod's historical character. "As an individual no doubt, his sins and deficiencies were many," Herod acknowl-edged in a moment of introspection.[83] As a soldier, he had cut down many by his sword, and as a king, he defended his throne from contenders. Hur-ston, too, conscious of Herod's controversial personality, deduced, however, "that a character does not have to be lovable to make good reading."[84]

Yet, according to Hurston's findings, the result of Herod's military and political actions was that the Jewish nation was advanced "to a degree of happiness which they never before had."[85] Although he lived and fought for the glory of Judea and Rome, Herod's historical legacy is one of infamy. He stood at the ideological crossroads of the first century and supported and openly espoused the philosophy that burgeoned into Christianity, but he stands accused of infanticide and the attempted murder of the Christ. Hur-ston's research and her biographical narrative pleads: "not guilty."

As with others who held the throne in Judea, Herod's leadership was undermined and his life was threatened. Many means were devised to dis-pose of Herod, as governor of Galilee, King of Judea, and as Procurator of west Asia: criminal charges, false accusations, politics, poison, and assassina-tion plots. The stratagem that Hurston focused on most acutely in the manu-script was that of false accusations. On more than one occasion, as Hurston's work reveals, Herod's enemies sought to dispose of him by lies and slander. Cleopatra, in collusion with Alexandra, accused Herod of killing Aristobu-lus, who was Alexandra's son and the young high priest. Aristobulus had died by drowning. Nonetheless, Alexandra had envisioned gaining the throne via her son. In the context of the narrative, Alexandra would do so, whether Aristobulus were alive or dead. Whatever the true circumstances of the drowning, Marc Antony, who presided over the case, pointed out to Cle-opatra that Herod was not at the scene of the drowning.

Failing in this, Alexandra, portrayed as being vigilant for every opportu-nity to remove Herod from her path to queendom, devised another strata-gem. She convinced her daughter Mariamne to accuse Herod of cruelty. The result proved to be the undoing of both Mariamne and her mother Alexan-dra. No longer blinded by love, Herod clearly saw his wife's hand in an attempt to kill him by a poisonous "love potion." He then recalled previous failed attempts she had made on his life.

> I have the memory of other attempts of you and your mother upon my life, such as the lying accusations to Antony through Cleopatra in the death of your brother. You sought to have my friend Antony take me out of your path to power for you. With your own mouth you accused me of the murder of your grandfather because I defended myself against the snare that he and your mother laid for me. These slanders you and Alexandra caused to be spread all over Jerusalem in the hope that the nation would rise and kill me.[86]

In spite of the smoldering ill will of the Orthodox priests and repeated plots against his life, Herod reigned successfully. For his friends and well-wishers outnumbered his enemies and disclosed all discovered conspiracies and plots. Unsuccessful in assassinating the man, his detractors satisfied themselves with assassinating his character. Only after his death would they be successful even in that. The death knell to what Hurston saw as Herod's true legacy was the accusation of the slaughter of the Innocents. By Hurston's reasoning, from a philosophical perspective, and by her calculations, from a temporal perspective, this purported event was an implausibility. Herod was partial to the Essenes and their philosophy, "So the doctrine of brotherly love, God the father of all mankind equally, and not just the Jews, gained ground in his reign. Not only would Christ never have been put to death under Herod," Hurston wrote, "but the Sanhedrin would not have dared to even start the commotion. As we Negros say, Herod would have been all over them just like gravy over rice." Moreover, Hurston asserted, "[T]he dates of Herod the Great were definitely established historically, 72–4 B.C. while no one can say when Christ was born, since he had no biographer, and there was no interest in the matter until generations later when Christianity was an established religion."[87]

Hurston perceived the accusations against Herod, during his reign and after his death, as grave injustices. The stance she took in her letters about Herod and in the Herod manuscript clearly illustrate that she was entirely in sympathy with King Herod.

Having been wrongly accused herself, it seems that Hurston keenly felt Herod's having been wrongly accused, both by his contemporaries who instigated his trials, based on "lies all lies," and by the long arm of New Testament biblical history. In her own case, she had to defend herself, in September 1948, against groundless charges of molesting a ten-year-old boy and two eleven-year-old boys. To establish her own innocence, she traced a network of lies to a faux friend—Richard D. Rochester. Because Rochester could not manipulate Hurston to serve his own ends in falsely accusing another, Rochester spitefully determined to punish Hurston for the perceived offense:

> [H]e demanded that I perjure myself by swearing that a man stole a car from Rochester so that he could put the man in jail, when he knew so well that it was not true. I refused and then he threatened me with a nation-wide bath of filthy publicity if I did not agree and so forth.[88]

Like Cleopatra, Alexandra, and certain ones among the Jewish priesthood who conspired and contrived with others to implicate Herod in concocted crimes, so, too, Rochester went about to find others to support him in his "campaign of slander." Among those he had enlisted was Mayme Allen, Hurston's landlady and mother of the ten-year-old boy of whom Hurston stood accused. The heinous charges were dismissed, yet Rochester was dogged in his intent to defame and destroy Zora Neale Hurston. Whereas Ms. Allen's charges were dismissed as groundless, Rochester invented yet other scandalous charges. He would later accuse her of smoking marijuana, indecent exposure, and voting fraud. Just as Herod's enemies used the courts in their schemes to destroy Herod, Rochester used the New York City court system in an attempt to deliver his promised revenge on Zora Neale Hurston. In a letter to Fannie Hurst, Hurston wrote:

> I can see the end of my troubles as far as my case is concerned, so I am reasonably calm on that score. In fact, I think that I have at last ferreted out the source of the matter and know my enemy and whom and how to fight. Things are now tangible, and my victory yesterday in the Small Claims Court was a much more important step than it might seem.... The Judge was right in there defeating the unholy purpose of Richard D. Rochester at every move. He helped me to prove himself that he did not come there to collect any 20.00 from me, but to use the court as a springboard to scandalize my name.[89]

Rochester promised Hurston "terror by slander." And this was her experience, as the morals charges, orchestrated by Rochester, became public record. "One inconceivable horror after another," Hurston wrote to the Van Vechtens. "It seemed that every hour some other terror assailed me, the last being the AFRO-AMERICAN sluice of filth. You should know that a Negro who works down in the courts secured the matter and went around peddling it to the papers."[90] Hurston despaired:

> My country has failed me utterly. My race has seen fit to destroy me without reason, and with the vilest tools conceived of by man so far. A Society, eminently Christian, and supposedly devoted to super-decency has gone so far from it's announced purpose, not to protect children, but to exploit the gruesome fancies of a pathological case and do this thing to human decency. Please do not forget that this thing was not done in the South, but in the so-called liberal North. Where shall I look in this country for justice?[91]

Hurston's soul revolted at the very idea of anyone associating her with such deeds. She wrote, "I swear to you, by anything and all things that I hold sacred that not one word of this foul and vicious lie is true. It is against everything in my soul and nature. There is no excuse for this most horrible crime of the century."[92]

The twist of the knife for Hurston was that the sordid and untrue story was exposed to the public by the Negro media and a Negro informant. Additionally, Mayme Allen, who instigated the morals charge, lived in the Negro community in which Hurston was working on behalf of her political party and on behalf of the community: "I would never have known such people," she wrote Hurst,

> but I was sent for to help out in the Republican campaign of 1946, and had to have an address in the District, and to work with as many common people as possible. I honestly did all that I could and look what happens. Nor have I received a word from one of them.[93]

Thoroughly disillusioned by these betrayals, Hurston found it difficult to even be in the presence of black folks. In this, too, Hurston found her situation comparable with Herod's. "As to Herod's reputed harshness," Flavius Josephus wrote, "Herod was the first man of the world in excusing offenses against himself. When seditious men were brought before him, he gave them a talk and dismissed them. Yet he was the first man in the world to punish unfaithfulness in his own family." Hurston wrote in response, "That is not hard for me to understand for I think that all of us expect greater fidelity out of our own than others."[94]

In the Herod narrative, Hurston addressed the issue of the sexual abuse of children. Her utter contempt of the idea of despoiling children, and of those who commit such acts, is expressed in Herod's reaction to Marc Antony's pedophilia. Upon Cleopatra's visit to Marc Antony in Tarsus in Cilicia, she brought with her a retinue of young males and females and made a "gift of pretty boys" to Antony.

Herod recoiled at the idea of participating in this practice:

> Herod had no wish to be present at such an orgy. His abhorrence of the practice all but choked him. Often a youth was mutilated for life during a single night of indulgence by some man of wealth and high office. On occasion, a boy was actually used to death. Why, Oh why did his friend Antony have to be cursed with such taste?[95]

Through indirect narration, Herod continues, his words giving expression to Hurston's own sentiments:

> Life to Antony had been most rewarding. Why then descend to such a brutish level? Perhaps the answer lay in the dissolute youth of the man. His own father, a man never overburdened with moral concepts had died while Marcus was a small boy, and his mother had married Lentullus, an abandoned wretch, if ever one lived, and the young Marcus had been very fond of this dissolute scoundrel. And now, like a maggot crawling from its slimy spawning place, Antony contaminated the Roman world by his presence. He had been married to four wives now, and had been faithful to none. And this hour, without conscience, he was brutally handling and corrupting young boys, some scarcely fourteen years old. Somebody should cleanse the earth of the scoundrel![96]

By example and by precept, Antipater taught his sons not to corrupt the young, who were innocent and vulnerable, but to protect them. Herod's impulse, therefore, was to "rush in upon Antony with his naked sword." But the same right hand in which he would hold his sword was the same hand he had extended in friendship. Then he knew, too, "If he killed Antony, he could not even hope to escape with his own life."[97]

Who would protect Zora Neale Hurston and defend her in her innocence? Who would shield her from "the twisted mind" of Richard D. Rochester? Hurston reasoned in a letter to Van Vechten that she had always "believed in the essential and eventual rightness" of America. She had "fought the good fight" and "kept the faith." Yet, she found that "there were those who care nothing about fairplay where a Negro is concerned."[98] She genuinely believed that her loyalty to America would have been honored and that the American justice system would have protected an innocent person from false and scandalous charges. But neither did Alexander Miller of the Children's

Society nor New York City District Attorney Frank Hogan conduct a proper investigation before Hogan issued a warrant for her arrest. Hurston contested:

> They have committed the foulest crime of the century. For leaving the havoc that they have wrought upon me as a public figure...AND I SWEAR TO YOU BY ALL THAT I HOLD SACRED THAT NOT ONE WORD OF THIS VILE CHARGE IS TRUE. I INVITE YOU, BECAUSE I VALUE YOUR TRUST, TO ASK QUESTIONS AND INVESTIGATE TO TEST MY INNOCENCE. DO THIS FOR THE SAKE OF MY MEMORY.[99]

Hurston looked to her friends for comfort and aid in establishing her innocence and in clearing her name. A published and internationally renown author who also augmented her income through freelance writing and public speaking, Hurston was concerned about the damage to her reputation, thus to her livelihood. Also prolific in her contributions to black culture and American society, Hurston was well aware that she had "had some influence on her own time" and was, therefore, concerned about her historical legacy, and thus her appeal to Carl Van Vechten.

Hurston imagined a lifetime of effort rendered null, an international reputation destroyed. She had "resolved to die," she told Van Vechten and Hurst. "Now [my] soul is dead, and I care about nothing any more," she wrote to Hurst.[100]

> You must believe me when I say that I have ever, and do love my country. If it chooses to destroy me in so foul a manner, let the deed lie upon the city and the national conscience, for the truth will certainly be known somehow. I believe in the unchangeable laws that govern the universe. Even if I am dead, the truth is bound to be known in time.[101]

Hurston appealed first to her trusted friend Van Vechten and then to universal law to clear and restore her name. Her earlier resolution to die transmuted into her resolution to take sword in hand and fight. In one sense, then, "Herod the Great" became a story about truth and justice, a battle waged to defend the good and protect the innocent: the restoration of a good name. Although Hurston was totally exonerated of the charges by March 14, 1949, Rochester's campaign of slander had taken its toll. This woman who had fervently declared, "I will to love," now knew hate. She met it, too, in the flesh, and had been adversely affected by it.

Gradually, Hurston began recovery from the trauma of these nightmarish experiences. As late as February 1951, though, she was still reflecting on the devastating affects of the ordeal. She wrote to literary agent Jean Parker Waterbury, "You can be sure that I am back to myself again at last. It was a very long journey through a dark wilderness, but I have come home again. It is only in these last weeks that I can see how lost I was."[102] Hurston felt that she had finally reached a "calm balance," a still point. By July, her equanimity of spirit began to move in the direction of her characteristic enthusiasm. "I am the happiest I have been in the last ten years" she breathed to friends and associates. She had moved from Belle Glade to Eau Gallie, to "the one spot on earth" that felt like home to her. In her letter to Jean Parker Waterbury, Hurston had addressed the "assorted scripts" she intended to mail to her agent, then declared, "I am tackling Herod" before I [s]tart on the newspaper just as sure as you snore."[103] She was occupied with domestic tasks, "[d]igging in my garden, painting my house, planting seeds, and things like that."[104] Yet, even in this springtime state of mind, she had occasion again to wonder at the deceit and dishonesty of which humans are capable. She discovered that her outline for an article on President Taft ("A Negro Voter Sizes Up Taft") was purloined by a representative of her then-literary agency, Ann Watkins, Inc., and was given to another Watkins author. In spite of her suspicion of more deceitful schemes and covetous and envious pretenders, Hurston reaffirmed her "unshakeable belief in the mill of the gods":

> In the most terrible hours of my life, I have imagined a cosmic funeral, and [seen] the bier of God pass by.
> "So God Himself is dead," I have murmured through burning tears, "and untruth and injustice is supreme."
> "Ah, no," I am able to hear after a while. "An empty casket passes you. He but gives opportunity for the proud and presumptuous the chance to destroy themselves. Be calm in your unchanging trust, and truth shall be avenged."[105]

Although the world might be a family of Hurstons, Zora Neale Hurston was an idealist and had an ardent sense of justice. In one way or another, her works resonate with this moral imperative: "God balances the sheets sooner or later." Truth and justice would prevail. Three years before the 1948 charges, Hurston shared with Van Vechten that the story she was "burning to write," was "the story of the 3,000 years struggle of the Jewish people for democracy and the rights of man." Her letter outlined this struggle from ancient to modern times:

> The Jewish people have suffered and still suffer from the slander of their own priests. I do not mean that the present Rabbis do it. I mean that Gentiles have formed their own opinion of the Jews through what is taught in Sunday Schools, and the slander of their oppressors is taken for granted, and justifies our present-day prejudices.[106]

In her lengthy proposal, "Herod the Great" is mentioned only in passing, and only once. In a 1946 letter, Hurston indicated that she would write a play that dramatized the fall of Jerusalem to Titus. In 1948, she proposed a book, "Just Like Us," that returned to the subject of the struggle of Jewish people. Herod the Great would be the focus of but one chapter in this work. By 1951, three years after Richard D. Rochester, Herod I moved to center stage. In Hurston's re-conception of the manuscript, Herod is central to the text, and the struggle of the Jewish people becomes context. Herod's story simultaneously becomes Hurston's story.

In writing about Herod and his era, Hurston gained a more objective perspective of herself and her era and a better understanding of what had happened to her. For, as Boyd wrote in *Wrapped in Rainbows*, "Nothing in Zora's fifty-seven years of living could have prepared her" for what transpired.[107] Hurston was totally bewildered. Her foundation was rocked. Her world had tilted. In one letter at the outset of Rochester's campaign, Hurston expressed her complete discombobulation in response to the morals charge: "Horror of disbelief took me. I could not believe that a thing like that could be happening in the United States and least of all to me. It just could *not* be true! I must be having a nightmare."[108] Lie though it was, her nightmare was true.

Hurston's work on Herod coincides with her own personal revitalization after the Richard Rochester madness. "Herod the Great" became more than a biography of a life. "Herod the Great" was a lifeline. In Hurston's reconfiguration of what she saw to be the true portrait and legacy of Herod, she had the opportunity to examine and understand this thing that made her go out of herself. She explored more fully the phenomenon called human nature and probed more deeply into the human dynamic perceived of as resilience.

What is it like to be falsely accused, to endure calumny and public suspicion, to have your reputation disparaged, to have your good works overshadowed and obscured by little minds successful in their unholy purpose? Herod, too, felt his way was thwarted by jealous and unscrupulous beings motivated by "unholy ambitions." Yet, Herod prevailed. And like High John, he came out more than conquer. His enemies even petulantly complained, "From his very dangers, Herod drew splendor."[109]

What could Zora Neale Hurston learn from Herod? Harold Bloom wrote, "Your solitary Self's deepest desire is for survival whether in the here and now, or transcendentally elsewhere. To be augmented by the genius of others is to enhance the possibilities of survival, at least in the present and the near future."[110] Hurston's sense of self was augmented by the genius of Herod the Great. Herod marched into battle, his sword in his right hand, high above his head, liquid sun glinting off his naked blade. Hurston likewise declared that she would be tussling, sword in hand. She would run, not away from the lies and slander, but toward the truth.

As she initiated her own investigation to prove her innocence, she was also dedicated to proving the innocence of Herod the Great. It was the same struggle. And as she pieced Herod's life together, she gradually became fully present in her own. At the time she had written Burroughs Mitchell in October 1953 that she was "[u]nder the spell of a great obsession," she also wrote, "I have been passing through the most formative period of my whole life." As she continued her work on the manuscript, even after Scribner's rejection, Zora Neale Hurston maintained her optimism and sense of growth. In a June 1957 letter to Herbert Sheen, she wrote,

> As for myself, I have gone through a period that might appear outwardly unprofitable, but in reality extremely important. A taking-in period like the gestation of a prospective mother. Now, I am ready to give forth again. I feel that I have made phenom[e]nal growth as a creative artist. Yes, I am doing a book as well as some [s]hort stuff.[111]

Hurston was right in her assumption that what she experienced as a period of fecundity would appear outwardly unprofitable. This has been, in the end, the assessment of various literary critics. The years Hurston invested in the Herod biography didn't "pay off." The work, itself, is criticized as "disappointing." The July 21, 1955, letter from Mitchell, expressing Scribner's decision not to publish the manuscript offered some explanation:

> In spite of your subject and your clearly deep feeling about it, the book does not vividly recreate the man and his time.... There is a wealth of fine material here but somehow it has failed to flow in a clear narrative stream. We think the book would prove difficult reading for the layman.[112]

Contemporary critics tend to echo Mitchell's critique. Some expand on the analysis of style, judging the narrative as pedantic and inconsistent, but none speak to the "wealth of fine material."[113] The content of the manuscript, even the letters about it—which have been described as "dull"—demand attention, discussion, and scrutiny. Hurston indicated in her letters and introductions that there is much for the reader to learn from the life of Herod and this "first century of decision." There was much to learn about modern culture and politics, philosophical perspectives, religious practices, and personal prejudices. She contended that much of twentieth-century thought was rooted in the ideological movements and biases of that first century. Her work on Herod begs the questions: In whose intellectual empire does modern society hold citizenship? Of whose histories are we the intellectual custodians? Whose "manners" do we reproduce? Do these manners serve all humanity, or a select few? If the aim of philosophy is intended to free humankind from fear, who among us is free?

Herod was Hurston's example of a self-realized individual. How do other individuals begin to realize their genius and potential? How do we parlay our particular genius into a gift for the greater good? In *Dust Tracks*, Hurston wrote, "Consider that with patience and tolerance, we godly demons may breed a noble world in a few hundred generations or so."[114] What would need to happen for such a world to materialize? Hurston reached through time for some inspired thought on the matter and found the life of Herod instructive on many levels. In the research she conducted in the writing of "Herod the Great" and in the endeavor itself, she discovered, and discovered anew, "cosmic secrets" that gave her life and work meaning beyond the materiality of publication or compensation.

Certainly Hurston wanted her book published. She was a writer. She had a story to tell, *and* she had a truth to avenge. At the same time, she was at peace with the inner growth she was experiencing during the process of the writing. In the multiple revisions and search for a publisher, Zora Neale Hurston was following her bliss. In that, she was free and at peace.

Some interpreters of Hurston's life gainsay her optimism and prefer to describe her later years as "a time of collapse and confusion, 'a talent in ruins.'"[115] They find her unconditional optimism and consistent joie de vivre untenable in the face of material lack, financial insecurity, and unpublished manuscripts. Yet Valerie Boyd notes that even in a moment of fear that she might never again be published, Hurston wrote these words to herself in the journal she maintained for notes on Herod: "You are alive, aren't you? Well, so long as you have no grave you are covered by the sky. No limit to your possibilities. The distance to heaven is the same everywhere."[116]

And at the same time, Hurston's later years are reflective of a natural waning, a relaxed exhalation after a long, rich, and deep intake. After years of living a full and extended life, she could now draw into her Self. As this passage from the twenty-fifth section of the *Tao Teh Ching* states:

> To be great is to go on,
> To go on is to be far,
> To be far is to return.[117]

What is most amazing about Hurston is that, even in her years of apparent contraction, she continued to expand inwardly. Her insights deepened. Her clarity sharpened. The knowledge and wisdom she imbibed from negotiating the yin and yang of life flowered into the wisdom that allowed her to transcend the mundane. She had grown into the oneness of the individual merged with Source. She glimpsed time's dissolution into eternity. She was present to her "return with the earth to Father Sun."[118] What, really, did she need of the *things* that humans want most? "I am not materialistic," Hurston avowed.[119] Her thought and actions reflect the internalization of these spiritual principles espoused in the *Tao Teh Ching*:

> Attain to utmost Emptiness.
> Cling single-heartedly to interior peace.
> While all things are stirring together,
> I only contemplate the Return.
> For flourishing as they do,
> Each of them will return to its root.
> To return to the root is to find peace.
> To find peace is to fulfill one's destiny.
> To fulfill one's destiny is to be constant.
> To know the Constant is called Insight.[120]

A talent in ruins? That assertion is debatable and almost negligible, because talent is for a time, but genius is forever. Hurston's genius created ever-expanding circles of knowledge, experience, and perception that vibrated out from the black folk culture of Eatonville into Southern culture, American culture, world culture, and to life itself; from the period of her birth to infinity; from far horizons out to the rim bones of nothingness—like the ripple from a pebble dropped in an erstwhile still pond. The reflection therein invites us to take a closer look, and then look again.

Lucy Hurston is the daughter of Everett Hurston and niece of Zora Neale Hurston.

Valerie Boyd is the author of *Wrapped in Rainbows*.

Robert Hemenway is the author of *Zora Neale Hurston: A Literary Biography*.

Phyllis McEwen is a poet and artist. Here she is performing as Zora Neale Hurston.

Jack Connolly is a Zora-phile and board member of the Cultural Affairs Council for St. Lucie County.

Alice Jackson is a librarian at the Zora Neale Hurston Branch Library in Fort Pierce, Florida.

The Zora Neale Hurston Branch Library with glass mosaic benches designed by Fort Pierce artist Anita Prentice.

Zora Neale Hurston house, Fort Pierce, Florida. "This site possesses national significance in commemorating the history of the United States of America." (U.S. Department of the Interior)

The Zora Neale Hurston gravesite and *Dust Tracks* marker, in the Garden of the Heavenly Rest Cemetery, Fort Pierce, Florida.

Zora Neale Hurston Memorial stone, "She jumped at the Sun," Eatonville, Florida.

The Zora Neale Hurston National Museum of Fine Arts, Eatonville, Florida.

The Clock Tower at Eatonville City Hall commemorating Eatonville's centennial celebration.

The Eatonville Branch Library at Zora Neale Hurston Square.

SIX

Ancestral Spirit

I n her dedicatory essay, "On Refusing to Be Humbled by Second Place in a Contest You Did Not Design: A Tradition by Now," Alice Walker wrote:

> We love Zora Neale Hurston for her work, first, and then again (as she and all Eatonville would say), we love her for herself. For the humor and courage with which she encountered a life she infrequently designed, for her absolute disinterest in becoming either white or bourgeois, and for her devoted appreciation of her own culture, which is an inspiration to us all.[1]

Walker's essay underscores the significance of Hurston's ability to "trust [her] own self-evaluation" and to hold her own "against the flood of whiteness and maleness that diluted so much other black art of the period." Her ability to do so, Walker stated, "is a testament to her genius and her faith." This testament to Hurston's genius and faith is also a testament to her prophetic politics. Many critics have been and continue to be baffled by Hurston's politics. As Walker wrote in her essay, Hurston's politics "tend to confuse us."[2] Yet, when one probes Hurston's politics, one finds at its heart the very same uncommon sense of self that is so widely celebrated.

Most of Hurston's published writings during the late 1940s and the 1950s were political in orientation. Even the unpublished manuscript "Herod the Great" can be considered a treatise on political rule. Although Hurston found politics repugnant, she would pen several journal articles on Florida state politics and national politics, and she actively participated in political campaigns. Zora Neale Hurston was never at a loss for an opinion and was always concerned about the social and political fabric of America. One of her main reasons for writing political pieces, however, was that they generated the monies necessary to subsidize the writing of her book manuscripts and to sustain her while doing so. Whereas the shorter articles could be written more quickly and afforded her the much-needed income, the longer works required months and years, even decades to write, with no guarantee of publication and compensation.

During the latter 1940s and the 1950s, Hurston had invested her energy, time, and resources in writing three book manuscripts that were never published: "The Lives of Barney Turk," "The Golden Bench of God," and "Herod the Great." The central character in "The Lives of Barney Turk" was a youthful and adventurous white Florida farmhand. The novel follows his travels to Honduras in Central America and to Hollywood, California. By all accounts, her Scribner's editor Burroughs Mitchell liked the story and found it promising, encouraging Hurston's efforts and making suggestions for revisions. Hurston completed a draft of the manuscript by September 8, 1950. "Here's Barney Turk at last," she wrote to Mitchell. "I like the boy and wish him every success."[3]

Hurston spent the next six months revising the manuscript, but "Barney Turk" never met with success. Mitchell did not find the book publishable. Shortly afterward, Hurston reluctantly began work on transforming her novelette "The Golden Bench of God," into a book-length work. The rejection of "Barney Turk" was upsetting to Hurston and made her wary about plunging into another long-term project when the last one was financially unsuccessful and had depleted her coffers. Her agent Jean Parker Waterbury was enthusiastic about the novelette and thought it would work well as a novel. "But the very mention of 'novel' gives me a shudder," Hurston said. "You have no idea what I have been through in the last six months. After using the money that I earned otherwise to buy the leisure to work on Barney Turk, I found myself with a year's work gone for nothing, and me cold in hand."[4] Yet Waterbury convinced Hurston of the potential of the subject matter as a book publication. Hurston's novel was based on the life and work of Madame C. J. Walker and her daughter A'Lelia Walker.[5] Though reluctant at the outset, Hurston admitted to Waterbury her growing enthusiasm for the work: "I have caught fire on the novel," she wrote.[6]

Again, Hurston met with disappointment. Waterbury believed in the work and thought it publishable, but Mitchell did not, nor did Tay Hohoff, a Lippincott editor whom Waterbury asked to look at the manuscript. Although her financial situation was strained, Hurston wrote Waterbury that her nerves were in fine shape. Working in her garden among her flowers and vegetables had done her "a world of good." All else that she needed was her typewriter, which she had had to pawn to relieve the financial strain. "As soon as I can get hold of money to get my machine out of hock, I will be in high spirits."[7] By this time, Hurston had already begun work on her "great obsession."

Hurston accepted these rejections of her work rather matter-of-factly. Her reaction to an earlier rejection of a book manuscript titled "Mrs. Doctor" resulted in the protest article, "What White Publishers Won't Print." "Mrs. Doctor" was Hurston's look at "the upper strata of Negro life." She had completed two-thirds of the novel when her editors at Lippincott "decided that the American public was not ready for it yet."[8]

"What White Publishers Won't Print" lambasted the racist politics of white American publishers and producers who were interested only in the stereotypical representations of blacks as well as "any non-Anglo-Saxon peoples within our borders." Hurston interpreted the indifference as the symptom of a graver problem:

> This lack of interest is much more important at this time than it was in the past. The internal affairs of the nation have bearings on the international stress and strain, and this gap in the national literature now has tremendous weight in world affairs. National coherence and solidarity is implicit in a thorough understanding of the various groups within a nation, and this lack of knowledge about the internal emotions and behavior of the minorities cannot fail to bar out understanding.[9]

Black people, Hurston argued, expressed a unique, "natural endowment" and complexity of personality just like everyone else. The assumption that blacks and other ethnic minorities were "uncomplicated stereotypes" whose highest achievements and refined emotionality were a result of aping whites meant that people of color in America would neither be seen nor treated as human beings. The essential aspects of these arguments constitute the crux of all of Hurston's political writings and activities. Just as Hurston was appalled by the "lack of curiosity about the internal lives and emotions of the Negroes," she was offended and insulted by anyone—regardless of race or creed—who would dare conceive of and approach African Americans as some undifferentiated, thoughtless, and insentient mass. In "Why the Negro Won't Buy Communism," for instance, Hurston decried the Communist party as a "brand of up-to-date slavery." She resented the idea that party leaders viewed American Negroes as a downtrodden people who were to be deeply pitied and so gullible as to desire to join the ranks of the Communist party en mass. Hurston questioned the deep concern on the part of Soviet Russia for "*all* the darker peoples of the world."[10] Rather, she concluded, their vision of "world brotherhood" was an aspect of imperialist propaganda: "I soon saw that they did not love us just because our skins were black. The USSR was bent on world conquest through Asia. They saw in us a shoestring with which they hoped to win a tan-yard. A dumb, but useful tool."[11]

Generally appalled by their recruiting methods, Hurston was particularly incensed by their manipulations of some blacks by the promise of white mates. She referred to this phenomenon as the "white mare apparatus," and asserted, "Yes, it is true that mules will unhesitatingly follow a white mare anywhere and at any time. But it is known there's danger in arriving at conclusions by analogy. It is possible, and even probable that we might not be mules."[12]

Hurston was outraged at the assumption that black people were so dominated by their libido and lust for sexual relations with whites that they could be manipulated accordingly and blindly led into the fold of the Communist party. Likewise, she was outraged at the notion that blacks could only learn if they sat next to whites. The May 17, 1954, Supreme Court ruling in *Brown vs. Board of Education* overturned the 1896 *Plessy vs. Ferguson* ruling that upheld the "separate but equal" doctrine regarding public school education of whites and blacks and verily sanctioned Jim Crow politics. The promise of *Brown* was to unify the nation by desegregating public schools. Segregated schools, the Court argued, were "inherently unequal." Hurston questioned the validity of the judgment, especially because "unequal" came to imply that black schools were inherently inferior. Hurston's response to the ruling was expressed in her August 11, 1955, letter to the editor of the *Orlando Sentinel*. She opened the letter by saying, "I was not going to part my lips concerning the U.S. Supreme Court decision." But three months after the decision "no one seems to touch on what to me appears to be the most important point in the hassle."[13]

What, for Hurston, was the *most* important point? In the next paragraph, she stated, "The whole matter revolves around the self-respect of my people."[14] Why should black children be subjected to sit in school classrooms next to white children who had been taught that they were "FIRST BY BIRTH"? In a letter to Dutch writer and translator Magrit de Sablonière, Hurston conveyed that she was not racist. She had white friends who were genuine in their relations with her—the spirit of friendship was evident. She found no value, however, in physical contact with whites that was void of a mutual spiritual presence. "I actually do feel insulted," she wrote, "when a certain type of white person hastens to effuse to me how noble they are to grant me their presence." Zora Neale Hurston had herself integrated Barnard College and was the first black associated with numerous events, civic and professional organizations, and societies. "As a Negro," she wrote to Sablonière, "you know that I cannot be in favor of segregation but I do deplore the way they go about ending it."[15]

Hurston did not favor poor, ill-equipped, underfunded schools, but she did honor black intelligence, black administrators, and black teachers. Perhaps her own education at Hungerford Normal School in all-black Eatonville inspired her tendency to accentuate the positives of Negro schools and to minimize the comparative negatives. She assessed Negro schools in Florida as being in "very good shape and on the improve." She touted the work of Dr. D. E. Williams, "the driving force of Negro instruction" in the state, and commended his initiative to "improve both physical equipment and teacher-quality."[16] She had confidence in his ability to effect positive change in the future. Contrarily, Hurston allowed,

If there are not adequate Negro schools in Florida, and there is some residual, some inherent and unchangeable quality in white schools, impossible to duplicate anywhere else, then I am the first to insist that Negro children of Florida be allowed to share this boon. But if there are adequate Negro schools and prepared instructors and instructions, then there is nothing different except the presence of white people.[17]

It was not the specter of white people that outraged Hurston, but the "myth" that the greatest delight for blacks is association with whites. The *Orlando Sentinel* letter recalls Hurston's *American Legion* article, "Why the Negro Will Not Buy Communism," criticizing the Communist ploy of the "white mare apparatus." In the *Sentinel* letter, Hurston reported that she detected the tracks of that same "white mare" in the Supreme Court's decision: "Lead a white mare along a country road and slyly open the gate and the mules in the lot would run out and follow."[18] As the white mare had been used to the benefit of dishonest mule traders, Hurston was suspicious of who was to benefit from the mostly unilateral integration of blacks into "white" school systems. The Communist party, she wrote in the *American Legion* article, sought benefit by gradual world domination.

"This ruling being conceived and brought forth in a sly political medium with eyes on '56, and brought forth in the same spirit and for the same purpose, it is clear that they have taken the old notion to heart."[19] From what, she pondered, were Americans being distracted? While the South was up in arms in celebration of and in resistance to the Supreme Court's decision, she warned that "it had better keep its eyes open for more important things"—such as the loss of democratic rule. "One instance of Govt by fiat has been rammed down its throat" by virtue of the Court's ruling. "But what if," she postured,

it is contemplated to do away with the two-party system and arrive at Govt by administrative decree? No questions allowed and no information given out from the administrative department. We could get more rulings on the same subject and more far-reaching any day. It pays to weigh every [saying] and action, however trivial as indicating a trend.[20]

Although she highlighted what she perceived to be the racial politics of the decision, for Hurston national politics was "the *most* important point in the hassle." For as she stated in "Why the Negro Won't Buy Communism," "[i]t had been proved too many times and by different countries, that nationality is stronger than race."[21] Hurston felt it was her patriotic duty to introduce the issue of democratic governance into the debate. In this letter, Hurston called for blacks to embrace their pride and dignity as she encouraged all Americans to recall their spirit of democratic freedom.

Hurston saw other alternatives to America's dilemma regarding black public education: Why not enforce compulsory education for Negro children as it is done for whites? Would it not be effective to appoint truant offers for the next ten years and support the home life of Negro children? "Use to the limit what we already have," she suggested.[22] Even with the Supreme Court's decision, Hurston stated, "[i]t is possible that the end of segregation is not here and never meant to be here at present, but the attention of the South directed on what was calculated to keep us busy while more ominous things were brought to pass."[23]

"Growth from within. Ethical and cultural desegregation" is what Zora Neale Hurston favored and advocated.[24] The gap in understanding that Hurston alluded to in "What White Publishers Won't Print" was wide. Yet Hurston did not see that sacrificing the souls of black children and black neighborhoods was the solution.

From Hurston's experience, change was always an internal matter. One must make the journey inward. This was true of herself as well as her fictional characters. This inward journey, Hurston contended, was also an individual journey. Significant, lasting change would be generated on an individual basis, not only, if at all, by judicial declaration. Hurston saw her friend Sara Creech as a fine example of the ideal of interracial understanding. Creech, a civil rights activist was one of the founders of the Inter-Racial Council in Belle Glade, Florida. She was also creator of the first "anthropologically correct" black doll. Creech shared her ideas and marketing plans for the doll with Hurston. Hurston was impressed and pleased. In a letter that expressed her sentiments, Hurston wrote, "The thing that pleased me most, Miss Creech was that you, a White girl, should have seen into our hearts so clearly, and sought to meet our longing for understanding of us as we really are, and not as some would have us."[25]

The letter also lauded Creech's contribution to social change through the Inter-Racial Council. Hurston twice addressed the organization as a guest speaker and was acquainted with their work and progressive politics. The organization, Hurston wrote, "could be a model for the nation, and according to what I hear, you, Sara Creech are at the very heart of it."[26]

Creech's brand of activism confirmed Hurston's belief that individualist politics were central to any movement toward social change. "This follows a conclusion that I reached some years ago from observation," she shared with Creech. "That is, that the so-called Race problem will be solved in the South and by Southerners. I have noted that when a Southerner becomes convinced, he goes all out for correcting the situation."[27]

Hurston noted that others moved and acted from the heart. In an earlier July 1946 letter to Claude Barnett, Hurston lionized journalist and publisher John S. Knight. "He fights race hatred in a way that I like," she wrote. Unlike the superficial "friends of the Negro," Knight "does not approach the matter in the spirit that we are inferior wards of the nation, but as citizens being denied their rights." Knight was not offering a spurious and ulteriorly motivated "friendship," which was sure to melt like chipped ice on a hot Florida day.[28]

Hurston rejected the very idea of such patronage. "I want nothing done as a favor to me. I want it done as my RIGHT AS A CITIZEN!" What is not prejudicial is universal, thus substantive and enduring. Hurston wondered why others did not look more critically at the meager offerings handed out as personal favors: "Why those Negroes do not see that anything that is done under favoritism can be withdrawn?"[29]

Although Hurston has become something of an icon among progressives and particularly black feminist thinkers, "she was deeply conservative," said William Cobb in an article about Zora Neale Hurston, written for the NAACP's *The New Crisis* magazine. Like many Zoraphiles, Cobb found himself surprised and disturbed by Hurston's conservative politics. Cobb's exploration of Hurston's politics left him at a loss to find common ground between many of Hurston's ideas and his own. He reconciled the matter by concluding, "Icons are neat, but humans are famously messy." If we think of icons as human beings, he expounded, "we can better appreciate their talents in the context of their contradictions or shortcomings."[30] But if we probe Hurston further, we might see that perceived shortcomings reveal her acute farsightedness and apparent contradictions tend to dissolve.

COLLECTIVE WISDOM

In *Wrapped in Rainbows*, Valerie Boyd wrote that "death was not the end for Zora Neale Hurston. Instead, it was a new beginning—of her life as an ancestor, as a spirit."[31] The following interviews attest to the truth of Boyd's words. As Alice Walker put it, we love Hurston for her work and for herself.[32] Her works have taught and inspired us. The soft, yet poignant words and phrases of her novels wash over us and leave us awed. The stories and the tales she collected make us laugh, cry, and think, and leave us pleasantly astonished by our own collective wisdom. The work speaks of the woman. Then we are hushed. We find it impossible to imagine such a woman—brilliant, magical, vital, and bold. So we settle for knowing as much of the facts about her life as we can uncover.

But the facts can only tell us *about* the life that took form as Zora Neale Hurston. The essential Zora defies knowing in any factual sense, because the essence of life itself is ever the mystery. The spirit that vitalized Zora Hurston in life and compelled her to extraordinary achievement is as vital in "death." In traditional African society, the physical and spiritual realms are not separate. The departed continues to live in the spirit realm, yet remains part of the family and is aware of and takes interest in what goes on in the family. "They are the guardians of family affairs, traditions, ethics and activities."[33]

Just as the departed inquire about family matters and warn against impending dangers, so, too, do the living approach the departed for advice, instruction, and even blessings. Before she undertook the writing of Hurston's biography, for example, Valerie Boyd visited Hurston's gravesite and inquired:

I have come to this cemetery at the dead-end of North 17th Street to ask the novelist and anthropologist for her permission to write a book about her life.

From what I understand, Zora was that kind of woman. The kind you had to ask before you acted on her behalf. The kind you couldn't be too presumptuous about.

Still, despite a healthy respect for my ancestors, I am not in the habit of talking to the dead. But something about Zora remains vibrantly alive—and that living spirit has called me here on this day, some 40 years after her death.[34]

Zora Neale Hurston was and is that kind of woman and, as an ancestral spirit, she inspires, instructs, and guides those who are open to her presence and her magic. Certain natural phenomena cannot be known directly, but rather can be understood indirectly by virtue of the affects of their presence. In some sense, Zora Neale Hurston's life is like this. Even with all the facts that scholars have so carefully gathered, one still feels at a loss to grasp the essential Zora. Yet, through the fresh and engaging words of those who speak here, we can enhance our appreciation of this phenomenal woman.

THE ESSENTIAL ZORA

Lucy Hurston is the daughter of Everett Hurston, Hurston's youngest brother, and the niece of Zora Neale Hurston. She is Chair of the Sociology Department at Manchester Community College.

DP: Would you tell us about Hurston, about your own life in relationship to Hurston, and your life as a writer. But first, who is Zora Neale Hurston for you?

LH: Zora Neale Hurston is and has been the inspiration for the way that I have lived my life for the last couple of decades. The person who inspired me to go to college at the very untraditional age of thirty-one. Not return to college but go to college at thirty-one and complete my Associate's degree at Manchester Community College, my Bachelor's at Central Connecticut State, my Master's degree at Ohio State University. And for a brief while to pursue my doctorate at the University of Massachusetts at Amherst. She was the person who told me that social life and behavior among groups is important to study, to examine, and to expose.

DP: Exactly what about Hurston, or what circumstances in your own life made you decide to attend college.

LH: I had started writing some short stories. And I decided that if they were to be taken seriously that I would need to have some kind of credentials. So I went to the community college to take some composition courses by way of acquiring the credentials I would need, since I wanted to present my writing to a broader audience. At the same time that I sought admission, I was told that there was funding available for me to become a full-time college student. The counselors encouraged me to take advantage of this opportunity. And, initially, I resisted. I understood the value of funding at the college level, and I felt that those funds shouldn't be wasted on me. They should be awarded to a more traditional student who had more of his or her life ahead of them. The counselors disagreed with me and encouraged me to just try it. And so I signed up against my better judgment. I signed up full time and enrolled in five courses my first semester of college at the age of thirty-one, was in the middle of a divorce with two kids, and everything else. But I finished my first semester of five courses on the president's list. Five courses and I maintained a 4.0. I continued my college career for the next ten years. And for ten years I had a 4.0. I joined about seven honor societies: Alpha Nu Gamma, Kappa Alpha Delta, a number of honor societies over the course of my time.

DP: Are you still writing short stories? Have any been published?

LH: I published some, and I continue to write them. I just always feel like there's a story weld up in me with some measure of gravity that is just screaming to get out. Short stories encapsulated that need to go out now and longer, bigger stories that need to go out and there's a novel that I'm working on. I am about three and a half chapters completed with my novel. But in the meantime, while I am working on that, I've got these short stories that just need to get out.

DP: Can you share for us a little bit about the novel that you are working on?

LH: I have tentatively titled the novel "Pressed with Fullness." It's a story about a black woman with a son who is by herself. She owns a travel company and a quasi-formal research company. She frequents the Caribbean where she has two love interests. At the same time, she is challenged with attempting to teach her son, from a feminist perspective, how to be a young black man. I have already published my first book, so I understand more about how the publishing world works, and I know that that title will be changed.

DP: When do you anticipate being complete with your novel?

LH: You know, its spring 2005, right? I would like to see this year close with the completion of what's necessary for this volume to be done. So I would like to see the end of 2005 close with this. I just have so much else going on and so many irons in the fire. I hoped that this would be done by Christmas of 2004. And that hasn't happened. So hopefully within the next nine months to a year.

DP: The book you have completed is *Speak So You Can Speak Again*. This is a compilation of Zora Neale Hurston memorabilia, a CD, poetry, and more. What inspired you to do this?

LH: From start to finish, I wanted to capture the family's perspective. And I think we just felt that there was so much academic examination of

Zora's life, valid academic examinations, that, for the first time, the family ought to contribute to that discussion. And so through my volume, I interviewed other living family members who knew Zora and added to that physical memorabilia that my father left me about Zora. And then the vocal contribution of Zora to put together in this one volume this unique perspective, this intimate personal hands-on perspective of Zora. For the people who know her, this gives a unique take on her life. For those people who don't know her, it's a wonderful primer and introduction to who she was and all that she offers up as an examination of African American culture. And I think that since I was a young girl, this was the mission that my father set me on by virtue of his leaving me all of her material and cultural artifacts. And so it was a way for me to share with the rest of the world what I was fortunate enough to inherit from my father and the family—the understanding of who Zora was as a woman, as an anthropologist, as a novelist, as a folklorist, as an African American woman who descended from slaves. It was a way for me to share the material elements of her culture with another generation of people interested in African American history.

DP: *Speak So You Can Speak Again*. Tell us about that title.

LH: You know, it was the idea that Zora spoke to and about Afro-American culture through the way she did her work, by what she chose to examine, methodologically how she chose to examine it, geographically how she chose to examine it. So she was speaking at that time mostly to deaf ears. But a reexamination of her work in the 1960s and 1970s after her demise gave rise to her cause; to continue to pump that theme some thirty years later gives me pause. But the baton sits firmly in my hand. And I know she speaks to me as does my father through these venues so I know I have an obligation to speak not just for her but through her. And a reexamination of her work allows us as a people to speak again about our place in this venue. We know now much more about her work than we did during the time she was alive. So a reexamination of her work, through the material I compiled to have published allows her, some forty-five years after her death, to speak again. There is now data available to social scientists in general and anthropologists in particular who are able to examine specific areas of the African American experience on this continent as a result of work that she did in the 1930s and 1940s. We have that opportunity now, thanks to her efforts. We did not know enough to appreciate her efforts during her lifetime. So she does get to speak again.

DP: You wrote a story about your father and all of this material that he had for you. What is the title of that short story?

LH: "Dad and Luch." And Luch is the nickname that my father had for me. I was named after my grandmother Lucy Ann Potts. My father said he named me after her because he knew I would have something special to do in life. And the short story "Dad and Luch" is an understanding of the relationship between me and my father, his link to Zora, and the way that he passed on that link to me by giving me the boxes of the material that were left in the attic of our home in Brooklyn, New York. The story describes his demise, how he became the guardian of the family's heritage, and how he passed that baton specifically on to me. So it was a wonderful short story that showed my relationship not just to my father but to my aunt, and the perpetuation of the Hurston legacy.

DP: Your dad left you all this material and passed it on to you. But before his demise, you would go to the attic and go through the material and you'd get in trouble for it. What made you go into the attic knowing you were still going to get in trouble?

LH: I don't think I so much went to the attic as I was called to the attic. I'd like to think that Zora spoke to me. I was three at the time Zora died and even though I am named after her mother, my grandmother, everything felt like it had a connection. By eight, nine years old, I knew there was something up there for me. And it was at about nine years of age that I was hauntingly called to the attic. And I would go through all of these papers and books and photographs, and I found comfort there. If you want to look for the initial response to a spiritual calling, that's where it was. I don't know what made me different from my siblings. I have two sisters and a brother. I don't know what made me different, but I knew from as far as I can remember time, that I was different. I was always on the outside looking in at this undefined thing going on in my family with my mother, my father, my siblings. I was always on the outside looking in until I found Zora. And then there was this feeling that there was somebody else on the outside with me looking in. I found peace in that. I found comfort. I found validation in the fact that there was somebody else outside that box with me looking in. And I think that's when spiritually Zora and I joined forces. And it took probably another twenty years before I could frame it in any kind of way. But that's its origin. That's where it started.

DP: In what ways, in terms of your life and your literary work, do you see yourself similar to and different from your aunt?

LH: I am forever humbled by the fact that people link me to Zora. I feel a major responsibility in that my father, through Zora, has passed the baton to me. And I am humbled by the fact that my father felt I somehow could take that challenge. It makes me approach writing with major trepidation in every task that I do. Whether I am writing about Zora, whether I am writing about my family and my siblings, or whether I am writing in an academic venue as a sociologist, it gives me pause. It makes me very leery because I understand the major contribution of my aunt. Zora is a hard act to follow. And, as the closest living blood and genetic relative to her, to be the person that spearheads the cause and the champion of her accolades makes me feel full. But it also weighs heavy because I have the obligation not to break the link.

DP: You are a participant in the first annual Fort Pierce ZoraFest. Tell us about your coming to Fort Pierce.

LH: It was a spiritual homecoming. There was some reason that the connection was made, the invitation was offered, and accepted. It is truly this spiritual homecoming. Zora is here. I think what happened here, in Fort Pierce, at Lincoln Park Academy is more a spiritual bonding with what Zora was about, and what resonates of her as she left this physical earth exists in the formation of this festival more than any other in North America right now. It's just all the pieces of it fitted together more so than anything else I've been involved with in my adult life. The people that were here, Valerie Boyd, Stetson Kennedy. Everybody that's been here gives more of a fit in the connection than anything else I've been involved in as a Hurston in my adult life.... Her spirit is here.

DP: How does she live? How do you see Zora present to us today?

LH: I'll give you two ways—in how I see her in me and how I see her beyond me. Zora has the audacity to continue to interrupt and direct my life. And it's out of respect for who Zora was that I allow her to do so. It's as if I have an angel. I allow her to interrupt and direct my life and guide me to places like Fort Pierce. And then, too, Zora finds ways to stick her big toe into other places; she refuses to let others forget her. She continues to reinforce to us the importance of the contributions that she made as a trained anthropologist in our literature, in our folklore, in our fiction, in every other kind of way, even though she transforms it and makes a big Halle Barry on ABC, it keeps the conversation alive. The pros, the cons, the good, the bad, she stays in the forefront; much as she did alive, she does it now, she just won't go away.

DP: What about Hurston do you want people to know and remember?

LH: If there is anything that I want people to take away with them about Zora is that she would not and does not conform; that she shaped and framed who she was, what was important, and how she was going to participate and contribute to our understanding of African American life; that we were a viable and important contribution to an understanding of American social life; and that was not to be diminished, overlooked, or undervalued. She maintains that mission via the current reevaluation of her work.

DP: Being her niece, a sociologist, and writer, what do *you* want to say to people? What do you want to impress on this generation and generations to come?

LH: As a sociologist, I would like people to appreciate what was, what is, and what can be—an understanding of the concept that there is more than one way of being and doing in this world. An expansion of an appreciation for the diversity of ways of being, be they along color lines, gender lines, be it about same-sex, interracial, or interfaith marriage, other ways of being and doing in communities of existence. And we don't have to convert or agree, but we must respect ways of being as social groups and we must respect the life of people.

Zora Neale Hurston's work began to receive renewed critical attention in the 1970s. Her reputation grew within the academy, but everyday folks, the ones she wrote about, knew very little about her. Even in her home state of Florida, few had even heard the name of Zora Neale Hurston. The Florida Humanities Council has supported sundry events, programs, seminars, performances, and festivals that have made the Florida public more aware of and knowledgeable about Zora Neale Hurston. Susan Lockwood, director of the Florida Humanities Council, is committed to continuing the Council's efforts in educating the public about Hurston and celebrating her life and achievements.

DP: What is the origin of the Florida Humanities Council (FHC)?

SL: FHC was established as one of the first state humanities councils by Congress through an appropriation to the National Endowment for the Humanities. We are a state affiliate of the NEH.

DP: What is the general purpose of the Council?

SL: To create a bridge between the academy and the general public and bring the humanities disciplines and research to the citizens of the state.

DP: How does the Council's focus on Zora Neale Hurston reflect its purpose?

SL: Our Council's Board focuses on Florida. Zora is part of the cultural heritage of the state and serves as a vehicle to learn about Florida history, literature, folklore, and more.

DP: What events, programs, and/or publications describe the Council's activities in relation to Zora Neale Hurston?

SL: FHC was the first funder of the Hurston Festival in Eatonville. There have been numerous grants funded—the most notable is the Hurston Heritage Trail in Fort Pierce. Several articles in the *Forum* magazine (the first in 1990) treat various aspects of her legacy. The Chautauqua presentations, through small grants and council-conducted programs, bring Zora, "in person" to scores of communities throughout the state. Many of the FCT programs for teachers include Zora via the Chautauqua presentation or through literary considerations of her writings.

DP: What individuals or audiences or communities do these programs target, both in terms of those who provide the programs, and those for whom they are provided?

SL: This would parallel the same audiences/communities generally targeted by FHC programs—Florida nonprofit organizations that are the delivery mechanisms for humanities programs and then Floridians, either full-time or part-time residents. Underserved audiences, teachers, and decision makers are of particular interest.

DP: What is the Council's objective in reaching audiences or communities targeted, that is, what does the Council want audiences to get from events and programs provided?

SL: Knowledge of Zora, the person, and her compelling story and then an understanding and appreciation of the Florida in which she lived. Like many cultural legacies of Florida, few people in the state know or appreciate her or her work.

DP: What characterizes the response of audiences and by what means does the Council measure or determine audience response?

SL: [Phyllis] McEwen "as Zora" is one of the most frequently requested of the Chautauqua programs. Audiences rave about her portrayals on evaluation forms. Teachers who attended the workshop which used *Their Eyes Were Watching God* as a text, returned to their classrooms ready to implement it with students.

DP: Will the Council develop future programs that focus on Zora Neale Hurston? If so, why so? What motivates the continued focus on Hurston?

SL: FHC is currently developing a proposal to NEH that, if funded, will bring teachers from around the country to Eatonville in the summer for a week-long seminar on Hurston. Several Board members have suggested a statewide FHC project which focuses on Hurston.

Phyllis P. McEwen describes herself as a Chautauqua-style actress-scholar. She is also an educator, former librarian, and poet. She has traversed the state of Florida regaling audiences with her performance as Zora Neale Hurston.

DP: Can you begin by telling us what is a Chautauqua actress-scholar?

PM: Sure. The Chautauqua descriptive indicates that it is not just acting, and then the acting descriptive indicates that it is not just a scholar. It's a tradition that comes from the nineteenth century. It was started in Chautauqua, New York. The word Chautauqua is a Seneca word that really means beautiful lake … foggy lake. Back in the late nineteenth century, people initiated a cultural movement that would supplement public education because public education was just not that good. So they instituted lyceums and Sunday schools and Friday schools and they conducted them on these big, beautiful lakes, where the people would gather on a Saturday or Sunday afternoon and have scholars talk about the issues of the day. There was not a whole lot of radio and, of course, the silent pictures were just beginning. People just didn't have all the communication mediums that we have now. So it was a big deal. They created whole festivals around them. The biggest one, the one that is believed to have ignited the movement began in Chautauqua, New York, out on Lake Chautauqua.

DP: What characters would be portrayed?

PM: In the beginning, the purest form of Chautauqua was not really centered around characters, but around scholars who had knowledge on a particular subject. Sometimes musicians were featured. But it has evolved into mainly presentations of characters that people are interested in, and that is mainly determined by the preferences of the people in a particular geographic area. Florida has had Chautauqua for quite a long time ... and that's mainly for topics that are of interest to Floridians.

DP: Speaking of Florida historical characters, what characters have you portrayed?

PM: I've only portrayed Zora Neale Hurston and it's *enough* for *me*. Some people portray several characters, but I *only* do Zora Neale Hurston.

DP: Is that a *choice*?

PM: Well, I looked at doing some other characters and none of them seemed to be of interest or fitting. Then I realized that I had so many requests to do Hurston that I really didn't have room for another one in my head. I mean I couldn't think of anybody people would want to hear more than Zora Neale Hurston, really. And I've thought of others, but it just didn't feel right. She is so complicated, and there's so much about her and she is so misunderstood that it keeps me working, just to deal with her. It's like dealing with three or four other characters 'cause she has all these different careers and all these different aspects. So, I think I'm sticking with Hurston.

DP: How long have you been portraying Hurston?

PM: Almost seventeen years now.

DP: When did you begin?

PM: I think the very first performance I ever did was at the Columbia Restaurant in Ybor City and it was at a Board of Trustees meeting of the Florida Humanities Council. They had funded me to do this presentation and to get the costume and to do the research I needed. Then there was an anniversary of the Chautauqua in West Florida, so the Council put together a cast of characters and we started traveling. My first *major* presentation of Hurston was either in Arcadia, which has a traditional Chautauqua, or it was in Depuniac, where the big, original Florida Chautauqua is held. I was with Osceola, Claude Pepper, Bartolomeo de las Casas, you know, that Spanish priest who played a role in the killing of the Indians then the enslavement of Africans. And there was an actor portraying Harriet Beecher Stowe—who lived in Mandarin, Florida, for a brief time. Zora did not care for that priest (nor the actor that portrayed him). But Zora had connections with Claude Pepper, of course. She had written some things that mentioned Osceola, and they were fascinated with each other. She had mentioned Harriet Beecher Stowe, as well. So, when we had improvisational moments, it was a lot of fun for Osceola and Zora to get together and frighten Harriet Beecher Stowe. Of course, Zora was real mad at Claude Pepper; and she called him "Claude Peppercorn." But he was quite a gentleman, and they had a good time together.

DP: When was that?

PM: It was 1990 when we toured. That was the only time I had been a part of a large group of Florida characters like that. It was fun... and Zora *stood* out.

DP: What is the exchange like when the audience interacts with the Hurston personality? What is it that people are interested in, or concerned about?

PM: Well, there's a whole range of things that may happen at a Chautauqua. Now, we do them at libraries, museums, and churches, all over. I do a lot of Zora solo, but I also sometimes perform with two other actors who perform the characters of Harlem Renaissance figures James Weldon Johnson and Langston Hughes.... So, it kind of varies with the intent of what you're doing and whether the people really know who Zora Neale Hurston is. In some places, such as Miami or Fort Lauderdale, audiences are well informed and have read *everything* by Hurston. They really have a dialogue with her and challenge her. They don't just ask *general* questions. They want to engage her. For instance, they might ask: "Why did you have to kill Tea Cake?" "Where can we find your lost novels?" "Why didn't you think all the people in Eatonville wouldn't be angry about all the stories you wrote about them?" "Didn't you think that they... ?" You know, so... they really engage. Some have personal questions, for instance: "Why didn't you stay married to one person?" People often ask, "What inspired you, despite how hard your life had been at certain parts?" "How did you get past all the obstacles?" Because people are really inspired by her, even though a lot of people don't realize that her life wasn't the tragic story that it has been made out to be. General consensus has been that Zora Neale Hurston had a horrible, tragic life, and yet she was this genius. Well, that's changing now, especially since Valerie Boyd's book. So I get less and less of that. A lot of people ask about her titles, like *Their Eyes Were Watching God*, which is a good question to ask Zora. They ask a lot about race relations and they are really, really interested in why she opposed school desegregation.

DP: If you can recall, what *is* her response to what inspired her?

PM: If I'm portraying her during the WPA [Work Projects Administration] years—it varies with the time period—but usually, I ask her about it and she'll come out with something about her mother. And being that her mother left her so young, she held onto those words she gave her about "jumpin' at the sun." And that "jumpin' at the sun" is something that audiences really like to hear because that's out there in the public.

And then, there's always a lot about being in a town where you're not the other, where you have this beautiful time in your life when everything is self-sufficient and you're not on the other side somewhere looking out and having a chance to have your imagination and be in nature and that kind of thing. And then, of course, the inside journey that Hurston had was probably the biggest inspiration: that she was a genius and she was in touch with her spirituality and she knew what she came here to do from the time when she was really, really young, according to everything that I can tell. So, it's usually based in that. And she'll mention mentors along the way, carry on about Ms. Osgood Mason, if we're doing the Harlem Renaissance, but usually, you know, it's something about her formative years.

DP: What has it been like for you in portraying *the* Zora Neale Hurston for seventeen years?

PM: There have been times in my life when that's all I've done. You know, I've been a librarian and a poet and all kind of other things in between. But there have been periods of time when all I do is portray her. It's been like working for Zora Neale Hurston. Like going out and being an ambassador about her and her life and dealing with misconceptions, sometimes. I see there's a lot of love for her. A lot of times, people get confused and ask me to sign books.

DP: In her name?

PM: Yeah, and I always say, I love Zora. But sorry, 'cause I don't want her to be upset with me. If I do her character just right, and I'm present with the audience, they are so excited about having a genius like Zora Neale Hurston in their presence, and they'll run out and want to get all the books, if there are books available. If it's a library, they check them out immediately. If they can buy them, they buy all the books. I have seen the public opinion of Zora go from a sort of curiosity about some kind of a "wild woman" to a certain level of respect. Still there is some confusion, but I have really seen the respect grow from 1990 or so, from comments like, "You know how she was, even though she did this and this and this." But now her name is really out there, the festivals, and of course, Oprah's movie. So now people are beginning to accept that this is a really, really important person that was here.

DP: During your performances do you ever talk about the fact that as a *scholar* who was a genius, that she was also *Doctor* Hurston? I hear you use that title from time to time.

PM: That happened around 1948 or 1949, something like that. Morgan had bestowed an honorary doctorate upon her. If I am portraying Zora after that time, I'll include that. But, of course, I've given her an honorary doctorate for her whole *life*. She *came* here with one.... I would like to develop my presentation to deal with her more as the scientist that she was, focus more on the anthropology. Because that's just an aspect of her that I haven't fully dealt with. That and the erotic and bawdy side. I think that's something that would be really interesting. Some of the stuff was really rough and I usually don't include it because the audiences are usually mixed. If people come and are ready to hear about the things they do to the virgin before they get married or they get to hear the *whole* song of Uncle Bud, I think that would be something interesting as well. I also want to do a performance focusing on her storytelling skills, too. To round out my portrayal of Zora. A lot of my early work was mainly based on biography, which is not really the best way to deal with a character in a humanities program, because you need to deal with humanities issues. But there was so much confusion about Hurston's life until lately. You know, Valerie Boyd's book, I think, has really done a lot. But people had so many misunderstandings about her.

DP: Such as?

PM: Well, you know, this idea about her being this tragic figure. If she was so smart, why was she interred in an unmarked grave and forgotten? A lot of questions about the morals charges made against her later in life. "The Lost Years"—*what* was she doing as a young girl? All these kinds of things.... But, for whatever reason, things are rounding out. People are not as concerned about these questions. And, of course, the womanist writers, like you and Valerie have been filling in some; it's not filling in the blanks so much as *giving respect*. There's so much *disrespect* of women's lives and a lot of the questions and a lot of the "maybe this and maybe that" were disrespectful and misogynistic about Hurston; you know, all the questions about her romantic life, her sexual life, her financial life, a lot are based on that and I think writers like you have been—I don't know what the word is— deconstructing some of that whole idea that "a scribbling woman got something wrong with her anyway." I feel that dissipating. I like that.

DP: So what inspired you to take on this *ambassadorship*?

PM: Well, the Humanities Council asked me whether I could assume the personage of a historical African American woman for Florida history. They asked me to try Mary MacLeod Bethune, but the fit wasn't right. But when I tried the character of Zora Neale Hurston, I felt transported into being with Hurston, and it would feel right. I felt that my performance was received fairly well and that I did right by Zora Neale Hurston. I had a lot of personal feelings about Hurston that you all have *said* in your books, that I have just *thought*. You know, how could a woman write a book like this and be all these crazy things people say about her? That doesn't go together. How could a woman do some of the things she wrote about in her autobiography—whether they actually matched the facts or not—[they] didn't match the images projected onto her. I remember the first time Stetson Kennedy saw me do Zora, he pulled me aside and said, "She wasn't that happy and that... giddy." He said, "she had a miserable life." You know, I thought, "well, for a second, he touts himself as somebody that has *worked* with her, and maybe she did it like that *at work*. You know what I mean, he just *worked* with her, so ... And I had a feeling about *that*. And it was a *strong*, intuitive feeling that I *follow*. And I was so pleased when you all published research that matched what I had just intuited. You all have scientifically researched it and analyzed it and you come up with that and I have feelings like that about her. So I would like to think she anoints me with it. We don't know about that, but it really feels right and when I hear criticism about my portrayal of Hurston, I try to look at it and deal with it for what it is because I really feel like it's something that I'm supposed to do. And obviously, it was, because I have done it for so long.

DP: What kind of "negative" criticisms have people made of the portrayal?

PM: Kennedy said it was too happy. Some people say I don't look like her because of my skin color. Hurston has talked about how she looks different to different people. So, she has that quality. And I tell them, "I'm not impersonating her, I just want to give you an experience of her." Some insist that she was some rude woman. I have had arguments onstage about that woman with the straw hat and I *knew* that wasn't Zora. When Valerie said that wasn't her.... I had been telling people this all along. If you know anything about Zora Neale Hurston, you would know that picture was not an image of Zora ... all that bagginess and the style is different. Those people would claim, "Oh you just want to have this idealistic view of her." And I said, "She's an *ideal* woman. You know, that's why it seems so great because *this* is a *great* woman: she's beautiful, she's foxy, she's brilliant, she got *around* and had fun. She just did and that's just the way it is. I can't help it if I'm portraying a fabulous *woman*.

DP: What's the thing you *most* want people to really *get* about her?

PM: Well, it used to be what a great person she is. But I found that there is something deeper. I want people to start talking about her to other people or start talking about the things that are important to Hurston. Once I did the whole Zora Neale Hurston performance as a WPA worker in Hawthorne and I focused on the history of the WPA and the way the government can come in and actually create programs that help people. People started asking me, "Where is this WPA 'cause we need to enroll in this?" and "Does the WPA know about Katrina?" You know, all that kind of stuff. And they started saying, "Why *don't* we have this in government, what has *changed*?" I like it when *issues* come up and I can use Zora Neale Hurston's life *as a vehicle*. So, I want to *continue* the fact that this is a genius that was among us and we have a lot of her work. But I also want to *use* this brilliant character to have people engage in dialogues about school desegregation: Was she right or wrong? When we do the Harlem Renaissance, was it a *successful* movement? Did a New Negro *really* emerge? And where are these New Negroes now? Who are the New Negroes? Just more humanities-oriented questions.

DP: I know that Hurston's character has inspired what you do. Does that inspiration transfer into your everyday life? And if so, how?

PM: Yes, it does. I feel that her *courage* to do things when the resources didn't look like they were there and when she had to make decisions that wouldn't match popular opinion and she made them anyway. Like her *Orlando Sentinel* letter about school desegregation. That courage to be true to yourself, that integrity is something I try to work with, like when I get really scared, I think, well, you know, Zora Neale Hurston didn't even have the twenty-first century on her side, or the twentieth century, much. They were going through so much violence. I mean, we go through all of that today, too. She did things that would be *easy* for me to do now, and she *did* them then. So, I like that. When people don't *understand*, and you really think you have something that's *brilliant*, the way she handled *that* is something that I liked. I think people had not a clue about a lot of things she was saying and doing. Not that it stopped her from putting it out there. When they weren't received, well, she went on to the next thing. It was almost like, "This is here for y'all when you're ready for it." You know? I've experienced that a little bit in some ways and it's *inspiring* to look at the way she does that. And the *energy* she had with all her output: That's something I'm looking at now. "Don't keep it in. Put it out there."

In the spring of 2008, Eatonville will host its nineteenth annual Zora Neale Hurston Festival of the Arts. N. Y. Nathiri first organized the festival as an integral part of the efforts of the Association to Preserve the Eatonville Community, Inc. (PEC) to have Eatonville, Hurston's hometown, commemorated as an historic community. In 1987, Eatonville celebrated 100 years of existence, "the oldest incorporated Black municipality in the United States." The Festival supports the goals of the PEC as it continues the legacy of Zora Neale Hurston in making known to the world the "greatest cultural wealth on the continent."

In the spring of 2005, Fort Pierce hosted its first, annual ZoraFest. Hurston's sun set in Fort Pierce, Florida, which is also the place of her burial. Fort Pierce was a safe harbor for Zora Neale Hurston, and her life, in turn, has inspired Fort Pierce in its own celebration of the author and of the people, the history, and the culture of Fort Pierce. Jack Connolly is a member of the Board of Cultural Affairs Council for St. Lucie County. He also is a member of the committee for ZoraFest.

DP: What generated the idea for the festival? What occurred or transpired that had Fort Pierce decide to create ZoraFest?

JC: When we learned who Zora Neale Hurston was and that she was buried here, that she lived here, we were looking for a way in which to celebrate Hurston while, at the same time, presenting Fort Pierce in a historic light. There are many people here who knew her, and we found that we have a treasure trove of information about her. She was dubbed the "Genius of the South," the "Literary and Cultural Genius of the South." And as a result, we decided to go ahead with ZoraFest. The first year we put it on, we called it the homecoming. We had many fine guest speakers, among whom, Dr. Plant, you were one. We have been going ever since. Initially, the festival was held over a two-day period. Four to five hundred people attended. Last year, we held the festival for four days, with about 4,000 people in attendance. This year, we are expanding to an entire week. We are confident that the number of people in attendance will increase as well. Word of mouth is a wonderful thing. It's a major means of spreading the word about the festival. "You have got to get to the Zora Festival" is the byword of those heading the advertising committee.

DP: ZoraFest, then, also brings recognition to the historic culture of Fort Pierce?

JC: That is part of it. But Zora is the main event. Our research revealed to us what a wonderful literary person she was. In addition, there was her anthropological work and theatrical productions, and in fact, she was considered the queen of the Harlem Renaissance. We, little by little, began to see how great she was. So we acted upon those things.

  We tried to get in touch with people in Notasulga, Alabama, where she was born. We called there to see if we could possibly get that group to join us since Notasulga was Hurston's actual birthplace and Fort Piece was the place where she last worked and where she passed. There is a Zora Neale Hurston Festival in Eatonville where she spent her youth. Then she moved with her brother up to another part of Florida. After acquiring more education, she moved up to New York.

DP: What response did you get from Notasulga, Alabama?

JC: Well, we called the mayor of Notasulga. And she was very interested, but no collaborations materialized.... Perhaps in the future we can have more involved collaboration with the people in Alabama. So we have continued on with this worthy thing. So basically we tried to focus on Zora's contributions to Fort Pierce. But, then, we can't have the end of Zora's life without going to the middle and beginning.

  She is beginning to be very well known. Almost every college teaches something about her. The governor declared the month of April, I believe it was in 2004, as national reading month, and he suggested a book to be read. That book was *Their Eyes Were Watching God* by Zora Neale Hurston. I went to a library where I live, and I noticed a poster with Oprah Winfrey on it. She had a copy of *Their Eyes Were Watching God*, in the original edition, and the poster was dated 1988. She was touting the book then. And I think a lot of people possibly had not even heard of Zora Neale Hurston at that time. But now she has come round to the fore where she belongs. She will only get bigger because she is what she is. Now she's just become more famous for what she has done.

DP: What impact do you see the festival having in Fort Pierce?

JC: I'll start with the schools. We have worked with the school system of Port St. Lucie County to include a children's program as a concurrent part of ZoraFest. During the school year, we have a writing contest, poetry. This year we also plan an art contest. The students' work will be awarded prizes. The winners of the first prizes will have an opportunity to either read or have someone else read their winning piece of literature about Zora. I anticipate, this year, seeing what kind of music will be presented because Zora did love music. I'd like very much for us to create a song or jingle. When I say "us," I mean people in general. If we had done something like that in the past, I think that children would be singing it and humming it today just like they do jingles from television or the radio.

   We had a party for her on January 7 at the library that is dedicated to her—the Zora Neale Hurston Library in Fort Pierce. I think that it meant more to the children who began to realize or ask who she was and what she was. And they really began to think in terms of Zora, what she had done. And of course, Zora did write children's books, so she was involved a great deal in literature on all levels and all ages. And I know we're going to do that again. We're going to do it this year on January 6 and 7. We're going to have another birthday party for her. I intend to form a committee of young people who will suggest certain things they'd like to see done. And, I believe if we involve the children with something like this in the beginning, they will be prone to participate in the ZoraFest on their own volition. We will have many activities for them—writing, various arts and craft, face painting. The usual things you would find at a street fair, but always indicative of Zora. I don't think that in this day and age we would want to lose sight of the fact that this is *a Zora Neale Hurston festival*.

DP: Tell me about the Heritage Trail.

JC: The Heritage Trail was a concept of Jon Ward, who was the executive director of Cultural Affairs for St. Lucie County. The Heritage Trail is in Fort Pierce and it marks the places in which Zora Neale Hurston lived and worked while in Fort Pierce: *The Chronicle*—the newspaper; the school—Lincoln Park Academy, where she taught; the house which was given to her to live in by Dr. Benton who was a prominent physician in the town and whose children still live here. Actually one of them, Attorney Margaret Benton, is in charge of the Martin Luther King, Jr., Foundation for this area, and the other sister, Arlena Benton Lee, is on the ZoraFest Committee. She organizes all the ground transportation and accommodations for guest participants. There involvement is a major contribution. They bring a lot of valuable ideas and attract a lot of people to the festival. We have people here in town who still remember her when they had her as a substitute teacher. In fact, one of them constantly tells me this one thing they well remember about Zora—her hats and the fact that whenever it was quiet time in the classroom she was writing, writing, writing. She was constantly reading to the children, and as she read, she was very dramatic in the way she read. And as one of them put it, they never really knew who she was, what background she had come from. By then she had been part of the Harlem Renaissance, which had ended. But no one *really* knew who she was, just that there was something special about her. Because now they do know and they are very happy, but a little sad that they didn't know then. But then Zora might have been a private person who didn't want people to make a big fuss about her anyway.

DP: You earlier mentioned that the Heritage Trail had won an award.

JC: We won the award given by the Florida Redevelopment Association. And it recognizes our work for the "Zora Neale Hurston Dust Tracks Heritage Trail." The trail marks those places associated with Hurston's life and legacy. Places also like the Backus House. We had a famous artist here [Beanie Backus]. And he loved jazz as did Zora. And they would frequently get together at his home to listen to jazz. We tried to incorporate all these things that mean something in relation to Zora, into ZoraFest.

   After the Harlem Renaissance ended, Zora came back to her roots here in Florida. And from what I learned about her, you can't help but want to honor the person, so from my point of view, I am very glad she did come back. When I got settled down here, I learned more about her. Here we are today.

DP: Who is she for you, Jack?

JC: It's a difficult question. I find myself at times going over to the grave to see that everything is being taken care of nicely around the grave and literally talking to her, asking her questions like I expect her to answer me. And I have to admit, once in a while, I feel I have to ask her certain things. Like at the birthday party, I came over to suggest what we were going to do and I hoped she didn't object to it. When we had the actual street fest and when it was all over, I actually went over to ask if she was pleased with us. I don't know what she is to me, but she is so much to me. It's hard to put it into words. I guess I never thought about it. I mean she is there and I go there. And I enjoy being in a place where I feel her spirit. I always feel something special about being alive during the time she was alive. I was living in New York in the 1950s and 1960s. She passed in 1960, but I didn't know that at the time. So sometimes I think, wow, I *could* have met and known this wonderful person. But that didn't occur, and I'm sorry I did not have that opportunity.

DP: Nonetheless, it seems as though there is still a connection.

JC: I feel that if she were alive today I would definitely seek her and hope she would be my friend. I would enjoy being a friend of hers. I would listen to what she had to say and learn from what she had done.... There are a couple of things I'm curious about, that I would like to ask questions about.

DP: What are they?

JC: They are really Zora questions. I am interested in knowing certain parts of her life that seem to have been skipped over because no one knows anything about them, and I would like to know what she was doing during those times. I know some people say she had a very positive attitude about things. She did not believe in retribution. She believed in getting on with it. But no matter what, a person is a person; they're human. And once in a while you have to have your negative feelings. I'd be interested in knowing if there is anything she would have changed that she did or things that she wished she could have done but didn't. But that's kind of difficult because there are so many things she did with her life. It's hard to believe one person could accomplish so much in one life. I guess she didn't have time for regrets. But I know one thing, I would be careful where I walked. I wouldn't want to walk on her garden because that was one thing she loved. Whether it was a window box in the city of New York or a garden outside her modest home or wherever, that's one thing she had. In fact in a letter she wrote to someone, she said, and I am paraphrasing here: "I now know I am home because I just planted a garden today. Can you picture me without a garden?" And its true. As modest as it may have been, she would not be without her little garden growth. From seeds to full bloom, it was Zora.

Alice Jackson is a librarian at the Zora Neale Hurston Branch Library in Fort Pierce.

AJ: I am the Assistant Branch Supervisor and Children's Librarian here at the Zora Neale Hurston Branch Library. We have been in existence since 1991. So we have been here for sixteen years. I have been here since it first began. We first started in a little mobile truck. We needed to put a library in the northwest section of town. And we had converted a book mobile that used to go around town. We would set it up at the Goodwill Presbyterian Church with children's books, adult books, lots of paperbacks, and we sat it there to see what kind of response we would get. We served patrons out of this mobile truck for almost five years.

    The land that we built the branch on was donated to us by the Friends of the St. Lucie County Library System. So it was Friends that donated the land. A combination of state funds and county funds built the facility itself.

DP: How did this library become the Zora Neale Hurston Branch Library?

AJ: In the late 1970s, 1980s there was this big revitalization of Zora Hurston. Everybody was all excited about Zora. Since Alice Walker had come into town and found the grave, and had it marked, people began to get this interest in Zora.… We began researching old newspapers— *The Chronicle* where she used to work. We started looking at these things, trying to find out who was this Zora Hurston. People began to talk more about her. They started to bring more articles to us, from Atlanta, Miami, Tampa, anywhere there was something written about Zora. They were bringing this data to that little mobile branch we had.

We needed a name for the library itself. We really didn't want to name it Lincoln Park Academy because most things in the black community have that name: Lincoln Park Community Center, the Lincoln Park school. We really wanted to give it some distinction that would bring people from everywhere to the branch itself. We were located at the Goodwill Presbyterian Church. The minister there at the time was really supportive of the library system. And he said, "Why don't you use the name Zora Neale Hurston." I said, "Zora Neale Hurston?" We thought about it and concluded that if we used her name it wouldn't offend anybody else in the town. You have to be careful when you name a building after someone in town. You don't want to step on anyone's toes. So that was the perfect literary person we could use at the time. I told our director at the time, Susan Kilmer, who took it to the Florida Board. They voted on it, and it was a go. That was how the library was named.

From there, people had to learn about her. In the beginning when we used her name, patrons assumed it referred to me because I was the face they saw all the time. They thought it was my library. "No, it's not my library. My name is Ms. Jackson. The library was named after Ms. Hurston, who was a writer."

So we began to educate people about who Zora was. The community really did not know who she was. From there, we started talking about the house. And the same day that we dedicated the building after it was built, the house became a historical fixture. So there was a kind of momentum building. We had the library that was built. No other library in the state had the name at the time—the Zora Neale Hurston Branch Library. The house was here, as well as her gravesite. Fort Pierce had a major contribution to make.

We have a lot of people that come from everywhere just to see the library. They want to see the house. They want to see the grave. And Zora and I have something in common because we were both born on January 7. And I was like, my goodness, does that mean something? So a lot of the times the doors to the building open up. And when people come in, they comment, "ooh, the doors open up." So it's our little pet thing that its Zora coming in to check things out because the doors do open. On occasion, you can be standing there, and they just open up, and we all figure it's her walking in and they close up. And later on they open up again and, we say, "she's gone back out." And we feel like it's just her watching over us. The library is built in an area that was called Vietnam. It was a high crime area. We just feel like we have been protected. We haven't had any major happenings. It's been smooth running. It's like she watches over the branch. We work at night. And we're not afraid because of the area we're in. And it's just that people respect the fact that the library is sitting here. And I think they take care of it considering it's been here this long.

DP: Who is Zora for you on a personal level?

AJ: Zora, on a personal level to me, was this sassy person that wanted things her way. She reminds me of myself. She spoke up; she did her own thing. She does remind me a lot of myself. I think I speak for the library about the naming. I think I wanted to have that. When we say Zora Neale Hurston Library, this is the place. We want to be user friendly. Zora had her own place in history, but we want this library to have its own distinction. We don't want it to be like every other library. We want that special feel because a lot of the times when people come in, they say that they experience a more people-friendly atmosphere. We want you to feel this library. We want you to feel the books, feel something different when you walk in here. That's the way we feel—the way I feel.

DP: You want them to feel Zora.

AJ: Yeah. Because we truly believe that she walks in here. We truly believe that she was a person who existed, she was a person who cared, she was a person who wanted you to know about stories, she was a person who wanted you to know how things exist, no false pretenses. This is it. This is what you get. That's what we want. That's how we want you to feel when you come in. Specific. To the point. This is what we offer. No false pretenses. We smile at you, this is it. This is what the Hurston Library is about.

DP: What do you perceive to be the most important contribution Hurston and her legacy has made?

AJ: She has made me look at literature in a way that makes me want to share it; I want to share it with the kids. You want to tell a story. I tell stories a lot. I look at the children, and I let them feel the story. I don't just read the book to them. If I could just tell a story, I'd try to do that as one of my pet projects once I'm retired. I think I'll just come back and volunteer. But I'd do things with storytelling because there's so much to tell about our history. I think that Zora told a lot about family stories. And I truly believe children should learn about their roots. A lot of the times I'll tell children to know their family's name, know their family background, know their grandmother's name, know their grandfather's name. How could you learn about Langston Hughes, how could you learn about Colin Powell, how could you learn about Alice Walker, how could you learn about Maya Angelou, if you don't know your own family? So Zora told about her family story. She wanted people to know about her mama, her daddy, about her. She was about family as well. But how can you know about other people, if you don't know your own family first? So there are things about the history around Fort Pierce that kids need to know. They should know about themselves first, then venture out into knowing other things. Once you know about you and why you are here and why you exist, the importance of you, then you can go out and reach for the stars.

Videotaped excerpts of biographers Robert Hemenway and Valerie Boyd at the second annual "ZoraFest: The Mystique of Zora Neale Hurston."

RH: I thought I would talk a little bit about Hurston, and share with you some of the things I like to share about Hurston when I speak about her. Then I'll address the topic of Zora Neale Hurston and Voodoo.... I am not the expert on Zora Neale Hurston. I can tell you what Zora Neale Hurston recorded with her experience with the Voodoo doctor in New Orleans. The thing about Zora Neale Hurston, from a biographer's perspective that is very difficult to make people understand is how difficult it is to get down to the essence of Zora Neale Hurston. She was such a complex and complicated person. And I tend to find that one of the best ways to do this is to tell you a story that may be impossible. It's also quite possible that it is true. But it's a story that we associate with Zora Neale Hurston. And the story is that Zora Neale Hurston was collecting folklore in South Carolina in the 1930s–1935, 1936. And she was in this small town in South Carolina. As a matter of fact, it was such a small town that it had only one street car, or no street car and one stop light. And Zora is there on a kind of hot, sunny afternoon, no traffic at the one stop light in the small town. And Zora needed to get from one side of the street to the other, so she walked against the light to get to the other side. And coming out of the shadow was a rather large sort of menacing white policeman who looked over to her. He stopped her and he said, leaning over her with his height and his bulk, "Girl what are you doing walking against the light?" And Zora said quickly, "Why officer, I saw the white folks go on green; I figured the red was for us."

Now, to me, that illustrates Zora Neale Hurston, because it shows Zora Neale Hurston being who she was: very quick witted. Being somebody who understands cultural transactions on very complicated levels, because Zora Neale Hurston says this to this white policeman, who she didn't much appreciate as menacing and frankly didn't appreciate being called a girl. She was a grown woman. What she is basically saying to that policeman is, "I know that you know that this segregation stuff is really stupid; that this notion that their would be one light for white folks and one light for black folks shows how really absurd this culture is as is this protocol that we have built in this culture that is going to put black people over here and white people over there. To me, that shows the complexity of Hurston's thoughts about these things. She was the kind of a person who, as one African American contemporary told me, when Zora was there she was the party. She was the kind of person that if she was here today, she would be in the middle of the room because she liked the center of attention. And she would be telling the stories, not some academic chancellor who happened to write a book about her. She was that kind of a very dynamic person....

There is another example I can give you of her ability to express herself, which grew directly out of the African American folk experience and the way that people expressed themselves in that experience. I think you need to know that Zora Neale Hurston graduated from Barnard College, one of the most distinguished women's colleges in the United States. Barnard College was at that time the women's division of Columbia University. And it's now somewhat independent, but still closely associated with Columbia University. Zora was the one black person at Barnard College. She said she was the first black person admitted to Barnard College. I haven't confirmed that, but I'm pretty certain that she was the only black person in her particular class, which is the class of 1927. Barnard College was very close to Columbia University. The president at that time was somebody like me: a white academic named Nicholas Murray Buckman. Nicholas Murray Buckman was, like me, a known scholar. He was an administrator. He had a popular presence on campus. And as Hurston once described him, she said, "Nicholas Murray Buckman is a cross between a duckbill platypus and a dictionary gone crazy from the hills."

Now what does that mean? I don't know what that means, but it says certain things to me. The image of a duckbill platypus is somebody who is talking a lot. And I think to a certain extent that's what Nicholas Murray Buckman did. And that's what chancellors, presidents of universities tend to do. They are out talking a lot. And he had apparently a good-sized vocabulary. And the dictionary going crazy through the hills suggests that kind of vocabulary.

So what I'm trying to get at in describing Zora Neale Hurston to people is that you have to have the sense of language. You have to have a sense of humor. You have to have the sensibility to negotiate the racial context and the racial protocols imposed on people of color during the time in which she was living.

She was somebody who was absolutely committed to her project. And her project was the analysis, reporting, and celebration of African

American folk culture. She thought that the African American folk culture was the greatest art of the country. And she desperately wanted it to be presented and realized by people with whom she interacted. That's why she wrote a book about folklore. That's why she put it on the Broadway stage: an evening of folklore called "From Sun to Sun." It's also called "The Great Day." It was called various things when she produced it in various parts of the country. But the idea was to educate people about African American folklore and African American culture. She also was a writer, of course. And to experience black people in their environment, in their linguistic environment, that was so special. She very much wanted that it not be left on some dusty shelf. She wanted it to be out and in people's minds and have them thinking about it.

She was absolutely fearless about collecting folklore. She went to turpentine camps. Places filled with people who didn't go to Sunday school every day, particularly on Sunday. She was around some pretty hard charging men. She packed a pistol sometimes in her purse. There is one picture of her actually with a shoulder holster and a pistol in her shoulder holster. She would come into a turpentine camp, and say, "I'm Zora Neale Hurston. I'm here. I'm on the run because my man in Jacksonville got arrested and they're looking to kill me and kill him. And I just wanna hang out and lay low for awhile." And the next thing she'd do is go to the juke joints while on the job and say to some of the guys hanging around the juke joints, "Do you know any blues, any stories." And she would collect those stories and those blues. She would say, "Wait a minute, let me sing you a blues and see if you can relate to it. I should make clear to you that I'm not a singer. But I just want to share one of the songs with you." I know this one case where she sang this blues at a juke joint and she got more verses to the blues song. I'll try to sing like that experience. She basically said, "Okay let's sing some blues." Here is one that I know:

Well you may go, but my slow drag will bring you back,
But you may go and this will bring you back.
Well, I've been in the country and I've lived in town
I'm totally shame from the head on down
Well you may go, but this will bring you back.
Well some folks call me a total shaker, but its a dogone lie
I'm a backbone breaker.
Well you may go, but this will bring you back.

If you could imagine a pelvic thrust on *this*, then you get a pretty good idea of the kind of style and fun that Zora Neale Hurston could generate. But the point I want to make is that she was collecting this folklore in the most dire and roughest kinds of environment because she knew that's where it existed, that it wouldn't come from some kind of educated and polished folks in a school yard.

One of the places she gathered folklore from was New Orleans. She went to New Orleans deliberately looking for Voodoo. She looked for people who had an association or claimed to have an association with Marie LaVeau. She found a man named Luke Turner, a two-headed doctor in New Orleans.... When she found him, she said, "Why don't you teach me what you know. I want to learn about Voodoo...." But Turner resisted for a long time. Then finally he said okay. He gave her a preparation, a series of things she had to do to prepare herself to enter into the study of Voodoo. And that took nine days. And at the end of the nine days he said, "You have to come back to me with three snake skins and clean underwear, and a sock on your right leg and no sock on your left leg, and prior to coming you have to sleep at night with the right stocking on, and your left foot bare." And in 1929 she went to Luke Turner's house, did all of these things. He took the three snake skins and said, well "okay," and made one of them into a turban around her head. He also had the snake skin put around her loins. And put another snake skin over her back. I should explain that the first thing he had her do when she came to his house in 1929 on that Monday morning was take off all her clothes. And she did. He put these snake skins around her, painted a sun in the middle of her forehand and on each of her cheeks. He painted a lighting symbol that went from the right shoulder to the left buttock. And then he took her into a room where she lay with her navel touching the snake skin. And that's where she stayed for the next sixty-nine hours. From early Monday morning to Thursday evening, that's where she stayed in that room with her navel touching that snake skin with only a pitcher of water near her head. Not eating anything, being indoctrinated into Voodoo. As she reports in *Mules and Men*, she had nine visions during those sixty-nine hours. And at the end, she not only felt purified, but she also came to realize that this Voodoo is something that is very, very serious. When Luke Turner came in at the end of that period of time, one of his assistants brought in this galvanized tub—like people used to do before there was running water—you took a bath with one of those tubs in the kitchen on Saturday nights sometimes. And she had to step into the tub and step out of the tub because it was filled with water, and the idea was that you had to pass through water in order to complete the ritual. He pricked her fingers so that blood dropped into a bottle of wine. She drank the wine and Turner drank the wine. And he eventually took her to the altar in his house. She put on a white robe—remember she was naked this entire time. And there were other things that marked the end of the Voodoo initiation that Zora Neale Hurston received from Luke Turner. She stayed with Turner for the next three months, learning his techniques and his ideals.

The thing I always find so fascinating about this is that this was a graduate from Barnard College. This is someone who was trained by

Franz Boaz as an anthropologist, one of the leading anthropologists at that time. And yet she was willing to take the kind of risk that comes to a young woman, a young attractive woman coming into a house, taking off her clothes, submitting herself to the ritual that he was demanding she go through, in order to learn the secrets of Voodoo. To me, that says everything about Zora Neale Hurston, as does the way she crossed against the red light....

From a follow-up e-mail interview.

RH: What inspired me to write the Hurston biography was *Their Eyes Were Watching God*. I thought that anyone who could write such a book was the kind of person that I wanted to know more about. So I started doing research and seven years later had a manuscript. The other compelling fact about Hurston was that just when you figured you had something nailed, knew why Zora seemed to want to do a particular thing, you discovered that the real reason for Zora's action was more complicated than it appeared. In other words, this was a very complex lady, who masked a lot of the real reasons for her actions, and each time you pursued her real motives, you learned something new, both in relation to her and to others. It was that realization, that these things—conjure, writing, collecting folklore, are really, really complicated. And Zora can lead you to that complexity if you have the patience and the courage to follow her. She is quite a leader.

When Valerie Boyd attended the Hurston Festival in Eatonville, she heard Robert Hemenway, who spoke early that day, say that "it's time for a new biography to be written about Zora Neale Hurston, and it should be written by a black woman." Boyd accepted the challenge.

VB: I wrote this biography of Zora Neale Hurston: *Wrapped in Rainbows*. I actually started the research in 1996. The book was published in January 2003. It's only been out for a couple of years in paperback. Because I had written this biography about Zora Neale Hurston, when Oprah Winfrey turned *Their Eyes Were Watching God* into a television movie, everywhere I went people would say, "What do you think about the movie, what do you think about the movie?" ... I just want to give a little summary about the book and how the book came to be and how it found it's way to film. Zora wrote *Their Eyes Were Watching God* while she was in Haiti studying Haitian Voodoo. Zora got a Guggenheim Fellowship to study Voodoo in Haiti. And she also spent some time, before going to Haiti, in Jamaica.... She was very much excited to get the fellowship.... But also, it saved her from a destructive relationship; a relationship that she was very much into, but had decided it was not good for her. She was in a relationship with a man,

20 years her junior, named Percival McGuire Punter. They started dating when he was twenty-three and Zora was forty-four.... She called Percival Hunter the real love of her life. It was a relationship she knew couldn't last.... The character Tea Cake was inspired by Percival, the younger man with the older woman Janie. That was the inspiration that she took from that relationship. And within seven weeks, she wrote *Their Eyes Were Watching God*. That's incredible.

Like many of you I was awed by Hurston's work. When I read *Their Eyes Were Watching God*, I was blown away. I wanted to know how could someone write this kind of book—not even knowing that it was seven weeks, just wanting to know the story behind the story. To create a character like Janie Crawford in the 1930s who still spoke to me so urgently. It was the early 1980s when I read this book. I was a freshman at Northwestern University. I was seventeen years old. I was embarking on that journey to know myself; the same journey that Janie is on throughout the novel. And of course when we meet Janie, she is sixteen. I totally related to Janie and loved the story and wanted to know about the woman behind the story. And that's how my interest in Hurston began. That's how I became a Zora-head.... That's when I started getting t-shirts and coffee mugs, and was really immersed in Zora's story. I find in going about and in talking about this work that everyone has a Zora story. I'm sure you all have stories about how you were introduced to her. In many cases, it was *Their Eyes Were Watching God*.

I was doing a radio show on NPR, and I was going on and on about how important this book was to black women. And a caller phoned in and said, "I'm a white man. I loved *Their Eyes Were Watching God*. Don't leave me out." That was a great lesson for me to realize that this novel transcends culture and race and gender lines. This novel is about human beings loving each other and forgiving each other and fighting with each other and doing all the things that we do as human beings. It transcends those other things, even though it's very black. It's very much a black story. It is very specific. But the specificity of it is what allows it to have that universal appeal. It's about us trying to find better ways to live our lives, and to live them in unity.

In March 2005, what was interesting about talking with them [Oprah Winfrey and Danny Glover] is that they were both fans of the novel. Oprah Winfrey said that when she first discovered *Their Eyes Were Watching God*, she was making *The Color Purple*. Danny Glover was on the set with her and he was talking about how he had read the book sixty-four times. And she responded, "Oh my god, you read it sixty-four times. I need to read it." And that's how she discovered *Their Eyes Were Watching God*. She had the same reaction that we did. She was blown away by it. She loved the book. Oprah Winfrey loves *Their Eyes Were Watching God*. The movie is an interesting work of art on its own, in that it introduced a whole new generation of people to Zora Neale Hurston.

The Department of Africana Studies at the University of South Florida offers a semester-long course that focuses exclusively on Zora Neale Hurston. It may be the only course of its kind in American colleges and universities. In the spring of 2006, the students enrolled in this course were asked to complete an end-of-semester survey. Among the several questions posed, students were asked, "Who is Zora Neale Hurston for you?" The students enrolled were African, African American, Caribbean American, white American, Latino, Hispanic American, female, male, heterosexual, gay, lesbian, Christian, Muslim, agnostic, and younger than and older than twenty-one. These are their responses.

WA: She is a great writer who brought to light a lot of issues that the African American culture faced in her time. She was not scared to write about real-life situations and this makes her stories popular. Zora Neale Hurston was a leader of her time. She led African Americans to believe it was okay to write about the things that really interested them and not just what the Jim Crow laws allowed them to write about. Hurston was a great teacher who took it upon herself to collect stories from different people and places and then share them with the world through her novels.

GA: A woman who has inspired me with her writings as well as her life.

HG: Zora is a genius of her time and of our time, she has created a way to teach us how to teach others about problems and issues in life. She has taught us many lessons that assist us in relating to her and to others who, we were originally taught, were so much unlike. Through her works she has displayed the obvious without focusing or centering the whole story on exclusively one serious issue. Zora Neale Hurston is a genius and master of creating genius within others.

SI: Zora Neale Hurston is a black woman who was ahead of her time and kind of like me, interested in so many different subjects and tried them all. She didn't just stop at writing or anthropology, she saw her potential and went for the gold. Most people who have an interest in life could learn a lot from her but they would have to think critically and outside of the box, not just read her literature but learn about her life and other things that she did while she was alive and "resurrected" just like we did in the course.

LR: For me, Zora is someone to be looked up to and admired because of her undaunted accomplishments and her faithfulness to the folk in her writing, even when others were criticizing that same faithfulness. I plan to be a high school English teacher, and I think of all the things I can teach my students by presenting Zora and her works to them. I can teach them things of a literary basis: plot, theme, structure, Aristotelian tragic protagonist, and more. Plus, I can teach them to think about society and how they participate in it, as Dr. Plant has taught me this semester.

EF: Zora Neale Hurston is a role model. A person who is indeed, something positive for both men and women, black and white. Her works are ones that need to be studied and carefully read. She is a person who will always have a positive reflection in my life, because she was in a negative situation, (Jim Crow laws and in the South, a woman and African American), and still was able to accomplish what many people today cannot.

FW: Zora is like a mentor for me. I know that sounds crazy, but she has inspired me beyond my wildest dreams. I recognized her struggles against racism, sexism and classism, and that made me realize that although I face another issue (heterosexism), it's still possible to accomplish my goals.

YR: Zora Neale Hurston is this great Floridian, writer, and anthropologist that fought for her beliefs and got best of her time and let the world know through her writings.

MK: Zora Neale Hurston to me was a revolutionary woman in her time. I enjoy reading the stories, plays and other things she wrote, as well as learning about her life and the things she felt and believed and how she fought for them and didn't follow the crowd.

DP: Zora Neale Hurston is a pioneer among black women writers, and even most writers in general. She laid the outline for those who followed her to be noticed and respected because she wrote what she felt. She wrote about how *she* viewed life around her, not what she was "supposed" to see according to other so called "greats."

DR: Zora Neale Hurston was a phenomenal woman. She told it like is was in her perspective. She wrote many books and related to many of her characters. She had goals in mind and never gave up or let anyone hold her back from achieving them. She was quite outspoken and she got in touch with her roots. Hurston is an author that is not to be forgotten because her achievements set the bar for many other individuals that followed in her footsteps.

JM: Hurston is a strong and independent-spirited woman who followed her gut instincts. She was a woman ahead of her times. She knew the importance of portraying reality through her works, regardless of what literary critics might say about her. I find her to be a brave, independent, intelligent "genius."

TJ: A woman of great worth and accomplishments. A strong woman of insight and a woman of her people. Someone who gave her all, and then some, for what she believed in. She is an independent woman who could never submit to anyone. A woman of love and compassion. A Genius of Life!

SK: Zora Neale Hurston was an accomplished writer. If that were all she was, that would be a lot. However, she was much more. Her other abilities keep adding. I think I admire her most as a woman who was able to keep true to her own vision, despite attacks by right and left, black and white.

CSC: She is a strong, courageous, independent, and victorious African WOMAN! She broke the cycle... and I commend her for her strength and determination. She is a motivator for me.

SS: A defining voice for African American women.

AP: To me, Zora is a writer, a teacher, an anthropologist, a poet, and apparently a Hoodoo priest. She is a fascinating individual and for the most part she was misunderstood. She is definitely someone to look up to and admire. She had a passion for her work and for the most part I think she was a down-to-earth individual. Zora is who I want to be and not what I want to be. I would love to write and live life like she did, but I am afraid of not succeeding.

RM: Zora Neale Hurston for me is boldness, strength, creativity, adventurous, odd, simple-like, sensitive, and beautiful.

AC: A genius of the South. I feel like Zora Neale Hurston was a true pioneer. She was a true hero for women and people of color. She was extremely determined to fulfill her dreams and would stop at nothing to reach her goals. She is extremely inspiring, and I look forward to reading more of her work outside of this course.

ES: Zora is (forgive the cliché) a touchstone for me, a kind of role model. I love her philosophy (I am a Spencer fan). I love her unwillingness to be other people's sheep or mouthpiece or robot. She struggled with whatever stereotypes (men/women/fair/dark/kinky/straight/you name it), but she absolutely refused to let them define her ultimately. I love that she did not sell out, regardless of what people think. I loved that she loved herself, regardless of where that came from. I loved her sense of humor and her affectionate and unadorned anecdotes and stories from the people she knew and the cultures she lived and visited in. Her essay "What It's Like to be Colored Me" speaks to me entirely. I have always felt like an outsider and no one has ever quite put it the way she does in that work. It's like "I am who I am without any defining from you!"

MP: Zora Neale Hurston was a genius in the respect that she believed the problems of race in her day could be solved.

JC: To me Zora was a very interesting writer who greatly contributed to the literary world. She decided to write about the reality of the African American people and not try to be politically correct or political in any way.

KT: She was a woman with a voice. A mysterious woman who faced so many obstacles, yet stayed true to herself. A wondrous, intelligent being, a comet.

KW: For me, Zora Neale Hurston is not only a literary genius. She is a woman who is sure of herself and writes whatever makes her happy. She is a person who decides for herself what she will and will not allow herself to get tangled up in. For instance, the whole race problem. She didn't want to really address it, so she rarely did. In one letter that she wrote to Countee Cullen, in the book *Zora Neale Hurston: A Life in Letters*, Zora addresses the race issue. But she never allowed it to consume her life—many people do. Hurston took the road less traveled and carved out her own destiny; I admire and strive for that. She has inspired me to find and share my genius.

OC: She is an anthropologist who had a vision ahead of her time.

KM: Zora is a pioneer, genius, role model, writer, anthropologist, teacher, thinker, philosopher—need I say more? I feel blessed to have learned so much about and from such amazing women (both Zora and D. Plant)!

RH: Zora Neale Hurston is an inspiration to me. She did not allow anyone to determine who she was with labels. She was true to herself no matter the circumstances. She took advantage of every opportunity she was given and did not worry herself about what she didn't have but more about what she did have and how she could take full advantage of those opportunities. She is truly an inspiration, role model even.

ES: Zora Neale Hurston for me is only one thing. A symbol of authenticity, a quality that many strive for, but few achieve.

IE: Zora Neale Hurston was a woman who was able to consciously point out the hypocrisy and stereotypes/limitations in society. Zora was able to analyze and ostracized what society wanted her to be. Although Zora was not able to shed all the stereotypes/limitations of being black, a woman, and Southern, she tried to point them out to others and enforce the need to be human, nothing more. Zora is in the same struggle as me, and her life has presented a way to become aware and overcome the stereotype/limitation of being black, woman, and Southern. Zora's life shows me that a struggle is not waged to be black, woman, or Southern but to become human. Zora's life, letters, and works show people being people even when others try to limit the experience. Zora is a person that finds the humanity in others as she struggles to find the humanity in herself, the same fight that I and others are trying to do.

NO: A woman who succeeded in making herself known and opening doors for others. She wrote many interesting books and influenced me to pursue my dream of writing.

AS: I truly see a lot of the conflicts Zora Neale had in her life, especially her familial origins and subsequent trials emanating from them, parallel to mine. I still feel young so she represents time for me, in that I feel like I can make social change in an original way. Not to say that she was old when she got started (all right, that thought did cross my mind) but to say her soul was always old. Maybe this means wisdom, intelligence, knowledge, depth, courage, creativity, expansion. But to me it means individuality.

NB: Zora Neale Hurston to me is a lot more than the titles that are given to her. She is a woman of great strength that did what she wanted without conforming to what society's idea of a woman should be. I will most definitely agree that she is the "genius of the south," because to me her writing skills were complex and like no other. She was original.

Conclusion: Sankofa

R umors of Hurston's having died penniless were not exaggerated, but
they were inflated. She did die penniless. But she often lived penniless, too.
Her letters to friends and associates speak to the problematic financial situations that figured into her folklore fieldwork and writing projects. As an
anthropologist and a writer, being without money was an occupational haz-
ard. Seldom was Hurston employed in positions that tendered a steady, reliable income, especially during the latter part of her life. Between 1927 and
1936, her anthropological expeditions were financed by patron Charlotte
Osgood Mason or by fellowships that allowed a steady income, but only for
a year or two at a time or less, and never beyond a maintenance level. The
folklore concerts and dramatic presentations in which she invested so much
of her time and energy (and her own meager resources) often left her in
debt. Her novels and the royalties from her novels generated some income,
but despite her phenomenal success as a writer and anthropologist, Hurston
never became financially wealthy.

> The largest royalty payment she ever earned from any of her books was
> $943.75. Her $100-a-week salary at Paramount in 1941 was the highest wage
> she was ever paid. And the $1,000 she received with her Anisfield Award [for
> *Dust Tracks on a Road*] was among the largest lump sums she ever handled.[1]

Earnings from these sources were invariably used to repay accumulated
debts, finance anticipated folklore collecting and anthropological expeditions, and provide self-support while she worked on yet another manuscript.
Publishers were sometimes late in paying her for articles submitted; at other
times she wasn't paid what she was owed. For instance, when Hurston's literary agent Jean Parker Waterbury sent her a $100 advance check, Hurston
"had exactly four pennies" to her name. She had been living on what savings
she had while she worked on one of her book manuscripts, "The Lives of
Barney Turk," but editor Mitchell Burroughs wrote Hurston of his regrets on

finding the novel unsuccessful. By then, her article "Why the Negro Won't Buy Communism" had been accepted for publication by the *American Legion Magazine*. Hurston's expectation of the $600 payment was daily disappointed. "I am all too weary of going to the Post Office and turning away cold in hand and having to avoid folks who have made me loans so that I could eat and sleep. The humiliation," Hurston confided, "is getting to be much too much for my self-respect, speaking from the inside of my soul."[2]

Although she never had a lot of money, Hurston was always generous with whatever she had. She would inquire into Langston Hughes's financial affairs, asking whether he needed any money and coaxing him to "ask ME first when you get strapped."[3] She might accommodate friends for a couple of weeks or so on her houseboat, the *Sun Tan*, or give a party for a friend just arriving home from international travels. If she were "flush with funds," she might mail parcels of pecans, citrus fruits, or gardenias to friends, family, or associates.

Some of her critics, contemporaneous and present-day, consider Hurston to have been "improvident"—as though being materially "provident" expresses some intrinsic virtue and entails a guarantee against future dispossession. Certainly nothing about economic deprivation or scarcity is romantic. Most of us who peer through the years of Hurston's life would wish her a less onerous economic situation. She herself protested the depressed feeling that attended the need to seek financial assistance. She admitted that she had "no talent for business nor finance" and that she was "not materialistic."[4] In the early 1930s, Hurston's collaboration with Robert Wunsch and John Rice of Rollins College in Winter Park, Florida, resulted in a venue to produce a concert and a play featuring African American folklore and folk life. Her patron Charlotte Mason questioned why Hurston would do that "instead of something that would bring [her] an immediate return." Hurston responded,

> I saw a chance here to make our dreams come true if only I could forget the flesh pots of my own personal comfort long enough to get a foothold. I have that now, Godmother. The small amount of personal comfort I have given up is so little to pay for what will come back to me. Perhaps I shall never roll in wealth. That is not the point. If we can give real creative urge a push forward here, the world will see a New Negro and justify our efforts. That is pay.[5]

For Hurston, the dream was the truth and she would work tenaciously to realize it, and often at her own expense.

Hurston conceived of money as a means to an end; it was currency, nothing more. And she would exchange every penny she garnered (sometimes along with those that may have been loaned to her), even sell her car and pawn her typewriter for the opportunity to collect what she called the "wealth of the continent"—Africana folklore—and to present this wealth through musical productions, dramatic presentations, novels, short stories, essays, and articles. In this, her providential eye *was* on the future, our future, humanity's future. To the extent to which critics associate wealth with money, we miss the capital with which Hurston was so enriched—social capital, intellectual capital, cultural capital, as well as the spiritual capital that is so often overlooked. "Zora Neale Hurston, every time she went about, had something to offer," declared Editor C. E. Bolen. "She didn't come empty."[6] She gave everything she had; there is only honor and glory in that. To Hurston, living life fully was paramount. Encouraging her first husband Herbert Sheen to travel with his new wife, she exhorted, "All you can take with you is the experiences of your life. You can't take your bank account." She confidently told him that if she should "die without money, somebody will bury me."[7]

And so it was. Zora Neale Hurston's pink-gowned body rested in a steel, pink-and-white casket barely visible for the glorious effusion of flowers. As an elderly neighbor proudly stated to Alice Walker, "We put her away nice."[8]

Hurston did not arbitrarily settle into Fort Pierce, Florida. In December 1957, C.E. Bolen, owner of the Fort Pierce Chronicle, "made a special trip [to Merritt Island] to talk to her."[9] At his invitation, Hurston accepted a position at his weekly newspaper as a columnist. She moved into a concrete-block home at 1734 School Court, owned by her physician, Dr. Clem C. Benton. Dr. Benton was no stranger. He had grown up in Goldsboro, a little town not far from Eatonville, and knew the Hurston family.[10] Over the ensuing years, their reacquaintance would bloom into a warm friendship of mutual admiration and respect. When Dr. Benton learned of Hurston's financial situation, he ceased collection of the $10.00 per week rent charge. He elected, rather, to pay her frequent visits and to routinely pick her up for three o'clock Sunday dinners with him and his daughters Arlena and Margaret.[11]

Dr. Benton's acts of kindness were more than chivalry. Although he read and was impressed by Hurston's writings and awed by her personality and accomplishments, it was not her celebrity that moved him. Dr. Benton was awed at how Hurston's phenomenal mind "just worked all the time."[12] He appreciated her genius and her profound presence. He knew he was in the company of an extraordinary human being, and he was touched by her essence, by the essential Zora Neale Hurston.

Just as Dr. Benton's acquaintance with Hurston harkened back to Eatonville, Marjorie Silver Alder, a white resident of Fort Pierce, Florida, recalled Hurston from her days in New York during the Harlem Renaissance and "was a great fan of hers." In spite of the racial segregation that divided the minds and addresses of the residents of Fort Pierce, Alder, a local radio and newspaper journalist and correspondent for the Miami Herald, befriended Hurston. Hurston became a regular guest at Alder's frequent dinner parties; they visited each other often and had long and passionately involved conversations on a wide variety of topics. When some of Alder's white guests affected displeasure with the idea of socializing and sharing a meal with a black person, both Hurston and Alder ignored the "party poopers."[13]

After these dinners, Hurston would collect the leftovers and take them home. She would use them to entice neighborhood children to her steps.

"[I]n the manner of the disciples feeding the multitudes," Alder reminisced, Hurston would feed the children, all the while teaching them of their rich heritage and gifting them with a sense of pride in being black people.[14] She took them for walks, told them stories, and encouraged them to write. After Hurston returned from her September 19, 1958, hospital stay, these same children would visit with Hurston and aid her in the least conspicuous way possible, a token of their care and respect. Hurston had been diagnosed with hypertensive heart disease. The condition left her breathless and with weak and swollen legs, but Hurston wouldn't acknowledge anything but strength. "So the children visited daily, almost as if their hostess were not ill."[15] Thus, she was rarely alone.

One of the great ironies of life is that the initial inhalation necessarily anticipates the final exhalation; Hurston's passing, her actual death, was unremarkable. As she herself stated, "we all must go."[16] What is remarkable is that Zora Neale Hurston lived to be sixty-nine years old, "three years older than the life expectancy for the average Black American woman."[17] Moreover, she lived a full and exceptional life. In her own parlance, she had gone to the horizon and back. Many of her dreams, as an anthropologist, a folklorist, a dramatist, and a novelist, were realized. Her autobiography and her letters frequently bubbled with the joy of successes and triumphs over disappointments.

On October 16, 1933, for example, when Hurston learned of J. B. Lippincott's acceptance of her first novel manuscript *Jonah's Gourd Vine*, Hurston had just finished directing a successful folk concert in Sanford, Florida, for the Seminole County Chamber of Commerce. She had been paid $25 for her work and was given a money order that would be honored at any store. Hurston elected to buy some much-needed shoes. While being fitted, she read the telegram from Lippincott asking her to respond to the terms outlined for *Jonah's Gourd Vine*. She was so excited to wire her acceptance that she "tore out of that place with one old shoe and one new one on and ran to the Western Union office. Lippincott had asked for an answer by wire and they got it! Terms accepted. I never expect to have a greater thrill than that wire gave me," she exuded in *Dust Tracks on a Road*. "You know the feeling when you found your first pubic hair. Greater than that."[18]

Among other successes, the critical acclaim of her theatrical production *The Great Day*, the publication of *Jonah's Gourd Vine*, and the December 1934 invitation to apply for a the Rosenwald Fellowship to support her doctoral study had Hurston proclaim that "life has picked me up bodaciously and throwed me over the fence."[19] These events inspired confidence in the work she was doing and determination in her artistic vision. The publication of *Jonah's Gourd Vine* indicated to Hurston that, as a novelist, she could, indeed, write the kind of story she wanted to write, versus the kind of story she was supposed to write. Hurston wanted to explore what made a man or woman "do such-and-so." The novel's publication and recommendation as a Book-of-the Month Club title validated Hurston's literary ambitions.[20] As *Jonah's*

Gourd Vine was her literary debut, *The Great Day* was her debut as a theatrical producer of authentic African American and Afro-Caribbean folklore, and its production carried a similar significance.

Hurston often "exceeded her own expectations." Along with the highs, though, were the lows, but this was "the stuff of life." Accordingly, Hurston "had her lumps, too." But she was defeated neither by tragic events nor by dire circumstances. As she proclaimed herself, Hurston was a conscious being. As such, she never identified herself with her circumstances—personal or political. As author and lecturer David Hawkins stated in *Power vs. Force: The Hidden Determinants of Human Behavior,* "external events may define conditions, but they don't determine the consciousness level of human response." The level of one's consciousness correlates with one's perception. Hawkins wrote, "By taking responsibility for the consequences of his own perceptions, the observer can transcend the role of victim to an understanding that 'nothing out there has power over you.'"[21]

In spite of the force of racist ideology and practice, in spite of the force of patriarchal dominance, in spite of the force of economic injustice, in spite of all the forces that could conspire to keep a good woman down, Zora Neale Hurston had the power to rise up, push through it all, and walk *her* chosen path. Hurston understood well the difference between power and force. The former is internal, eternal, spiritual, and constant. The latter is external, temporal, physical, and conditional. She was aware that power and perception go hand in hand and that her reaction to external circumstances was a direct reflection of her internal self-concept. "Who we become, as well as what we see," stated Hawkins, "is determined by *perception*—which can be said, simply, to create the world."[22] When we visit the world Hurston created in her writings and her legacy, we glimpse the possibility of humankind, just as Hurston glimpsed the infinite possibility that resonated in the world created by "the folk." She knew intuitively and experientially that power did not lie in laws and lynchings, and that only true power would nullify the unjust law and transform the unconsciousness that inspired hateful deeds.

One of the uses of literature for life, Harold Bloom asserts, is to augment one's awareness and widen and clarify one's consciousness.[23] If our individual lives and our collective worlds are to evolve toward an enlightened existence, then it is necessary to aspire to higher levels of consciousness. Many of the social and political conditions of Zora Neale Hurston's time have continued into the present. For instance, recalling W.E.B. Du Bois' prediction that the problem of the twentieth century would be the problem of the color line, historian John Hope Franklin stated "categorically" in his book *The Color Line: Legacy for the Twenty-First Century* that the problem of the twenty-first century will also be the problem of the color line. The words are hollow screams thrown up from strangled voices at the bottom of a well that is one hundred years deep. The promise of the continuation of these conditions will be fulfilled only if individually and collectively we do not choose alternative realities. Inspiration and wisdom to create life-affirming realities can be drawn from the literature with which Zora Neale Hurston gifted us as well as from her own example. Hurston wrote in *Dust Tracks on a Road* that the dark days of slavery were certainly sad, but there was nothing she could do to change them. So she made a conscious choice to turn her thoughts and energies to the present and "settle for from now on."[24] Fear and dire predictions, which are based on the past, are but a kind of mental slavery. One can reify the fear or choose to create what one desires. Just as these malleable conditions have persisted, ingenuity is humankind's constant companion. The capacity for empowerment and the ability to create anew is ever present. "Recognized geniuses may be rare, but genius resides within all of us," wrote Hawkins.

> There's no such thing as "luck" or "accident" in this cosmos; and not only is everything connected to everything else, no one is excluded from the universe— we're all members. Consciousness, like physicality, is a universal quality; because genius is a characteristic of consciousness, genius is also universal. It follows that that which is universal is available to each and every person.[25]

ANCESTRAL LIGHT

Hurston's legacy can be conceived of as a touchstone to ignite the genius we each have within us. In her book *Soul Talk*, Akasha Gloria Hull reminded us that the ancestral spirits of our forebears are there for us. In the chapter titled "Talking to Ancestral Light: Communications from the Other Side," she related that "[w]ithout fail, the communication is beneficent, soothing, comforting, and inspirational."[26] The cultural icon of the sankofa bird is an image that symbolizes this dynamic of communication. The body poised forward and the head turned backward, the sankofa bird has a grain or seed between its beak. The typical interpretation of this symbol is that one must look back, that is, one must know one's past so that one can chart the future. Another interpretation is that when an individual looks back, she may find that she has overlooked and neglected something essential to her well-being, something that must be retrieved and integrated into her present existence. Zora Neale Hurston is that seed, that genius that we, as a people, had thrown away.[27] Bloom informed us that "[o]ur recognition of genius is always retroactive."[28] But because genius is "always above its age," it manifests itself in time.

Having retrieved Hurston from oblivion and having begun the work of integrating her legacy into our lives, perhaps we are now ready to move out from under or own shadows, as Hurston herself was once described as a woman half in shadow. Many describe Hurston as a woman ahead of her time. But as Hawkins stated, the cosmos does not make mistakes. Hurston's ability to live the life she did in the circumstances she faced is exemplary and instructive. From the vantage point of the first half of the twentieth century, Zora Neale Hurston stands as a lighthouse, her beams dissipating the darkness, the confusion, and the illusions that would otherwise obscure the shoreline and safe entry into our own harbors. As Hurston often exclaimed: Let there be Light!

Notes

INTRODUCTION

1. Alice Walker, *In Search of Our Mothers' Gardens* (San Diego: Harcourt, Brace, Javonvich, 1983), 92.

2. Zora Neale Hurston, *Dust Tracks on a Road* (1942; repr., New York: Harper Perennial Modern Classics, 2006), 227.

3. Valerie Boyd, *Wrapped in Rainbows: The Life of Zora Neale Hurston* (New York: Scribner, 2003), 398.

4. Boyd, *Wrapped in Rainbows*, 433.

5. Akasha Gloria Hull, *Soul Talk: The New Spirituality of African American Women* (Rochester, VT: Inner Traditions, 2001), 1, 7–8.

6. Ibid., 5, 18, 19.

7. Chögyam Trungpa, *Cutting through Spiritual Materialism* (Boston: Shambhala Publications, 1973), 11.

8. Alice Walker, *We Are the Ones We Have Been Waiting For: Inner Light in a Time of Darkness, Meditations* (New York: New Press, 2006), 103.

9. Hurston, *Dust Tracks*, 250.

10. Walker, *We Are the Ones*, 2–3.

CHAPTER ONE

1. Zora Neale Hurston, *Dust Tracks on a Road* (1942; repr., New York: Harper Perennial Modern Classics, 2006), 212.

2. Hurston says this of her mother at Lucy Hurston's death, *Dust Tracks*, 66.

3. Hurston, *Dust Tracks*, 226.

4. Valerie Boyd, *Wrapped in Rainbows: The Life of Zora Neale Hurston* (New York: Scribner, 2003), 431.

5. Hurston, *Dust Tracks*, 265.

6. Boyd, *Wrapped in Rainbows*, 433.

7. Ibid., 15–16.

8. Hurston, *Dust Tracks*, 8.

9. Zora Neale Hurston, *Jonah's Gourd Vine* (1934; repr., New York: Harper Perennial, 1990), 75.

10. Hurston, *Dust Tracks*, 74.
11. Ibid.
12. Ibid., 20.
13. Ibid., 21.
14. Ibid.
15. Boyd, *Wrapped in Rainbows*, 18.
16. Hurston, *Dust Tracks*, 19.
17. Ibid., 1.
18. Boyd, *Wrapped in Rainbows*, 21.
19. Ibid., 21–22.
20. N. Y. Nathiri, *Zora! Zora Neale Hurston: A Woman and Her Community* (Orlando: Sentinel Communications, 1991), 123.
21. Boyd, *Wrapped in Rainbows*, 22.
22. Ibid., 35.
23. Hurston, *Dust Tracks*, 12.
24. Ibid.
25. Ibid., 68.
26. Ibid., 13.
27. Ibid.
28. Ibid., 14.
29. Ibid.
30. Ibid., 13.
31. Ibid., 29.
32. Ibid., 27.
33. Ibid., 28.
34. Ibid., 29.
35. Ibid., 46.
36. Ibid., 48.
37. Ibid., 53–54.
38. Ibid., 61.
39. Ibid., 29–30.
40. Ibid., 41.
41. Ibid., 34.
42. Ibid., 27–28, 58.
43. Ibid., 66.
44. Ibid., 67.
45. Ibid.
46. Boyd, *Wrapped in Rainbows*, 52–53.
47. Hurston, *Dust Tracks*, 70.
48. Ibid., 79.
49. Ibid., 80.
50. Ibid., 71, 81.
51. Zora Neale Hurston, *Their Eyes Were Watching God* (1937; repr., Urbana: University of Illinois Press, 1978), 112.
52. Hurston, *Dust Tracks*, 42.
53. Ibid., 69–70, 81–82.
54. Ibid., 84–85.
55. Ibid., 85.
56. Ibid., 88–89.

57. Ibid., 94.
58. Ibid., 96.
59. Ibid., 97.
60. Ibid., 75–78.
61. Ibid., 99–100.
62. Ibid., 100.
63. Ibid., 101, 103.
64. Ibid., 109, 116.
65. Ibid., 118.
66. Ibid., 119.

CHAPTER TWO

1. Zora Neale Hurston, *Dust Tracks on a Road* (1942; repr., New York: Harper Perennial Modern Classics, 2006), 35.
2. Ibid., 36.
3. Ibid.
4. Ibid., 37.
5. Ibid., 38, 39.
6. Ibid., 40.
7. Ibid., 41.
8. Ibid., 121–22.
9. Ibid., 122.
10. Valerie Boyd, *Wrapped in Rainbows: The Life of Zora Neale Hurston* (New York: Scribner, 2003), 74.
11. Hurston, *Dust Tracks*, 122.
12. Boyd, *Wrapped in Rainbows*, 75.
13. Hurston, *Dust Tracks*, 124.
14. Ibid., 127.
15. Ibid., 129, 127.
16. Ibid., 129, 130.
17. Boyd, *Wrapped in Rainbows*, 80.
18. Hurston, *Dust Tracks*, 130.
19. Boyd, *Wrapped in Rainbows*, 80.
20. Hurston, *Dust Tracks*, 130–31.
21. Ibid., 137, 204.
22. Boyd, *Wrapped in Rainbows*, 84.
23. David L. Lewis, *When Harlem Was in Vogue* (New York: Vintage, 1982), 90.
24. Zora Neale Hurston, "John Redding Goes to Sea," *Opportunity* 3–4 (January 1926): 16.
25. Ibid., 21.
26. Nathan Huggins, *The Harlem Renaissance* (New York: Oxford, 1973), 72.
27. Ibid., 9, 78–79.
28. Zora Neale Hurston, "Drenched in Light," *Opportunity* 1–2 (December 1924): 374.
29. Hurston, *Dust Tracks*, 138.
30. Boyd, *Wrapped in Rainbows*, 97.
31. Zora Neale Hurston, "Spunk," in *The Complete Stories*, ed. Henry Louis Gates, Jr., and Sieglinde Lemke (1925; repr., New York: Harper Perennial, 1995), 26.

32. Boyd, *Wrapped in Rainbows*, 97.
33. Carla Kaplan, ed., *Zora Neale Hurston: A Life in Letters* (New York: Doubleday, 2002), 55, 68.
34. Hurston, *Dust Tracks*, 139.
35. Kaplan, *Letters*, 69.
36. Ibid., 75.
37. Langston Hughes, *The Big Sea: An Autobiography* (1963; repr., New York: Thunder's Mouth Press, 1987), 239.
38. Boyd, *Wrapped in Rainbows*, 117, 121.
39. Hughes, *The Big Sea*, 235.
40. Zora Neale Hurston, "Sweat," in *The Complete Stories*, ed. Henry Louis Gates, Jr., and Sieglinde Lemke (1926; repr., New York: Harper Perennial, 1995), 76.
41. Kaplan, *Letters*, 87.
42. Hurston, *Dust Tracks*, 141.
43. Zora Neale Hurston, *Mules and Men* (1935; repr., Bloomington: Indiana University Press, 1978), 6.
44. Hurston, *Dust Tracks*, 141.
45. Hurston, *Mules and Men*, 9–10.
46. Kaplan, *Letters*, 93, 97.
47. Hurston, *Mules and Men*, 3.
48. Kaplan, *Letters*, 100.
49. Hurston, *Dust Tracks*, 142, 143, 144.
50. Kaplan, *Letters*, 101.
51. Hurston, *Dust Tracks*, 204.
52. Lifeprints are moments in life, positive or negative, that leave their mark and are so arresting that all one's senses are heightened and impress on the mind every detail of that moment.
53. Hurston, *Dust Tracks*, 204.
54. Ibid.
55. Boyd, *Wrapped in Rainbows*, 150.
56. Kaplan, *Letters*, 101.
57. Hughes, *The Big Sea*, 296–98.
58. Boyd, *Wrapped in Rainbows*, 158.
59. Kaplan, *Letters*, 106.
60. Boyd, *Wrapped in Rainbows*, 159.
61. Kaplan, *Letters*, 111.
62. Hurston, *Dust Tracks*, 143.
63. Boyd, *Wrapped in Rainbows*, 162.
64. Hurston, *Dust Tracks*, 146, 153.
65. Hurston, *Mules and Men*, 162.
66. Hurston, *Dust Tracks*, 154.
67. Ibid., 154–55.
68. Ibid., 147–49.
69. Ibid., 145–48.
70. Hurston, *Mules and Men*, 4.
71. Kaplan, *Letters*, 114, 115–16.
72. Hurston, *Mules and Men*, 190.
73. Kaplan, *Letters*, 124.
74. Ibid., 124, 126.

75. Hurston, *Mules and Men*, 207, 209–10, 214–15.
76. Kaplan, *Letters*, 131, 156.
77. Ibid., 135, 137.
78. Ibid., 148–49, 150.
79. Ibid., 196.
80. Ibid., 193.
81. Hughes, *The Big Sea*, 334.
82. Kaplan, *Letters*, 194, 226.
83. Boyd, *Wrapped in Rainbows*, 225.
84. Kaplan, *Letters*, 222.
85. Ibid., 228.
86. Hurston, *Dust Tracks*, 281.
87. Kaplan, *Letters*, 238.
88. Hurston, *Dust Tracks*, 283.
89. Arthur Ruhl, "Second Nights," *New York Herald Tribune* (January 17, 1932).
90. Hurston, *Dust Tracks*, 284.
91. Kaplan, *Letters*, 253–54.
92. Ibid., 254.
93. Ibid.
94. Ibid., 259.
95. Steve Glassman and Kathryn Seidel, eds., *Zora in Florida* (Orlando: University of Central Florida Press, 2001), 131.
96. Ibid., 131.
97. "The Listening Place," *Winter Park Herald* (January 26, 1933): 5.
98. Glassman and Seidel, *Zora in Florida*, 136.
99. Kaplan, *Letters*, 325.
100. Hurston, *Dust Tracks*, 173.
101. Kaplan, *Letters*, 334, 342.
102. Ibid., 335.
103. Ibid., 151, 316.

CHAPTER THREE

1. Robert Hemenway, "Zora Neale Hurston and the Eatonville Anthology," in *The Harlem Renaissance Remembered*, ed. Arna Bontemps (New York: Dodd, Mead, 1972), 191.
2. Alice Walker, *In Search of Our Mothers' Gardens* (San Diego: Harcourt, Brace, Jovanovich, 1983), 87.
3. Ibid., 97, 100.
4. Ibid., 95
5. Ibid., 102.
6. Ibid., 105.
7. Walker, "Looking for Zora," in *In Search of Our Mothers' Gardens*, 107.
8. Jean Toomer, *Cane* (1923; repr., New York: Liveright, 1975), 13.
9. David L. Lewis, *When Harlem Was in Vogue* (New York: Vintage, 1982), 90.
10. Darwin Turner, "Introduction," in *Cane* (1923; repr., New York: Liveright, 1975), xvi.
11. The Harlem Renaissance or New Negro Movement was the African American cultural and socio-political movement, which began in the early 1920s and ended in the early 1930s, around the time of the Great Depression.

12. Toni Cade Bambara, "Some Forward Remarks," in *The Sanctified Church* (Berkeley, CA: Turtle Island, 1983), 7.

13. Carla Kaplan, ed., *Zora Neale Hurston: A Life in Letters* (New York: Doubleday, 2002), 229.

14. Ibid., 404.

15. Valerie Boyd, *Wrapped in Rainbows: The Life of Zora Neale Hurston* (New York: Scribner, 2003), 286.

16. Walker, *In Search of Our Mothers' Gardens*, 83.

17. Hemenway, "Zora Neale Hurston and the Eatonville Anthology," 191.

18. W. K. McNeil, "Pre-Society American Folklorists," in *100 Years of American Folklore Study* (Columbus, OH: Mershon Center, Ohio State University, 1988), 2.

19. Charles T. Davis and Henry Louis Gates, Jr., eds., *The Slave's Narrative* (New York: Oxford University Press, 1985), xxvii–xxviii.

20. Stephen Gould, *The Mismeasure of Man* (New York: Norton, 1981), 35.

21. John Hope Franklin and Alfred A. Moss, Jr., *From Slavery to Freedom*, 7th ed. (New York: Knopf, 1994), 206.

22. Anna Julia Cooper, *A Voice from the South* (1892; repr., New York: Oxford University Press, 1990), 228.

23. William W. Newell, quoted in McNeil, "Pre-Society American Folklorists," 3.

24. William H. Wiggins, Jr., "Afro-Americans as Folk: From Savage to Civilized," in *100 Years of American Folklore Study* (Columbus, OH: Mershon Center, Ohio State University, 1988), 29.

25. Zora Neale Hurston, *Dust Tracks on a Road* (1942; repr., New York: Harper Perennial Modern Classics, 2006), 143.

26. Audrey Smedley, *Race in North America: Origin and Evoluion of a Worldview* (Boulder, CO: Westview Press, 1993), 275–76.

27. Boyd, *Wrapped in Rainbows*, 132.

28. Langston Hughes, *The Big Sea: An Autobiography* (1963; repr., New York: Thunder's Mouth Press, 1987), 239.

29. Walker, *In Search of Our Mothers' Gardens*, 85.

30. Franz Boas, "Preface," in *Mules and Men* (1935; repr., Bloomington: Indiana University Press, 1978), x.

31. Hurston, *Mules and Men*, 3.

32. Ibid.

33. *Short Oxford English Dictionary*, 5th ed., vol. 1 (Oxford: Oxford University Press, 2002), 6, 999, 1636.

34. The only African Americans who were cotemporaneous with Hurston and similarly credentialed were Texas-born John Mason Brewer (1896–1975) and Arthur Huff Fauset (1899–1983). Brewer had earned a master's degree in anthropology and had conducted considerable fieldwork in Texas. He was well established within the field of anthropology. Brewer's major works, beginning with *The Word on the Brazos: Negro Preacher Tales From the Bottom of Texas*, in 1953, appeared decades after Hurston's work. Arthur Fauset earned a master's degree in anthropology and was a member of various folk societies, as was Brewer. Fauset's work, however, focused on African American religious institutions in the urban north.

35. Zora Neale Hurston, "The Sanctified Church," in *The Sanctified Church*, ed. Toni Cade Bambara (Berkeley, CA: Turtle Island, 1983), 103, 104, 105, 107.

36. McNeil, "Pre-Society American Folklorists," 5.

37. Simon Bronner, "The Intellectual Climate of Nineteenth-Century American Folklore Studies," in *100 Years of American Folklore Study* (Columbus, OH: Mershon Center, Ohio State University, 1988), 7.

38. Boas, "Preface," in *Mules and Men*, x.

39. Zora Neale Hurston, "Characteristics of Negro Expression," in *The Sanctified Church*, ed. Toni Cade Bambara (Berkeley, CA: Turtle Island, 1983), 49.

40. Jack Santino, "Folklore as Performance and Communication," in *100 Years of American Folklore Study* (Columbus, OH: Mershon Center, Ohio State University, 1988), 21.

41. Ibid.

42. Hurston, *Dust Tracks*, 145, 172, 279–80.

43. Walker, *In Search of Our Mothers' Gardens*, 87.

44. Kaplan, *Letters*, 170.

45. Kaplan, *Letters*, 169.

46. Ibid., 363.

47. Boyd, *Wrapped in Rainbows*, 278–79.

48. Kaplan, *Letters*, 370.

49. Boyd, *Wrapped in Rainbows*, 286.

50. Kaplan, *Letters*, 371.

51. Ibid., 363.

52. Ibid., 349–50.

53. Harold Bloom, *Genius: A Mosaic of One Hundred Exemplary Creative Minds* (New York: Warner Books, 2002), 4.

54. Kaplan, *Letters*, 235.

55. W. K. McNeil, "The Folklorist and Anthropology: The Boasian Influence," in *100 Years of American Folklore Study* (Columbus, OH: Mershon Center, Ohio State University, 1988), 55.

56. Carla Kaplan, ed., *Every Tongue Got to Confess: Negro Folk-tales from the Gulf States* (2001; repr., New York: Perennial, 2002), xxiii.

57. Hurston, *Mules and Men*, 4.

58. Kaplan, *Letters*, 90.

59. Ibid., 156–57.

60. Ibid., 149, 187, 190.

61. Boyd, *Wrapped in Rainbows*, 286–87.

62. Ibid., 284.

63. Kaplan, *Letters*, 373.

64. Boyd, *Wrapped in Rainbows*, 285.

65. Hurston, *Dust Tracks*, 205, 206.

66. Boyd, *Wrapped in Rainbows*, 287.

67. Hurston, *Dust Tracks*, 205, 209–10.

68. Ibid., 211.

69. Zora Neale Hurston, *Their Eyes Were Watching God* (1937; repr., Urbana: University of Illinois Press, 1978), 143, 144.

70. Hurston, *Dust Tracks*, 209.

71. Hurston, *Their Eyes*, 163.

72. Hurston, *Dust Tracks*, 212.

73. Kaplan, *Letters*, 375.

74. Zora Neale Hurston, *Tell My Horse* (1938; repr., New York: Harper and Row, 1990), 30, 31, 35.

75. Ibid., 25.

76. Boas, "Preface," in *Mules and Men*, x.

77. Hurston, *Tell My Horse*, 39.

78. Kaplan, *Letters*, 379.

79. Hurston, *Tell My Horse*, 113, 116.

80. Ibid., 201, 207.

81. Ibid., 204, 205, 209.

82. Kaplan, *Letters*, 387.

83. Ibid.

84. Ibid., 403, 404.

85. Hurston, *Tell My Horse*, 219.

86. Louis C. Jones, quoted in Bronner, *American Folklore Studies*, 97.

87. Bronner, *American Folklore Studies*, 98.

88. Boyd, *Wrapped in Rainbows*, 313.

89. Pamela Bordelon, *Go Gator and Muddy the Water* (New York: Norton, 1999), 15.

90. Boyd, *Wrapped in Rainbows*, 313.

91. Ibid., 313–14.

92. Borderlon, *Go Gator*, 15.

93. Boyd, *Wrapped in Rainbows*, 313.

94. Ibid., 315.

95. Ibid., 316.

96. Ibid., 315.

97. Ibid., 318.

98. Bordelon, *Go Gator*, 28.

99. Bordelon, *Go Gator*, 30, 35.

100. Ibid., 129.

101. Ibid., 43–44; Boyd, *Wrapped in Rainbows*, 323.

102. Zora Neale Hurston, "Speak So You Can Speak Again" (Becker and Mayer!, Ltd. Compact Disc Recording, 2004), in *Speak So You Can Speak Again*, by Lucy Ann Hurston (New York: Doubleday, 2004). Transcription by the author.

103. Bordelon, *Go Gator*, 46.

104. Ibid., 47.

105. Ibid., 35.

106. Ibid., 16.

107. Boyd, *Wrapped in Rainbows*, 325.

108. Ibid., 325–26.

CHAPTER FOUR

1. Carla Kaplan, ed., *Zora Neale Hurston: A Life in Letters* (New York: Doubleday, 2002), 424–25.

2. Valerie Boyd, *Wrapped in Rainbows: The Life of Zora Neale Hurston* (New York: Scribner, 2003), 327.

3. Kaplan, *Letters*, 424.

4. Ibid., 422–23.

5. Ibid., 450–51.

6. Ibid., 450.

7. Ibid., 455.

8. Ibid., 458.

9. Joseph Campbell, *Pathways to Bliss: Mythology and Personal Transformation* (Novato, CA: New World Library, 2004), xviii.

10. Pamela Bordelon, ed., *Go Gator and Muddy the Water* (New York: Norton, 1999), 69.

11. Zora Neale Hurston, *Dust Tracks on a Road* (1942; repr., New York: Harper Perennial Modern Classics, 2006), 41, 58.

12. Ibid., 143.

13. Bordelon, *Go Gator,* 70.

14. Hurston, *Dust Tracks,* 25, 215, 216.

15. Ibid., 221, 217.

16. Ibid., 222, 223, 225.

17. William James, *The Varieties of Religious Experience* (1997; Touchstone Edition, New York: Simon and Schuster, 2004), 372–73.

18. Lao Tzu, *Tao Teh Ching,* John C. H. Wu, trans. (Boston: Shambhala, 2005), 23.

19. Zora Neale Hurston, *Mules and Men* (1935; repr., Bloomington: Indiana University Press, 1978), 5.

20. Kaplan, *Letters,* 148, 154, 358, 485.

21. Ibid., 510, 574.

22. Ibid., 114.

23. Zora Neale Hurston, *Their Eyes Were Watching God* (1937; repr., Urbana: University of Illinois Press, 1978), 31.

24. Zora Neale Hurston, "Crazy for This Democracy," in *I Love Myself When I Am Laughing . . . ,* ed. Alice Walker (1945; repr., Old Westbury, NY: Feminist Press, 1979), 168.

25. Zora Neale Hurston, "My Most Humiliating Jim Crow Experience," in *I Love Myself When I Am Laughing . . . ,* ed. Alice Walker (1945; repr., Old Westbury, NY: Feminist Press, 1979), 164.

26. Hurston, *Dust Tracks,* 253.

27. Ibid.

28. Kaplan, *Letters,* 489.

29. Ibid., 489, 490.

30. Hurston, *Mules and Men,* 253.

31. Zora Neale Hurston, "High John the Conquer," in *The Sanctified Church,* ed. Toni Cade Bambara (Berkeley, CA: Turtle Island, 1983), 69.

32. Ibid., 70.

33. Ibid., 69.

34. Hurston, *Mules and Men,* 67–68; Hurston, "High John the Conquer," 70.

35. Hurston, "High John the Conquer," 75, 77.

36. Ibid., 69, 77.

37. Hurston, *Dust Tracks,* 14.

38. Hurston, "High John the Conquer," 70–71.

39. Of the different variations of this term, I choose to use "Vodou." In *Heritage of Power* (1998; rev. ed., San Francisco: MEP Publications, 2002), Susheel Bibbs gives an analysis of the etymology of Vodou that historicizes the practice and points us toward its original meaning and function. "*Voodoo, Vodoun,* or *Vodou* . . . is derived from *vodun* . . . in the Fon language of the Ewe/Fon people, who once lived in what is called old Dahomey." "Vodun" has two roots, "vo" and "dun/do": "*vo* is said to relate to *vau* (vɔ)—*sacrifice that follows.*" *Dun* (*Do*) "refers to part of a Yoruba scripted divination system called Odu Ifá," which was adopted by the Fon because of its effectiveness in conflict resolution (20–21, 29).

40. Kaplan, *Letters,* 391.

41. Zora Neale Hurston, *Tell My Horse* (1938; repr., New York: Harper and Row, 1990), 113.

42. James, *Varieties of Religious Experience*, 360.

43. Kaplan, *Letters*, 699; Hurston, *Tell My Horse*, 219.

44. Kaplan, *Letters*, 699.

45. Hurston, *Dust Tracks*, 217.

46. Kaplan, *Letters*, 137.

47. Ibid., 139.

48. Ibid.

49. Hurston, *Dust Tracks*, 226.

50. Kaplan, *Letters*, 699.

51. Ibid.

52. Hurston, *Dust Tracks*, 225, 226.

53. Ibid., 226.

54. Kaplan, *Letters*, 463.

55. *Saturday Review*, February 20, 1943, 11.

56. Maya Angelou, "Foreword," in *Dust Tracks on a Road*, xi–xii.

57. Hurston, *Dust Tracks*, 226.

58. Boyd, *Wrapped in Rainbows*, 354–55.

59. Kaplan, *Letters*, 478.

60. Zora Neale Hurston, "The Sanctified Church," in *The Sanctified Church*, ed. Toni Cade Bambara (Berkeley, CA: Turtle Island, 1983), 81.

61. Hurston, *Mules and Men*, 193, 195.

62. Ibid., 193.

63. Hurston, "The Sanctified Church," 58.

64. Hurston, *Mules and Men*, 207, 209.

65. Ibid.

66. Ibid., 210.

67. Kaplan, *Letters*, 131, 137.

68. Hurston, *Mules and Men*, 215.

69. Ibid., 201.

70. Ina Fandrich, quoted in Bibbs, *Heritage of Power*, 20.

71. Hurston, *Mules and Men*, 201.

72. Bibbs, *Heritage of Power*, 61.

73. James Ferguson, *The Story of the Caribbean People* (Kingston, Jamaica: Ian Randle Publishers, 1999), 135.

74. Luisah Teisha, quoted in Bibbs, *Heritage of Power*, 63.

75. Zora Neale Hurston, *Jonah's Gourd Vine* (1934; repr., New York: Harper Perennial, 1990), 89.

76. Ibid.

77. Ibid., 107–9.

78. Ibid., 117.

79. Ibid., 128, 135.

80. Ibid., 126.

81. Ibid., 136, 159, 168.

82. Ibid., 175–78.

83. Ibid., 182.

84. Ibid., 200.

85. Ibid., 113; Kaplan, *Letters*, 302.

86. Hurston, *Jonah's*, 122.

87. Ibid., 168–69.
88. Hurston, *Their Eyes*, 24.
89. Ibid., 25.
90. Ibid., 27, 28.
91. Ibid., 28–29.
92. Ibid., 45, 46.
93. Ibid., 51–52.
94. Ibid., 52, 53.
95. Ibid., 42.
96. Ibid., 31–32.
97. Ibid.
98. Ibid., 50.
99. Ibid.
100. Ibid., 49–50
101. Ibid., 69, 70.
102. Ibid., 50, 74.
103. Ibid., 113.
104. Ibid., 117.
105. Ibid., 118.
106. Ibid., 121, 122–23, 124.
107. Ibid., 65.
108. Ibid., 123.
109. Ibid., 139.
110. Ibid., 138.
111. Ibid., 141, 161.
112. Ibid., 192.
113. Ibid., 200.
114. Ibid., 171.
115. Ibid., 236.
116. Ibid., 286.
117. Ibid., 192.
118. Campbell, *Pathways to Bliss*, xxiii.
119. Joseph Campbell, *Myths of Light: Eastern Metaphors of the Eternal* (Novato, CA: New World Library, 2003), 25, 26.
120. Ibid., 23, 24.
121. Ibid., 44.
122. Ibid., 133.
123. Ibid., 31, 137.
124. Ibid., 171.
125. Ibid., 285.
126. Ibid., 286.
127. Hurston, *Jonah's*, 112.
128. Ibid., 128–29.
129. Hurston, *Their Eyes*, 133.
130. Hurston, *Jonah's*, 182.
131. Ibid., 89.
132. Hurston describes two spirit groupings and implies a third. The loa Guedè is an example of the third grouping; see Hurston, *Tell My Horse*, 116, 219. Bibbs clearly delineates three groups: Rada, Kongo (Petwo), and Creol/Kreyol. The last grouping represents a variety of old and new loa or spirits; see Bibbs, *Heritage of Power*, 26–27.

133. Hurston, *Jonah's*, 25.

134. Ibid., 122.

135. Zora Neale Hurston, "The Race Cannot Become Great Until It Recognizes Its Talents," *The Washington Tribune* (December 29, 1934): 3.

136. Hurston, *Dust Tracks*, 171.

137. Zora Neale Hurston, *Seraph on the Suwanee* (1948; repr., New York: Harper Perennial, 1991), 25.

138. Ibid., 11.

139. Ibid.

140. Ibid., 9.

141. Ibid., 4–5.

142. Ibid., 46, 56.

143. Ibid., 57.

144. Ibid.

145. Ibid., 126.

146. Ibid., 271, 272.

147. Ibid., 280.

148. Ibid., 306, 307.

149. Ibid., 307–8, 310.

150. Ibid., 349–50.

151. Zora Neale Hurston, *Moses, Man of the Mountain* (1939; repr., Urbana: University of Illinois Press, 1984), xxi.

152. Ibid., xxii.

153. Hurston, *Jonah's*, 147.

154. Hurston, *Tell My Horse*, 118–19.

155. Ibid., 29–30.

156. Hurston, *Moses*, 99.

157. Ibid.

158. Ibid., 54, 58.

159. Ibid., 73.

160. Ibid.

161. Ibid., 109–10.

162. Ibid., 101.

163. Ibid., 100, 101.

164. *Short Oxford English Dictionary*, 5th ed., vol. 1 (Oxford: Oxford University Press, 2002), 1747; Hurston, *Moses*, 80.

165. Hurston, *Moses*, 105.

166. Ibid., 134.

167. Ibid., 159.

168. Ibid., 315–16.

169. Ibid., 100.

170. Ibid., 327.

171. Ibid., 344–45.

CHAPTER FIVE

1. Carla Kaplan, ed., *Zora Neale Hurston: A Life in Letters* (New York: Doubleday, 2002), 771.

2. Zora Neale Hurston "Herod the Great," Volume I, "Introduction B," 2. Zora Neale Hurston Collection, George A. Smathers Libraries Special Collections, University of Florida, Gainesville.

3. Zora Neale Hurston, *Dust Tracks on a Road* (1942; repr., New York: Harper Perennial Modern Classics, 2006), 255, 256.

4. Ibid., 255–56.

5. Ibid., 215.

6. Matthew 2:8–16.

7. Matthew 2:1–2.

8. Kaplan, *Letters*, 729–30. Hurston's research is confirmed by contemporary biblical scholars. For instance, in his 2003 publication *Lost Christianities: The Battles for Scripture and the Faiths We Never Knew,* Bart D. Ehrman writes that "the New Testament had been written by the second century.... The Gospels that came to be included in the New Testament were all written anonymously; only at a later time were they called by the names of their reported authors, Matthew, Mark, Luke, and John" (3).

9. Hurston, *Dust Tracks*, 231.

10. Kaplan, *Letters*, 702. The sense of this letter is that Hurston, as she stated, had initiated the writing of the manuscript, but paused to sound Mitchell's interest as well as his approval to go forward. On the face of it, the letter appears to be the first letter of inquiry to Scribner's. However, an earlier letter, dated July/August 1951 (referenced above) suggests otherwise. This letter begins, "Dear Burroughs: You have no idea how I have struggled to shorten this work, and with a literary hop and jump place Herod on the throne and march on to the end of the work with no more than 80,000 words. But it just will not come out that way" (Kaplan, *Letters*, 665).

11. Kaplan, *Letters*, 664, 734.

12. Ibid., 702–3.

13. Kaplan, *Letters*, 529, 532.

14. Ibid., 602.

15. Hurston, *Dust Tracks*, 229.

16. Zora Neale Hurston, "The Race Cannot Become Great Until It Recognizes Its Talents," *The Washington Tribune* (December 29, 1934): 3.

17. Harold Bloom, *Genius: A Mosaic of One Hundred Exemplary Creative Minds* (New York: Warner Books, 2002), 6.

18. Kaplan, *Letters*, 734, 736.

19. Ibid., 736.

20. Ibid., 737.

21. Ibid., 741, 742.

22. Ibid., 784.

23. Robert Hemenway, *Zora Neale Hurston: A Literary Biography* (1977; repr., Urbana: University of Illinois Press, 1980), 340.

24. Ibid., 604.

25. Alice Walker, *In Search of Our Mothers' Gardens* (San Diego: Harcourt, Brace, Jovanovich, 1983), 86–87.

26. Kaplan, *Letters*, 838.

27. Hurston, *Dust Tracks*, 264–65.

28. Zora Neale Hurston, *Moses, Man of the Mountain* (1939; repr., Urbana: University of Illinois Press, 1984), 327.

29. Ibid., 346.

30. Zora Neale Hurston, *Their Eyes Were Watching God* (1937; repr., Urbana: University of Illinois Press, 1978), 25.

31. Hurston, *Dust Tracks*, 264.

32. Ibid., 227.

33. Kaplan, *Letters*, 422.

34. Bloom, *Genius*, 6.

35. Ibid., 6, 8.

36. Kaplan, *Letters*, 532, 730.

37. Hurston, "Herod the Great," Volume I, "Introduction A," 9.

38. Kaplan, *Letters*, 531, 702, 730; Hurston, *Dust Tracks*, 231.

39. Kaplan, *Letters*, 729.

40. Hurston, "Herod the Great," Volume II, "Introduction," 9.

41. Ibid., Volume I, "Introduction A," 10.

42. Ibid., Volume I, "Introduction B," 1–2.

43. Ibid., Volume I, "Introduction A," 11.

44. Ibid., Volume I, "Introduction B," 1.

45. Ibid., Volume II, "Introduction B," 1.

46. Ibid., Volume III, 2–3.

47. Ibid., Volume III, 19, 21, 33.

48. Ibid., 29, 30.

49. Ibid., 51, 55.

50. Ibid., 86.

51. Ibid., 68a, 69.

52. Ibid., 73–74.

53. Ibid., Volume IV, 104a, 105.

54. Ibid., Volume V, 238, 243.

55. Ibid., Volume I, 113, 166.

56. Ibid., Volume II, "Introduction B," 3.

57. Ibid., Volume I, "Introduction A," 3.

58. Ibid., Volume I, "Introduction B," 2.

59. Ibid., Volume I, "Introduction A," 2.

60. Ibid., Volume II, "Introduction A," 5.

61. Ibid., 5–6.

62. Ibid., Volume I, 131a.

63. Ibid., 132.

64. Kaplan, *Letters*, 732. In his 2006 publication *The Lost Gospel of Judas Iscariot*, Bart Ehrman's research posits the same conclusions that Hurston had reached regarding the philosophical thought of Jesus. According to Ehrman,

> the most important thing to know about the historical Jesus is that he was a first-century Jew who lived in Palestine. The second most important thing to know is that, like so many other Palestinian Jews of his day, he held views of God, the world, and humans' place in it that were deeply and thoroughly apocalyptic.
>
> ... [A]n apocalyptic form of Judaism was widespread in Jesus' time and place. The community of Jews known as the Essenes, who produced the Dead Sea Scrolls, were apocalyptic, as were many, if not all, Pharisees. So were the followers of the various Jewish prophets who appeared on the scene in Jesus' day, such as John the Baptist, who practiced a rite of baptism to prepare people for the coming end of the age.

Jesus of Nazareth began his public ministry by being baptized by John. If nothing else, this shows that he aligned himself with John's message in particular, as opposed to the message of other Jews living at the same time (153–54).

65. Kaplan, *Letters*, 703, 733.
66. Bloom, *Genius*, 5.
67. Hurston, "Herod the Great," Volume II, "Introduction C," 1.
68. Zora Neale Hurston, *Mules and Men* (1935; repr., Bloomington: Indiana University Press, 1978), 209–10.
69. Hurston, *Moses*, 351.
70. Kaplan, *Letters*, 730–31.
71. Hurston, "Herod the Great," Volume I, 147.
72. Valerie Boyd, *Wrapped in Rainbows: The Life of Zora Neale Hurston* (New York: Scribner, 2003), 337.
73. Hurston, *Dust Tracks*, 267–68.
74. Ibid., 202.
75. Hurston, "Herod the Great," Volume IV, 153.
76. Ibid., Volume III, 58.
77. Ibid., Volume I, 108.
78. Ibid., 115.
79. Ibid., 132.
80. Ibid., 155, 168-A-4.
81. Ibid., 168-A-3.
82. Ibid.
83. Ibid., Volume I, 114–15.
84. Kaplan, *Letters*, 702.
85. Hurston, "Herod the Great," Volume I, 168-A.
86. Ibid., 109.
87. Kaplan, *Letters*, 729, 733.
88. Ibid., 579.
89. Ibid.
90. Ibid., 571.
91. Ibid., 571, 572.
92. Ibid., 574.
93. Ibid., 575.
94. Ibid., 731.
95. Hurston, "Herod the Great," Volume IV, 163.
96. Ibid., 164.
97. Ibid.
98. Kaplan, *Letters*, 572, 574.
99. Ibid., 573.
100. Ibid., 574.
101. Ibid., 574–75.
102. Ibid., 643.
103. Ibid., 663, 664.
104. Ibid., 667.
105. Ibid., 667, 669.
106. Ibid., 529, 532.
107. Boyd, *Wrapped in Rainbows*, 387.

108. Kaplan, *Letters*, 571.
109. Ibid., 703.
110. Bloom, *Genius*, 5.
111. Kaplan, *Letters*, 755.
112. Boyd, *Wrapped in Rainbows*, 423.
113. See, for example, Kaplan's assessment in *Letters* (602), which repeats and concurs with Hemenway in *Zora Neale Hurston: A Literary Biography* (1977; repr., Urbana: University of Illinois Press, 1980), 345.
114. Hurston, *Dust Tracks*, 232.
115. Kaplan, *Letters*, 591.
116. Boyd, *Wrapped in Rainbows*, 427.
117. Lao Tzu, *Tao Teh Ching*, John C. H. Wu, trans. (Boston: Shambhala, 2005), 51.
118. Hurston, *Dust Tracks*, 226.
119. Kaplan, *Letters*, 755.
120. Lao Tzu, *Tao Teh Ching*, 33.

CHAPTER SIX

1. Alice Walker, "Dedication," in *I Love Myself When I Am Laughing . . . and Then Again When I Am Looking Mean and Serious* (Old Westbury, NY: Feminist Press, 1979), 2.
2. Ibid., 2, 4.
3. Carla Kaplan, ed., *Zora Neale Hurston: A Life in Letters* (New York: Doubleday, 2002), 632.
4. Ibid., 647.
5. Madam C. J. Walker was born Sarah Breedlove Walker (1867–1919). Through a dream, she had ascertained the ingredients for straightening and processing black hair. Madam Walker created a lucrative hair care business that made her one of the first black female millionaires in America. Her adopted daughter Alelia Walker inherited the business and the wealth it produced. A socialite and philanthropist, Alelia Walker was a committed patron of black arts during the Harlem Renaissance era.
6. Kaplan, *Letters*, 649.
7. Ibid., 678.
8. Ibid., 529.
9. Hurston, "What White Publishers Won't Print," in *I Love Myself*, 169.
10. Hurston, "Why the Negro Won't Buy Communism," *American Legion* 50 (June 1951): 15.
11. Ibid., 15.
12. Ibid., 57.
13. Kaplan, *Letters*, 738.
14. Ibid.
15. Ibid., 743, 747.
16. Ibid., 740.
17. Ibid., 738–39.
18. Ibid., 739.
19. Ibid.
20. Ibid., 740.
21. Hurston, "Why the Negro Won't Buy Communism," 59.

22. Kaplan, *Letters*, 740.
23. Ibid., 739.
24. Ibid., 740.
25. Kaplan, *Letters*, 629, 630.
26. Ibid., 630.
27. Ibid.
28. Ibid., 543.
29. Ibid.
30. William Cobb, "The Other Side of Zora," *The New Crisis* 110, no. 1 (January/February 2003): 66.
31. Valerie Boyd, *Wrapped in Rainbows: The Life of Zora Neale Hurston* (New York: Scribner, 2003), 433.
32. Walker, *I Love Myself*, 2.
33. John S. Mbiti, *African Religions and Philosophy* (London: Heineman, 1969), 83.
34. Valeria Boyd, "Zora and Me: Writing the Life of a Literary Legend," *The New Crisis* 110, no. 1 (January/February 2003): 30.

CONCLUSION

1. Valerie Boyd, *Wrapped in Rainbows: The Life of Zora Neale Hurston* (New York: Scribner, 2003), 418.
2. Carla Kaplan, ed., *Zora Neale Hurston: A Life in Letters* (New York: Doubleday, 2002), 648–49.
3. Ibid., 111.
4. Ibid., 755.
5. Ibid., 77, 276.
6. Robert Hemenway, *Zora Neale Hurston: A Literary Biography* (1977; repr., Urbana: University of Illinois Press, 1980), 348.
7. Kaplan, *Letters*, 755.
8. Boyd, *Wrapped in Rainbows*, 433; Alice Walker, *In Search of Our Mothers' Gardens* (San Diego: Harcourt, Brace, Jovanovich, 1983), 114.
9. N. Y. Nathiri, *Zora! Zora Neale Hurston: A Woman and Her Community* (Orlando: Sentinel Communications, 1991), 38.
10. Walker, *In Search*, 109.
11. Boyd, *Wrapped in Rainbows*, 429.
12. Walker, *In Search*, 310.
13. Boyd, *Wrapped in Rainbows*, 428.
14. Nathiri, *Zora!* 40.
15. Kaplan, *Letters*, 618.
16. Ibid., 679.
17. Boyd, *Wrapped in Rainbows*, 432.
18. Zora Neale Hurston, *Dust Tracks on a Road* (1942; repr., New York: Harper Perennial Modern Classics, 2006), 175.
19. Kaplan, *Letters*, 325.
20. Hurston, *Dust Tracks*, 171.
21. David R. Hawkins, *Power vs. Force: The Hidden Determinants of Human Behavior* (1995; repr., Carlsbad, CA: Hay House, 2002), 72, 242.
22. Ibid., 243.

23. Harold Bloom, *Genius: A Mosaic of One Hundred Exemplary Creative Minds* (New York: Warner Books, 2002), 12.

24. Hurston, *Dust Tracks*, 229, 230.

25. Hawkins, *Power vs. Force*, 197.

26. Akasha Gloria Hull, *Soul Talk: The New Spirituality of African American Women* (Rochester, VT: Inner Traditions, 2001), 55.

27. The second interpretation of "Sankofa" is based on my discussion with my colleague Dr. Edward Kissi, a professor of African history and genocidal studies.

28. Bloom, *Genius*, 12.

Selected Bibliography

Bambara, Toni Cade, ed. "Some Forward Remarks." In *The Sanctified Church*. 1934. Reprint. Berkeley, CA: Turtle Island, 1983.

Bibbs, Susheel. *Heritage of Power*. 1998. Revised ed. San Francisco: MEP Publications, 2002.

Bloom, Harold. *Genius: A Mosaic of One Hundred Exemplary Creative Minds*. New York: Warner Books, 2002.

Boyd, Valerie. *Wrapped in Rainbows: The Life of Zora Neale Hurston*. New York: Scribner, 2003.

———. "Zora and Me: Writing the Life of a Literary Legend." *The New Crisis* 110, no. 1 (January/February 2003): 28–31.

Bronner, Simon. *American Folklore Studies*. Lawrence: University of Kansas Press, 1986.

Campbell, Joseph. *Myths of Light: Eastern Metaphors of the Eternal*. Novato, CA: New World Library, 2003.

———. *Pathways to Bliss: Mythology and Personal Transformation*. Novato, CA: New World Library, 2004.

Cobb, William. "The Other Side of Zora." *The New Crisis* 110, no. 1 (January/February 2003): 66.

Cooper, Anna Julia. *A Voice From the South*. 1892. Reprint. New York: Oxford University Press, 1990.

Cunard, Nancy, ed. *The Negro: An Anthology*. London: Wishart and Co., 1934.

Davis, Charles T., and Henry Louis Gates, Jr., eds. *The Slave's Narrative*. New York: Oxford University Press, 1985.

Ehrman, Bart. *Lost Christianities: The Battles for Scripture and the Faiths We Never Knew*. New York: Oxford, 2003.

———. *The Lost Gospel of Judas Iscariot: A New Look at Betrayer and Betrayed*. New York: Oxford University Press, 2006.

Ferguson, James. *The Story of the Caribbean People*. Kingston, Jamaica: Ian Randle Publishers, 1999.

Franklin, John Hope, and Alfred A. Moss, Jr. *From Slavery to Freedom: A History of African Americans*. 7th ed. New York: Knopf, 1994.

Glassman, Steve, and Kathryn Seidel, eds. *Zora in Florida*. Orlando: University of Central Florida Press, 2001.

Gould, Stephen. *The Mismeasure of Man*. New York: Norton, 1981.

Hawkins, David R. *Power vs. Force: The Hidden Determinants of Human Behavior*. 1995. Reprint. Carlsbad, CA: Hay House, 2002.

Hemenway, Robert. *Zora Neale Hurston: A Literary Biography*. 1977. Reprint. Urbana: University of Illinois Press, 1980.

———. "Zora Neale Hurston and the Eatonville Anthology." In *The Harlem Renaissance Remembered*, Arna Bontemps, ed. New York: Dodd, Mead, 1972.

———, ed. *The Black Novelist*. Columbus, OH: Charles E. Merrill, 1970.

Huggins, Nathan. *The Harlem Renaissance*. New York: Oxford University Press, 1973.

Hughes, Langston. *The Big Sea: An Autobiography*. 1963. Reprint. New York: Thunder's Mouth Press, 1987.

Hull, Akasha Gloria. *Soul Talk: The New Spirituality of African American Women*. Rochester, VT: Inner Traditions, 2001.

Hurston, Lucy Anne, and the Estate of Zora Neale Hurston. *Speak So You Can Speak Again*. New York: Doubleday, 2004.

Hurston, Zora Neale. "Characteristics of Negro Expression." In *The Sanctified Church*, ed. Toni Cade Bambara. 1934. Reprint. Berkeley, CA: Turtle Island, 1983.

———. "Crazy for This Democracy." In *I Love Myself When I Am Laughing . . . and Then Again When I Am Looking Mean and Serious*, Alice Walker, ed. 1945. Reprint. Old Westbury, NY: Feminist Press, 1979.

———. *Dust Tracks on a Road*. 1942. Reprint. New York: Harper Perennial Modern Classics, 2006.

———. "Drenched in Light." *Opportunity* 1–2 (December 1924): 371–74.

———. *Every Tongue Got to Confess: Negro Folk-tales from the Gulf States*, Carla Kaplan, ed. 2001. Reprint. New York: Perennial, 2002.

———. "Herod the Great." Zora Neale Hurston Collection. George A. Smathers Libraries Special Collections. University of Florida, Gainesville, FL: n.d.

———. "High John the Conquer." In *The Sanctified Church*, ed. Toni Cade Bambara. 1934. Reprint. Berkeley, CA: Turtle Island, 1983.

———. "John Redding Goes to Sea." *Opportunity* 3–4 (January 1926): 16–21.

———. *Jonah's Gourd Vine*. 1934. Reprint. New York: Harper Perennial, 1990.

———. *Moses, Man of the Mountain*. 1939. Reprint. Urbana: University of Illinois Press, 1984.

———. *Mules and Men*. 1935. Reprint. Bloomington: Indiana University Press, 1978.

———. "My Most Humiliating Jim Crow Experience." In *I Love Myself When I Am Laughing . . . and Then Again When I Am Looking Mean and Serious*, Alice Walker, ed. 1944. Reprint. Old Westbury, NY: Feminist Press, 1979.

———. "The Race Cannot Become Great Until It Recognizes Its Talent." *Washington Tribune* (December 29, 1934): 3.

———. "The Sanctified Church." In *The Sanctified Church*, ed. Toni Cade Bambara. 1934. Reprint. Berkeley, CA: Turtle Island, 1983.

———. *Seraph on the Suwanee*. 1948. Reprint. New York: Harper Perennial, 1991.

———. "Speak So You Can Speak Again." Becker and Mayer, Ltd. Compact Disc Recording, 2004. In *Speak So You Can Speak Again*, Lucy Ann Hurston and the Estate of Zora Neale Hurston. New York: Doubleday, 2004.

———. "Spunk." In *The Complete Stories*, Henry Louis Gates, Jr., and Sieglinde Lemke, eds. 1925. Reprint. New York: Harper Perennial, 1995.

———. "Sweat." In *The Complete Stories*, Henry Louis Gates, Jr., and Sieglinde Lemke, eds. 1926. Reprint. New York: Harper Perennial, 1995.

———. *Tell My Horse*. 1938. Reprint. New York: Harper and Row, 1990.

———. *Their Eyes Were Watching God*. 1937. Reprint. Urbana: University of Illinois Press, 1978.

———. "What White Publishers Won't Print." In *I Love Myself When I Am Laughing . . . and Then Again When I Am Looking Mean and Serious*, Alice Walker, ed. 1950. Reprint. Old Westbury, NY: Feminist Press, 1979.

———. "Why the Negro Won't Buy Communism." *American Legion* 50 (June 1951): 14–15, 55–60.

———. *Writings by Zora Neale Hurston from the Federal Writers' Project: Go Gator and Muddy the Water*, Pamela Bordelon, ed. New York: Norton, 1999.

———. *Zora Neale Hurston: A Life in Letters*, Carla Kaplan, ed. New York: Doubleday, 2002.

James, William. *The Varieties of Religious Experience: A Study in Human Nature*. 1997. Touchstone Edition. New York: Simon and Schuster, 2004.

Kaplan, Carla, ed. *Zora Neale Hurston: A Life in Letters*. New York: Doubleday, 2002.

Lao Tzu. *Tao Teh Ching*, John C. H. Wu, trans. Boston: Shambhala, 2005.

Lewis, David L. *When Harlem Was in Vogue*. New York: Vintage, 1982.

"The Listening Place." *Winter Park Herald* (January 26, 1933): 2.

Mbiti, John S. *African Religions and Philosophy*. London: Heineman, 1969.

Nathiri, N. Y. *Zora! Zora Neale Hurston: A Woman and Her Community*. Orlando, FL: Sentinel Communications, 1991.

Ruhl, Arthur. "Second Nights." *New York Herald Tribune* (January 17, 1932).

Smedley, Audrey. *Race in North America: Origin and Evolution of a Worldview*. Boulder, CO: Westview Press, 1993.

Turner, Darwin. "Introduction." In *Cane*. 1923. Reprint. New York: Liveright, 1975.

Walker, Alice, ed. "Dedication." *I Love Myself When I Am Laughing . . . and Then Again When I Am Looking Mean and Serious*. Old Westbury, NY: Feminist Press, 1979.

———. "Looking for Zora," In *In Search of Our Mothers' Gardens*. San Diego: Harcourt, Brace, Jovanovich, 1983.

———. *We Are the Ones We Have Been Waiting For: Inner Light in a Time of Darkness, Meditations*. New York: New Press, 2006.

Index

Abuse, 112–13, 155–58
Accompong, Jamaica, 75–76, 127
Action, 17, 146
Activism(-ists), 2, 102, 168
Adler, Marjorie Silver, 8
Africa: Bahamas, 47; cultural
    institutions, 100–101; Moses, 125–26;
    tales, 76
African American churches, 67
African American folk culture. See Folk
    culture
African American folklore. See Folklore
African Americans, 4, 12, 48, 62, 125.
    See also Black folk(s); Black people
African continuum, 67–68
African culture, 46–47
African Diaspora, 76–77, 100
African(a) peoples: genius, 58, 87;
    humanity, 60–69, 100–101; spiritual
    battles, 108–9. See also Black folk(s);
    Black people
African society, 100, 169
African spirituality, 98, 126
Afro-Caribbean culture, 76
Alder, Marjorie Silver, 203–4
Alexandra (historical figure), 152–54
Alsberg, Henry, 79, 80, 95
Altadena, California, 98
Ambition(s), 15–16, 36, 51–52, 130, 160
America, 70, 78, 90; citizenship, 168–69;
    folk culture, 67–68; loyalty, 157;
    racism, 91–92; rightness, 157–58

"American Guide," 78–79
Ancestral light, 206
Ancestral spirit, 169–70
Anger, 94, 110
Anisfeld Award in Racial Relations,
    98–99
Ann Watkins, Inc., 159
Anthropologist(s): Boas, Franz, 38, 193;
    Hurston, 58–66, 77, 78, 83, 87–89,
    101, 120, 172, 174; Mason, Charlotte
    Osgood, 41, 53
Anthropology, 36, 52–53, 136; black
    folklore, 39, 58–60, 63, 65–69; race,
    60–61, 63–64, 68–69; religion, 3, 96
Anthropometric studies, 64, 65
Antipater, 143, 144–45, 152, 157
Archetypes, 92–96, 140
Arrest, 158
Art, 34, 100, 163, 184; folk lore, 66, 90, 191
"Art and Such" (essay), 81
Artifacts, 172–73
Artistic expression, 34, 37, 58, 100, 120
Artistry, 48, 108
Artists, 1, 37, 41, 120
Arvay Henson (fictional character),
    120–25, 129
Association to Preserve the Eatonville
    Community, Inc., 182
Audience(s), 27, 28, 87; Chautauqua,
    178–80; folk performance, 69, 70;
    The Great Day, 48, 50–51, 81; white,
    51, 98–99

Autobiography, 14, 98–100, 104
Awards, 34–35, 71, 77, 98–99, 184, 185.
    See also Fellowships
Aycock and Lindsay Co., 82

Backus, Beanie, 185
Bahamas, 46–47, 73
Baltimore, Maryland, 24–25, 30
Bambara, Toni Cade, 83
Bankruptcy, 49
Barnard College, 35–36, 166, 190
Barnicle, Elizabeth, 74
Beecher, Henry Ward, 62
Belief(s), 63, 94–95, 126, 149; Hurston's,
    3, 14, 96–98, 133, 159, 168, 196;
    research on, 38, 46–47, 89
Belle Glade, Florida, 139
Belo, Jane, 87, 90
Benedict, Ruth, 52
Benton, Clem C., 184, 203
Benton, Margaret, 184
Bethune, Mary McCloud, 51
Bethune-Cookman College, 85
Betrayal, 156–57
Bible, 29, 134–36, 135, 155
Big Sweet (lumber camp personality),
    43, 45
Biographical sources on Herod, 143–45
Birth(s), 58, 61, 62; biblical figures,
    134–35, 136, 143–44; Hurston, Zora
    Neale, 10–11, 30, 99; parents, 15;
    racism, 91, 166; siblings, 10, 13
Black church(-es), 67, 98
"Black Death" (short story), 33–35
Black expression, 44, 63, 69, 101
Black feminists, 169
Black folk(s), 65–66; attributes, 94;
    expression, 67, 69, 88; heroes, 92–96;
    ritual space, 87–88; soul-stuff, 52–53
Black folk culture, 100–101, 115–16,
    125; Loughman, Florida, 42; Mason,
    Charlotte Osgood, 41
Black folklore. See Folklore
Black folk plays, 85
Black folk traditions, 100, 109
Black people, 44, 204; spirit, 90–91;
    stereotypes, 41–42, 165; white mates,
    165–66
Black religion, 67

Black soul, 52–53
Black women writers, 139–40
Bloom, Harold, 72, 138, 142, 150, 205
Boas, Franz, 36–38, 46–47, 52, 58,
    63–65, 68, 76, 96–97
Boger, Columbus H., 12
Bolen, C. E., 203
Bonner, Simon, 78
Bontemps, Arna, 151
Books, 28–29
Bordelon, Pamela, 83
Botkin, Ben, 81–82
Boyd, Valerie, 3, 99–100, 169–70, 178,
    180, 193–95
Brer Rabbit (folk character), 76, 93
Brother Anansi (folk character), 76
Brown v. Board of Education, 166
Buckman, Nicholas Murray, 190
Burial, 7–8, 203

Calhoun, Mary, 12, 27–28
Camps, 42–45, 48–49, 82, 191–92
Cane (Toomer), 57, 58
Canzo, 76, 102
Car, 38, 42, 73
Carl Middleton (fictional character),
    121–22
Catholic Church, 97
Cemetery, 7, 55, 56–57, 170
Ceremonies, 76, 88, 101
"Characteristics of Negro Expression"
    (essay), 69
Characters, 116–25, 140–42
Charles Johnson's Civic Club, 57
Charles Scribner's Sons, 8, 133–34,
    138–39, 160–61
Chautauqua, 175–82
Chicago, Illinois, 51
Childhood, 15–18, 20, 29, 42
Children, 185, 188–89, 203–4; abuse,
    155–58; Hurston, John, split with,
    20–21
Children's books, 184
Christianity, 97, 141, 154; black religion,
    67; Herod and, 134–35, 149
Christmas, 42
Church(-es), 67, 97, 98, 106–8;
    sanctified, 67, 81, 87
Citizenship, 168–69

Clara White Mission, 82
Clark, Joe, 12, 55
Cleopatra, 157
Cobb, William, 169
Cocoa Beach, Florida, 139
Cocon Gris, 77
Collection, 45, 46, 52, 82–83;
    interpretation, 96–97; organization,
    46; purpose, 63–64; results, 47, 72;
    urgency, 38–39; use, 49. *See also*
    Folklore collecting
Collection methodology, 72–73; folklore,
    39; folk songs, 82, 191; objective
    observer, 39, 43; participant-observer
    approach, 43–45, 63–64; plan, 45
College students, 195–99
Color line, 205–6
Color prejudice, 35
Color Struck (drama), 35, 37
Columbia University, 52, 64, 70, 190
Common people, 78
Communist Party, 165–66, 167
Community empowerment, 125
Comparative analysis, 46–47, 64;
    religion, 87, 96–98; tales, 76
Compulsory education, 167–68
Conjure, 45–46, 101, 105–6, 126
Connolly, Jack, 182–86
Conquer(or), 95, 146
Consciousness, 99, 116, 119–20, 124,
    205
Contract with Mason, 41–42, 44, 46,
    58–59, 75
Correspondence. *See* Letters
Corse, Carita Dogget, 81, 83
Cosmic secrets, 42, 46–47, 88, 97, 136
Cosmos Club, 31
Courage, 2, 38, 182, 193; folklore
    collecting and, 191–92; "Herod the
    Great" manuscript, 137
"Crazy for This Democracy" (essay), 91
Creation, 106–7, 109, 128
Creativity, 67–68, 81, 88
Creator, 106–7, 128
Creech, Sarah, 168
Crigwa Players, 37
Crimes, 155–56
Criminals, 146–47
Critics, 2, 35, 48–49, 58, 59, 104

Cross City, Florida, 82
Crown, 45, 125, 130, 140; power, 46,
    101–3
Cultural artifacts, 46, 172–73
Cultural expression, 66–67
Cultural institutions, 100–101
Cultural transactions, 189–90
Cultural transformation, 125
Culture, 70–71, 148–49; diversity,
    52–53, 175; heroes, 92–96
Curiosity, 15–16, 77, 88–90, 128, 129;
    about Africans, 62; about Hurston,
    179; about Negroes, 27, 165
Curricula development, 85–86

Damballah (Vodou deity), 126–27
Dance, 48
"Dance Songs and Tales from the
    Bahamas," 47
Darwinian ideas, 60–61
Dating of student, 85
David McKay Co., 139
Daytona Beach, Florida, 51
Death, 169–70; Hurston, John, 31;
    Hurston, Lucy Ann Potts, 18;
    Hurston, Zora Neale, 7–8, 56, 78,
    203–4; Tea Cake, 115
Deity, 78, 126, 150
Delia Jones (fictional character), 37
Democracy: American, 70, 167; Jewish
    struggle for, 159; racism, 91–92, 99,
    167
Desegregation, 166–68
"Diddy-Wah-Diddy" (essay), 81
Diversity, 64–65, 70, 175
Divine being, 125–26
Divine power, 150
Divinity, 92–93, 97
Divorce, 48, 84, 97, 106
Doctor(s), 91; Hoodoo, 100, 102; two-
    headed, 43, 45–46, 105–6, 127, 189,
    192
Doctoral study, 47, 51, 204
Doctorate degree, 83, 179
Dolls, 168
Drama department, 51, 85–86
Dramatic interests, 47–49
Dramatic production, 37
Dramatization, oral tradition, 108–9

Dreams, 129–30
"Drenched in Light" (short story), 34
Drum(s), 46, 77, 104, 119
Drumbeat, 93–94
Duality, 93–96; political power, 127–28;
    transcending, 120, 124, 141
Du Bois, W.E.B., 37, 205
Durham, North Carolina, 84, 85–86
Dust Tracks on a Road (autobiography),
    98–100, 104

Eastern philosophy, 3, 116, 141, 148,
    149, 162
Eatonville, Florida, 11–12, 51, 55–56,
    78, 83, 92, 98, 166, 183; Festival,
    175, 182; fieldwork, 37–39; High
    John de Conquer, 115–16; John
    Redding Goes to Sea, 33; Jonah's Gourd
    Vine, 104–8; Their Eyes Were
    Watching God, 111–12
Eau Gallie, Florida, 138, 158–59
Education, 12; Chautauqua, 176–77;
    desegregation, 166–68; folklore, 66;
    Hurston's, 19–20, 27–32, 35–36
Embree, Edwin, 51, 52
Emotional state, 40, 113, 165
Employment, 19–24, 29–32; columnist,
    203; Federal Writers Project, 79–83;
    Hurst, Fannie, 35; Mason, Charlotte
    Osgood, 41–42, 58–59; substitute
    teacher, 185
Empowerment, 107, 109, 124–25; oral
    tradition, 128; personal, 116–20
Enemies, 44–45, 154–57
Enthusiasm, 71–72, 90, 158–59; field
    research, 73–74; Herod the Great,
    136, 164; school, 35
Epigraph on grave, 57–58
Equality, 12, 15, 33, 62, 111–12, 130,
    166
Equal opportunity, 12, 34
Essence, 88–90
Essenes, 149, 153, 155
Euro-Americans, 61–63
Everglades Cypress Co., 42
Every Tongue Got to Confess: Negro Folk-
    tales from the Gulf States (Kaplan,
    ed.), 72
Evolutionary model, 61–62, 64, 68

Expectations of parents, 15
Expression, 66–67; African American
    folk, 67, 69; artistic, 34, 37, 58, 100,
    120; black, 44, 63, 69, 101; religious,
    100; self, 111–13, 115–16
Extramarital affairs, 105–7

Faith, 92, 97, 122
Faithfulness, 152
Family, 13–14, 20–21, 39, 171–73,
    188–89
Fast and Furious (skit), 47–48
Fear, 94, 110, 149
Federal government, 70–71, 181
Federal Theatre Project, 71
Federal Writers Project (FWP), 78–83
Fellowships: Guggenheim, 71, 74–75,
    77–78, 102, 126, 193; Rosenwald, 51,
    52, 204; Woodson, 37–38
Fiction, 103–8
Field notes, 38, 81
Fieldwork, 46–47, 58–59, 67; Bahamas,
    46; collection, 39, 72–73, 82, 191;
    Florida, 37–39, 42–45, 48–49, 82,
    191–92; Haiti, 59, 67, 74, 76–78;
    Harlem, 36, 65; intimate
    relationships, 74–75; Jamaica, 74, 75–
    76; methodology, 39, 43–45, 60–61,
    63–64, 72–73; New Orleans,
    Louisiana, 100–103; plan, 45; Works
    Projects Administration, 81–82
Finances, 49–50, 201–3
Fire!! (publication), 37
"Fire and Cloud" (short story), 126
"Fire Dance" (performance), 47, 81
Fisk University, 40, 51, 70
Florida, 37–39, 42–45, 50–51, 72,
    79–83. See also names of specific
    localities
Florida Baptist Academy, 18–20
Florida Guide, 80–83
Florida Humanities Council, 175–76,
    180
The Florida Negro (WPA guide), 79–83
Florida Redevelopment Association, 185
Folk, 33, 58, 66–67, 96
Folk aesthetic, 34
Folk artistry, 48
Folk community, 35

Folk concerts, 49–51, 81, 204
Folk culture: African American, 33, 67, 191; American society, 70; black, 41, 42, 115–16, 125; framework for studying, 68–69
Folklife, framework for studying, 68–69
Folklore, 4, 66–67, 81; African American, 88; anthropology of black, 39, 51–53; back soul, 52–53; cosmic secrets, 88–90; fieldwork, 58–59; genius, 60–61; High John de Conquer in black, 92–96; movement, 70; performance of Florida, 81; pioneering efforts, 62; publication, 60; survivalistic nature, 61. *See also* Fieldwork
Folklore collecting: courage, 191–92; financing, 202–3; genius, 60–61, 74; Mason, Charlotte Osgood, 41–42; New Orleans, 45–46; plan, 45; recordings, 82–83; South Carolina, 189–90. *See also* Collection; Collection methodology
Folklorist(s), 61, 66–69, 74, 78, 88
Folksongs, collection methodology, 82
Folktales, 76; African origins, 67–68, 76; Negro, 67–68; recording sessions, 82–83; spiritual interests, 90; symbolic characters, 93–94; telling, 16–17. *See also* Stories
Folk-Tales from the Gulf States, 47
Folk traditions, 33
Force-power distinction, 205
Form, 88–89
Fort Pierce, Florida, 7–8, 55, 133–34, 139, 174, 182–86, 203–4; ZoraFest, 174, 182–86, 189–94; Zora Neale Hurston Branch Library, 186–89
Franklin, John Hope, 205
Freedom, 94, 125; desegregation, 167–68; High John de Conquer, 120–25; manna and struggle for, 130, 141; model of, 4–5; spirit of, 120–25
Friends(-ship), 8, 73, 106, 151–52, 158, 166, 168
Friends of the St. Lucie County Library System, 186
"From Sun to Sun" (stage production), 191
Funeral, 8, 203

Garden, 2, 185
Garden of Eden, 113–14, 117
Garden of the Heavenly Rest Cemetery, 56–57
Generosity, 49, 202
Genesee Memorial Gardens, 7
Genius, 61; African(a) peoples, 58, 87; biographical inwardness, 150; black folk, 65–66; fieldwork, 60–61; folklore, 88; Hurston, 1–2, 53, 58, 70–71, 142, 162, 206; idealized forerunners, 142; individual(s), 61; oral tradition, 100–101, 115–16; of people, 1; vitality and enthusiasm, 72–73; Zora Festival, 183
Genius of the South, 57–58
"Georgia Dusk" (poem), 57, 58
Gilbert and Sullivan Theater Co., 24–25, 29, 64
"The Gilded Six-Bits" (story), 51
Glover, Danny, 194
God(s), 88–90, 96–98, 106–7; Herod and Moses, 150; Vodou, 77, 119; wager with, 29, 42. *See also* Universal Spirit
"Go Gator and Muddy the Water" (essay), 81, 87–88
Go Gator and Muddy the Water: Writings by Zora Neale Hurston from the Federal Writers Project (Bordelon, ed.), 83
Goodwill Presbyterian Church, 186, 187
Grave, 55–58, 169–70, 185, 187
The Great Day (stage production), 48–51, 191, 205
Greatness, 145–48
Great Race theory, 60–64
Greeks, 144, 148–49
Green, Paul, 70, 86–88
Grover, Edwin Osgood, 50, 74
G Street Barber Shop, 31–32
Guede (Vodou deity), 78
Guggenheim fellowship, 71, 74–75, 77–78, 102, 126, 193

Haiti, 59, 67, 74, 76–78, 102–3
Halpert, Herbert, 82
Harlem fieldwork, 36, 65
Harlem Renaissance, 32, 33, 36–37, 49, 58–59, 62, 185

Harper Brothers, 133–34
Harris (fictional character), 126
Harris, Joel Chandler, 68
Hattie Tyson Pearson (fictional
    character), 105–6, 126
Hawkins, David, 205
Health of Hurston, 8, 29–30, 73–74,
    133, 204
Hemenway, Robert, 3, 55, 60, 62,
    189–94
Herod I, King of Judea, 133–62, 143–48,
    157
"Herod the Great" (manuscript), 133–34,
    136–39, 158–61, 164
Heroes, 88, 92–96, 142
Herskovits, Melville, 36, 52
High John de Conquer: heroic figure,
    92–96, 106, 109, 115–16, 126, 160;
    tale, 120–25
High John de Conqueror (play), 86–87
High school, 30–31
History, 37–38, 135–36, 144–45, 188
Hogan, Frank, 158
Hohoff, Tay, 164
Holmes, Dwight O. W., 30, 31
Holt, Hamilton, 50
Holy union, 109, 111, 117
Homelessness, 21–22
Hoodoo, 45–46, 76–77, 100, 101–3,
    126, 192
Hoodoo doctors. *See* Two-headed
    doctors
Hoodoo Queen, 57, 102
Hopefulness, 14–15
Horizon, 18, 118, 153; trip to, 15, 33,
    42, 95, 114
Howard University, 31–32
Hughes, Bernice, 31
Hughes, Langston, 38, 40–41, 44, 47, 65,
    151, 202
Hull, Akasha Gloria, 3–4, 206
Humanity, 53, 64–65, 120, 136; African
    Americans, 62; African(a) peoples,
    60–69, 100–101; ideal, 140–42, 151
Humor, 190
Hungerford Normal and Industrial
    School, 12, 27–29, 166
Hunting party, 75–76
Hurst, Fannie, 8, 35, 36, 52, 71, 151

Hurston, Alfred, 9
Hurston, Amy, 9
Hurston, Benjamin Franklin, 13, 39
Hurston, Clifford Joe, 8, 13
Hurston, Everett Edward, 13, 170,
    172–73
Hurston, Hezekiah Robert (Bob), 10, 18,
    19, 23–24, 39
Hurston, Issac, 10
Hurston, John, 9, 12–13, 15, 22–23, 88,
    135; daughters, 11; death, 31; Moge,
    Mattie, marriage, 18–19; rejection of
    Zora, 19–20; split with children,
    20–21
Hurston, John Cornelius, 10, 38
Hurston, Lucy, 170–75
Hurston, Lucy Ann Potts, 8–10, 13–15,
    18, 95
Hurston, Mabel, 8
Hurston, Richard (Dick) William, 10, 20
Hurston, Sarah Emmeline, 10, 19, 30
Hurston, Vivian, 8
Hurston, Wilhemina, 23, 83
Hurston, Winifred, 83
Hurston, Zora Neale: ancestral spirit,
    170–99; anthropologist, 58–66, 77,
    78, 83, 87–89, 101, 120, 172, 174;
    arrest, 158; autobiography, 14,
    98–100; awards, 34–35, 37–38, 71,
    77, 98–99; belief, 3, 14, 96–98, 133,
    159, 168, 196; birth, 10–11, 30, 99;
    Chautauqua portrayal, 175–76;
    childhood, 15–18; courage, 2, 38,
    137, 182, 191–93; death and burial,
    7–8, 56, 203, 204; divorce, 48, 84, 97,
    106; doctor degree, 179; education,
    27–32, 35–36; employment, 19–21,
    23–24, 35, 41–42, 58–59, 79–83, 98,
    185, 203; enemies, 44–45, 154–57;
    enthusiasm, 35, 72–74, 136, 158–59,
    164; folklorist, 61, 66–69, 74, 78, 88;
    free spiritedness, 15–16; genius, 1–2,
    53, 58, 70–71, 142, 162, 206; grave,
    55–58, 169–70, 185, 187; health, 8,
    29, 73–74, 133, 204; homelessness,
    21–22; idealism, 140–42; income, 25,
    32, 82, 83, 98, 158, 164, 201–3; inner
    life, 88–90, 94–95; joy, 23, 71, 204;
    leader, 102, 193, 195; learning,

27–29; marriage, 39–40, 83–84; memorabilia, 171–73; moral charges, 155–58; optimism, 161–62; parents, 8–10, 13–15; personality, 150–62; relationships, 74–75, 153; risk taking, 139–40; schools, 12, 19–20, 23–24, 29–32; seeker, 101–2; siblings, 15, 17; social scientist, 39, 46, 60, 65, 102, 136, 172, 179; tragic figure, 180–81; visions, 20–21, 22, 42, 192; work, 40, 62, 72–75, 84, 88, 136, 137, 153, 172, 175; writing, 31, 32–35, 58–59, 103–8, 137–38

Ideal, 140–42, 153; black leadership, 125; characters, 151; interracial understanding, 168; women, 181
Idealism, 140–42, 153; Herod, 138, 144, 152
Idealized forerunners, 142
Ideals of democracy, 99
Identity, 95, 99, 109; American, 70, 78; black folk traditions, 109; Hurston risk taking, 139–40; oral tradition, 108–9
Ideology, 62–63; New Negro Movement, 36–37, 37, 120; religion, 98
Imagination, 88–89
Income, 25, 32, 82, 83, 98, 158, 164, 201
Independence, 130
Individual(s), 64, 116, 120; genius, 61; Herod as ideal, 138; ideal, 140, 142, 144; identity, 92, 109
Individualist politics, 168
Inferiority, 35, 62–64; blacks, 60–61, 91, 166–69; women, 122, 124
Infidelity, 105–7, 118–19
Initiation rites, 46, 76, 101–3, 192
Inner life, 88–89
Inner strength, 124–25
Innocence, 134–35, 153–54, 157–58
"The Inside Light—Being a Salute to Friendship," 151
Inside search, 116–20
Inspiration, 170
Integrity, 152
Interracial understanding, 168
Intimacy, 151

Intimate relationships, 74–75
Intraracial prejudice, 35, 48
Introspection, 116–20
Inward expansion, 161–62
Inward journey, 168
Inwardness, 150
Isis Watts (fictional character), 34
Israel, 130, 141

Jackson, Alice, 186–89
Jacksonville, Florida, 18–20, 38, 47, 82, 84
Jamaica, 74, 75–76
James, William, 89, 96
Janie Mae Crawford (fictional character), 75, 109–16, 117–18, 119–20, 141, 194
J.B. Lippincott and Co., 8, 51, 164, 204
Jefferson, Thomas, 61
Jesus Christ, 93, 106–7, 134–35, 149, 155
Jethro (fictional character), 129–30
Jew(s), 25
Jewish people, 136–37, 154–55, 159
Jewish priesthood, 134, 145–47
Jewish sects, 148–49
Jews, 87, 134, 143–44, 155
Jim Crow, 2, 11, 38, 79–81, 91, 166
Jim Meserve (fictional character), 120, 122
Jody Starks (fictional character), 75, 111, 118–19
John Buddy Pearson (fictional character), 98, 104–8, 118–19, 120, 126
John concept, 92–96
John de Conquer (heroic figure). See High John de Conquer
John Golden Theater, 48, 69
"John Redding Goes to Sea" (short story), 32–33, 140–41
Johnson, Charles Spurgeon, 32–34
Johnson, Georgia Douglas, 32, 57
Johnson, Guy, 52
Johnson, Hall, 48, 49
Joint Committee on Folk Art, 81–82
Jonah's Gourd Vine (novel), 51–52, 104–8, 126, 137, 204–5

Jones, Thomas, 51
Josephus, Flavius, 143–45, 150, 156
Journey, 125–31
Joy, 4, 23, 71, 122, 204
Jump at de sun, 14, 105, 178–79
"Jungle Scandals" (skit), 47–48
Justice, 130, 134, 156–59

Kennedy, Stetson, 80, 83, 180–81
Knight, John S., 168
Knott, Sara Gertude, 70
Knowledge, 29, 64, 113–14, 128, 140

Language, 43, 48, 64, 68–69, 190; black
    vernacular, 33, 67, 104. *See also*
    Word(s)
Larraine (fictional character), 121–22
Laughter, 36, 93–94, 95
LaVeau, Marie, 45, 102–3, 192
Leader(s), 129–30, 193; Hurston, 102,
    193, 195; Moses, 125, 140
Leadership, 70, 130; Herod, 143,
    146–47, 154; Moses, 125, 140
Letters, 14, 19, 90, 204; field notes, 38,
    44; "Herod the Great," 133, 136–37,
    139, 150, 155, 161; publishers, 51
Letters of recommendation, 52, 71, 74
Lewis, Kossola Cudjo, 40, 47
Library, 184, 186–89
Lies: crimes, 155–56; *Dust Tracks on a
    Road*, 99; fieldwork, 38; folklore
    collecting, 191; Herod's enemies, 154,
    155; listening, 16, 42; Moses, 127;
    participant-observer approach, 43;
    Tea Cake and death, 115; telling, 30,
    99; Walker use, 56
Life, 96–98, 141, 142, 169–70
Light, 40, 206
Lightning, 46, 150, 192
Lincoln, Abraham, 61–62
Lincoln Park Academy, 8, 174, 187
Lincoln Park Nursing Home, 8
Lippincott, Bertram, 51
Listening, 42, 114–15; conversations, 19,
    29; folklore, 66; lying sessions, 16
Literary ambitions, 51–52
Literary critics, 161–62
Literary works, scientific knowledge,
    59–60

Literature, 25
Little Negro Theatre, 37
"The Lives of Barney Turk" (unpublished
    manuscript), 164, 201–2
Locke, Alain, 32, 33, 41, 92–93
Lockwood, Susan, 175–76
Logan Killicks (fictional character),
    110–11
Lomax, Alan, 74
Loughman, Florida, 42–45
Love, 74–75, 115–16, 117, 153
Lucy (lumber camp personality), 44–45
Lucy Ann Potts (fictional character),
    104–6, 118–19
Lumber camps, 42–45

Macedonia Baptist Church, 9, 13, 18, 69
Mack, John, 19, 30
Macon, Georgia, 40
Magazine, Alabama, 45
Magic, 46–47; Christianity, 97; medicine
    man, 127; song and, 109
Maitland, Florida, 11–12
Maria (fictional character), 123–24
Mariamne (historical figure), 152–54
Marriage, 111, 117, 121–23; Hurston,
    John, and Mattie Moge, 18–19;
    infidelity, 22; parents, 9–10; Price,
    Albert, III, 83–84; Sheen, Herbert
    Arnold, 39–40, 48; *Their Eyes Were
    Watching God*, 109–16
Mason, Charlotte Osgood, 41–42, 46,
    47–48, 49, 58–59, 68, 69, 73, 202
Master-slave duality, 93–94
Matthew (Gospel), 135, 143
Mayer, Annie Nathan, 35–36
McEwen, Phyllis P., 176–82
Meharey Medical School, 23
Memphis, Tennessee, 23–24, 29, 31
Mentor, 129
Mentu (fictional character), 128
Merritt Monument Co., 57
Methodology: Boas, 63–64; collection,
    39, 72–73, 82, 191; comparative
    analysis, 46–47, 64; fieldwork, 43,
    60–61, 63–64, 67; objective observer
    method, 39, 43; participant-observer
    approach, 43–45
Miller, Alexander, 157–58

Mimicry, 69
Mind, 94–95, 116–25, 120–21, 138
Ministry, 107–8
Miriam (fictional character), 127
Missionary Baptist Church, 88
Missionary work, 122, 130
Mitchell, Burroughs, 139, 161, 164, 201–2
Mobile, Alabama, 40
Moge, Mattie, 18, 21, 22–23
Money for school, 29–30
Moral charges against Hurston, 90, 155–58, 160
Morgan Academy, 30–31
Morgan College, 30–31, 83
Moseley, Mathilda, 55–56
Moses (biblical figure), 7, 95, 100, 125–31, 150
Moses, Man of the Mountain (novel), 83, 125–31
Movies, 98
"Mrs. Doctor" (manuscript), 165
Muck, 114–16
Mule Bone (play), 47
Mules and Men (folklore work), 52, 59, 60, 65–66, 68, 72, 93, 139
Music, 25, 69, 87
"My Most Humiliating Jim Crow Experience" (essay), 91
Mythology, 27–29, 69, 93

Nanny (fictional character), 116–17
Nashville, Tennessee, 51
Nathiri, N. Y., 182
National Folk Festival, 51
National Folk Festival Association (NFTA), 70–71
Nationalism, 99
Nature, 66–67, 96–97, 127, 128–29; two faces of, 141
The Negro: An Anthology (Cunard, ed.), 100
Negro community, 156
Negro culture. *See* Black folk culture; Folk culture
Negro media, 156
Negroness, 38–39, 48
Negro Problem, 34, 168
Negro spirituals. *See* Spirituals

Negro Units, 71, 79
"A Negro Voter Sized Up Taft" (article), 159
Neurasthenia, 68
Newell, William W., 63
New Negro Movement, 32, 33, 36, 37, 120
New Negro Theatre, 47
New Orleans, Louisiana, 40, 45, 100–103, 192
Newspaper columnist, 203
New spirituality, 4–5
New York City, 34, 91, 155–56
Night school, 30
North Carolina College for Negroes, 84, 85–86
Notasulga, Alabama, 8–10, 183
Novelist, 58–59
Nugent, Bruce, 36–37, 64–65

Objective observer method, 39, 43, 63–64
Odum, Howard, 52
Ole Massa (folk character), 94
Opportunity (journal), 33–35
Optimism, 161–62
Oral tradition, 61; dramatization, 108–9; empowering element, 125, 128; genius, 100–101, 115–16
Orlando Sentinel (newspaper), 166
Osceola, Florida, 177–78
Outward unprofitability, 160–61

Paradise Lost (Milton), 23
Paramount Pictures, 98
Parents, 9–10, 13–14
Participant-observer approach, 43–45
Passion, 4–5, 136–37, 139–40
Patterson, Sarah Peek, 56
Pay, 71, 94, 95, 204
Peace, 125, 130
Pennies, 27–28, 40, 201
Pepper, Claude, 177–78
Performance(s), 48; African American folk culture, 191; Chautauqua, 177–78; Florida folklore, 81; folklore, 69; *The Great Day*, 48–51. *See also* Dramatic production; Theater
Personality, 150–62, 180–81

Philosophy, 3, 99, 116, 141, 149, 162
Phoeby (fictional character), 115–18
Pickens, William, 31
Playwriting, 47–48, 86–87
Pleasant, Mary Ellen, 102
Poetry, 13, 61, 98, 108
Political power, 127–28
Political writings, 163–64
Politics, 68, 81; *Dust Tracks on a Road,* 98–100; Hurston views on, 163–64; publisher racist, 165–68; racial and national, 167–68. *See also* Desegregation; Negro Problem; Racism
Polk County, Florida, 45
Potts, Lucy Ann. *See* Hurston, Lucy Ann Potts; Lucy Ann Potts (fictional character)
Potts, Richard, 8–10
Potts, Sarah, 8–10, 16
Poverty, 9, 122–23, 202
Power, 92, 95–96, 127–28, 205; leader-ruler distinction, 130; personal, 112–13, 116–17; salvation, 118–19; spoken words, 115–16; Vodou, 103; word and prayer, 104–8
Prayer, 104, 118–19
Preacher(s), 13, 104–8, 118, 119
Preaching, 88, 104–8, 119, 135
Price, Albert, III, 83–84
Priest(s), 177; Jewish, 134, 143, 145–46, 148, 154–55; oral tradition, 127–28; Voduo, 76, 102, 103
Primitive cultures, 62–63
Promised Land, 125
Propaganda, 34
Protection: camp research, 38, 43, 191; Haiti, 78; justice system, 157–58; marriage, 111
Public and Hurston, 175–76, 179
Publication, 31; *Dust Tracks on a Road,* 98–99; Federal Writers Project, 79–83; fieldwork, 72; Herod research, 150; *Jonah's Gourd Vine,* 51, 98–99, 204; *Mules and Men,* 52; in *Opportunity,* 33–35; in *Stylus,* 32; *Their Eyes Were Watching God,* 59
Public education, 167–68, 176–77

Publishers, 51, 165–68, 201
Punter, Percival McGuire, 74–75, 194

Race, 4, 25, 34, 60, 64; problem, 34, 168
"The Race Cannot Become Great Until It Recognizes Its Talent" (essay), 120
Race consciousness, 2, 4, 120
Racial relations, 25, 41–42, 98–100, 190; hierarchy, 61–62; protocol, 14–15, 190
Racism, 19, 83, 90–92, 165–68, 205–6. *See also* Jim Crow
Rada deity, 126–27
Railroad camps, 48–49
Randolph, Forbes, 48
Rape, 122
Reading, 27–29, 183
Reality, idealism, 138
Recordings, 44, 46, 82, 87
Reichards, Gladys, 36
Rejection(s), 19–20, 142, 160–61, 165
Relationships: friendships, 151–52; men to women, 111–13; strife, 141
Religion, 89, 96–98, 118–19
Religious expression, 100
Religious practices, 3, 45–46, 76–77, 100–103
Republican Party, 156
Restoration from trauma, 158–60
Rhythm, 94
Rice, John, 202
Ridding horse, 15–16, 95
Righteousness, 134
Rights of citizens, 168–69
Risk taking, 139–40
Ritual(s), 53, 76; of death, 18; Fire Dance, 48; Hoodoo initiation, 101–3, 192; insult, 113–14; space, 87–88
Roberts, Carrie, 29
Rochester, Richard D., 155–56, 157, 160
Rollins College, 50–51, 70, 202
Romance, 152–53
Roosevelt, Franklin Delano, 70, 78
Rosenwald fellowship, 51, 52, 204

Salary, 79–80, 81–82, 83, 98
Salvation, 118–19
Sanctified church(-es), 67, 81, 87

Sanford, Florida, 22, 51, 204
Sankofa bird, 206
Santino, Jack, 69
Scandal, 155–58
Scholarly societies, 37–38
School(s), 12, 19–20, 23–31;
    desegregation, 166–68; ZoraFest, 184
Scientific community, 60–61
Scientific investigations, 59–60
Search, 116–20
Secret rites, 58
Secret societies, 77
Secrets of nature, 127
"Seeing the World As It Is," 133–34
Seeker, 88–90, 101–2
Segregation, 19, 68, 166–68, 189–90,
    203. See also Jim Crow
Self, 159–60; awareness, 116–17;
    confidence, 92; evaluation, 163;
    expression, 111–13, 115–16;
    knowledge, 188–89; realization, 109,
    111, 125, 129, 161; respect, 166;
    support, 21–22, 84
Seminole County Chamber of
    Commerce, 204
Seraph on the Suwanee (story), 120,
    129
Sexual abuse scandal, 155–58
Sexuality, 165–66
Sexual promiscuity, 104–6, 110
Sheen, Herbert Arnold, 32, 39–40, 48,
    75, 97
Shepherd, James, 85
Silence, 118–19, 127
Singing, 191
Singing Steel (drama), 51
Slander, 154, 156
Slaughter of innocents, 134–35
Slavery, 8–9, 82, 92, 130, 165, 206
Smith, Bessie, 40
Social acceptance, 35–36, 203
Social behavior, 64
Social change, 168
Social conditions, 82
Social dynamics, 73
Social life, 32
Social pyramid, 61
Social science, 60–63
Social scientist(s), 60

Song(s), 93–94, 109, 191; collecting,
    69, 82
Soul, 90, 94–95; black, 52–53, 58–59;
    winning, 95–96, 130
Source of Life, 96–98
South: African culture, 62, 76, 100;
    collecting in, 38–42, 82; genius of, 57
South Carolina, 189–90
Southern culture, 41, 162
Southerner(s), 65, 168, 198
Soviet Russia, 165
Sparta, Georgia, 57
Speak So You Can Speak Again (Hurston,
    L), 171–72
Spears (play), 35
Spirit, 2, 14, 88; ancestral, 169–70; black
    people, 90–91; poverty of, 123
Spiritual battles, 108–9
Spiritual concepts, 88–89
Spiritual development, 13–14
Spiritual empowerment, 125
Spirituality, 3–5, 98, 125, 126
Spiritual power, 101
Spirituals, 48, 69; recording, 87
Spiritual state, 40
Spiritual world, Dust Tracts on a Road,
    100
Spoken words, 115–16
"Spunk" (short story), 34–35
St. Augustine, Florida, 39
Stereotypes, 41–42, 165
St. Lucie Country Welfare Agency, 8
Stories, 19, 128, 169, 191; African
    background, 76; collecting, 43, 46,
    59, 69, 72, 190; Hurston's, 16, 37, 58,
    140; ideal figures, 142; presentation,
    68. See also Folktales
Story Magazine, 51
Storytelling, 68, 188, 204
Stowe, Harriet Beecher, 177–78
Strength, 17, 36, 95–96, 124–25, 153
Strokes, 8
Struggle, 4–5, 110, 125, 135, 141
Students, 35, 85, 195–99
The Stylus (literary publication), 32
Subjectivity, 138
Submission, 112–13
Success, 118
Sun, 14, 23–24, 40, 127, 192

Sunrise, 95, 124–25
Sunset time, 20
Superiority, 124–25
Supreme Court, 166, 167
Surrender, 124
"Sweat" (short story), 37
Symbols, 40, 46; lightning, 150; marriage, 122; sun, 14

Taft, William Howard, 159
Talent in ruins, 161–62
Tales. See Folktales; Stories
Tannebum, Frank, 87, 90
Tao Teh Ching, 162
Tea Cake (fictional character), 75, 114–15, 117, 194
Teachers, 27–28
Teisha, Luisah, 102
Television, 193
Tell My Horse (folklore collection), 60, 80
Terror by slander, 156
Theater, 32, 37, 47–49, 51; Gilbert and Sullivan Theater Co., 24–25; Negro, 37, 44, 50, 86; North Carolina College for Negroes, 85–86
Theatrical presentation, 53
Their Eyes Were Watching God (novel), 59, 75, 77, 83, 109–20, 183, 193–94
Their Eyes Were Watching God (television movie), 193
Toomer, Jean, 57–58, 66
Tradition, 87–88; folk, 33, 70, 109; folklore, 66, 68; identity, 109; oral, 61, 62–63, 100, 108, 115, 125, 128; religious, 81, 89, 100; spiritual, 67, 103–4, 126–27
Transcendence, 93, 120, 124, 141
Transcendent, 87–88, 97, 162
Traveling, 73
Trickster figures, 93–94
Trungapa, Chögyan, 4
Truth, 99, 137–38, 158–59, 202
Turner, Lorenzo Dow, 32
Turner, Luke, 45–46, 101–3, 150, 192
Turpentine industry, 82, 191–92
Two-headed doctors, 43, 45–46, 105–6, 127, 192
"Two Women in Particular," 151

Uncle Remus: His Songs and Sayings (Harris), 68
Universal Spirit, 2, 88, 117. See also God(s); Source of Life
University of North Carolina, 70, 86
University of South Florida, 195

Van Vechten, Carl, 8, 35, 71, 74, 158
Vernacular, 33, 67, 104
Vision(s): childhood, 20–21, 22, 25, 42; Hoodoo initiation, 192; marriage, 117
Vitality, 72–73, 96, 153–54
Vodou, 76–77, 100, 101–3, 189; divinities, 119, 126–27
Vodou doctors. See Two-headed doctors

Walker, Alice, 1, 4–5, 55, 62, 163, 169, 187
Walk Together Chillun! (play), 71
Washington, D.C., 31–32
Waterbury, Jean Parker, 164, 201
West Indies, 74
"What White Publishers Won't Print" (article), 165, 168
Wheatley, Phyllis, 61
White(s), 60–62, 91, 165–66; men, 9, 10, 194; publisher racism, 165–68; supremacists, 79, 90–91; women, 121–22
White mare apparatus, 165–67
"Why the Negro Won't Buy Communism" (article), 165–66, 202
Wife, 110–13
Williams, D. E., 166
Will-to-freedom, 90–91
Winfrey, Oprah, 179, 183–84, 193, 194–95
Winning, 95–96, 130
Winterpark, Florida, 50
Womanist writers, 180
Women, 111–12, 117–18, 120–22, 180–81
Wood folk, 15
Woodson, Carter G., 37–38
Word(s), 17; prayer, 104–8; spoken, 13, 100, 115–16; written, 133–34
The Word, 93, 118, 122; Indian philosophy, 149; preaching, 13, 106, 108

Work, 40, 72, 110, 136; anthropological, 65–66, 96; intimate relationships, 74–75; romance, 153
Works Projects Administration (WPA), 71, 79–83, 181
World, 33, 94–95
World War II, 98–99
Wrapped in Rainbows (Boyd), 193–95
Writer(s), 58–59, 79, 137–40, 180. *See also* New Negro Movement
Writing(s), 32–35, 59, 163–64

Written word, 133–34
Wunsch, Robert, 50, 51, 202

Yale University, 51

ZoraFest, 182–86, 189–94
Zora Neale Hurston Branch Library, 184, 186–89
Zora Neale Hurston Dust Tracks Heritage Trail, 175, 184–85

About the Author

DEBORAH G. PLANT is an associate professor of Africana studies at the University of South Florida and the author of *Every Tub Must Sit on Its Own Bottom: The Philosophy and Politics of Zora Neale Hurston.*